Addie Moe
726-2968

D1130443

Developing Quality Systems

Developing Quality Systems

A Methodology Using Structured Techniques

Brian Dickinson

Second Edition

McGraw-Hill Book Company

New York   St. Louis   San Francisco   Auckland   Bogotá
Caracas   Colorado Springs   Hamburg   Lisbon
London   Madrid   Mexico   Milan   Montreal
New Delhi   Oklahoma City   Panama   Paris
San Juan   São Paulo   Singapore
Sydney   Tokyo   Toronto

Library of Congress Cataloging-in-Publication Data

Dickinson, Brian, date.
  Developing quality systems.

  Rev. ed. of: Developing structured systems. c1981.
  Bibliography: p.
  1. System design. I. Dickinson, Brian, date.
Developing structured systems.
QA76.9.S84D53   1988   004.2'1   88-12869
ISBN 0-07-016803-2

1234567890   DOC/DOC   8921098

ISBN 0-07-016803-2

Printed and bound by R. R. Donnelley & Sons Company.

To Mrs. D.[2]

Contents

Acknowledgments

At the time I was preparing the first edition of this book, many of my colleagues were against the idea of methodologies. In fact, even the tools of Structured Analysis, Design, and Information Modeling were still in their infancy. However, as the tools have become increasingly used and refined over the last few years, many of the skeptics have come to realize that the tools do not manage themselves and that a project manager needs a practical frame-work in which to coordinate these new tools and techniques, and their deliverables.

After the first edition went to press, a friend and colleague of mine, Tom DeMarco, initiated an ongoing series of long distance "pro and con" papers which he called "Dueling Methodologies." I was set against a colleague who took a stand against methodologies. The ensuing debates refined my ideas about why methodologies were important and crystallized the concept which I called the "Adaptation Assumption."

I had frequently observed that people in data processing were taking the new tools and techniques that were emerging in the late seventies at face value, assuming that they were ready for immediate use, whereas the developers of the tools and techniques were assuming that users would **adapt** the tools rather than simply **adopt** them as is.

The series of "Dueling Methodologies" debates went on for several weeks and made me realize the significance of these hidden assumptions and that this same issue would arise in many organizations as they came to discover that the tools needed to be adapted and controlled rather than simply "plugged in."

I acknowledge those debates for revealing a major adaptation assumption of my own—that everyone in the industry saw the need for a methodology as self-evident. I found out that this belief was just not true. So I am grateful to the participants, especially Steve Mc-

Menamin, Tom DeMarco, and III, and all those who worked for Yourdon Inc. at the time and were part of the debates.

I would also like to thank the many concerned students who, over the years, have given me feedback about their use of this methodology and their suggestions about additional topics for this edition such as software package selection, information modeling and prototyping.

I would like to thank Gretchen Becker and my colleague, Tony Stubbs, for helping me with this second edition, and proving that any significant deliverable is a process of iteration.

And last but not least, I am grateful to my wife, Kristen, who helped with the revisions and spent many arduous weekends making all second edition text changes.

— *Brian Dickinson*

Preface to Second Edition

Software Quality Via Software Engineering

For the second edition, I have retitled this book "Developing Quality Systems" to reflect the need for a focus on *quality* as the end product.[1] I see quality as inextricably bound up with viewing system development as an engineering discipline.

In the last few years in the data processing industry, there has been a significant interest on the subject of Software Engineering. The new job title of "Software Engineer" has emerged, and office posters on software quality have begun to appear (unfortunately many times without any substance to back them up).

To me, "Software Engineering" implies a new discipline, a new approach to software development that won't allow what I call the "What's a few bugs between friends?" syndrome that I see in so many system development efforts.

What concerns me is that so many organizations seem to revamp their business software each time some new implementation technology arrives (e.g., hardware, system support software) when, in fact, the business hasn't changed at all. For example, in banking we continue to deposit, withdraw, inquire, and transfer funds regardless of the implementation—manual teller, automatic teller machine, home banking, etc.

It seems, however, that when the technology changes, either the existing system is rebuilt or another parallel system is built to accommodate the new technology. This of course causes its own synchronization and redundancy problems for data as well as processing. For the DP community to force this on the business community is ridiculous. This approach would be fine if we intended to

---

[1] The first edition was entitled *Developing Structured Systems*.

build "throwaway" systems with very short payback lives, but today's systems represent large business investments of time, money, and resources.

I believe that today we have the tools and techniques necessary to build engineering-quality zero-defect systems that can last as long as the business that uses the system—not just as long as the hardware or implementation technology lasts. The methodology presented in this book is intended for use by professionals who want to build such systems.

I am constantly amazed when I hear the frequently asked question in my management seminars—"How can we shortcut these new techniques?" If the system you are building is intended to last, then the quality has to be put in as you build it. Attempting to shortcut quality leads to less respect, both internal and external, for the team, and ultimately for the company that produced the poor quality product.

Clearly, an "engineering-quality" approach will lengthen a system's life span, but as an added benefit I believe that when actual testing time is taken into account in the old way of developing systems the

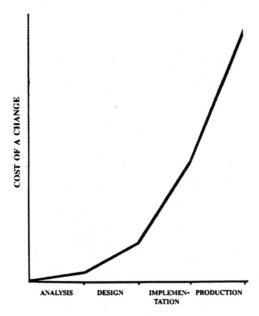

Figure P-1 The cost of error correction during the system life cycle.

new software engineering methods should also shorten the system development lifecycle.

Figure P-1 shows that correcting an omission in the final stages of the development lifecycle (where I see it typically performed) will cost significantly more than correcting it in an earlier stage.

If we acknowledge this, we are drawn to conclude that building quality in from the very first stage of the development lifecycle rather than testing out defects at the end should actually save significant time and money and should deliver a superior product overall.

I think this obvious fact has been relatively ignored by planners of system development efforts. As a result, Users and DP managers are conditioned to correct analysis requirements deficiencies after software construction rather than before. Therefore, DP departments rarely track the cost of removing defects, and the coding phase of the effort is usually expected to be large. If we define quality as "conformance to requirements," then obviously quality must be built into each stage of the development life cycle and not inserted after the fact.[2]

Since writing the first edition of this book, I took some time off and built my own house (I mean actually swinging a hammer and developing muscles). What amazed me during and especially after building this house was the similarity between house building and software building. Having been in DP for nearly twenty years before starting the house building project, I had enough "war stories" from DP projects to use as comparison.

I found that "quality" was required and had to be demonstrated at all stages of the house project. For example, land recording/surveying, ground surveys, architectural drawings, blueprints, structural calculations, heat loss calculations, etc., all had to be externally approved prior to any construction. Moreover, local government staff also inspected every stage of the construction itself. Any aspect of the construction failing to meet the national and local building code standards had to be brought up to code by law. And of course, as each day went by, the cost of making a change (modifying the plumbing, raising the ceilings, etc.) went up dramatically.

If the DP industry continues to deliver haphazardly built software based on poor definitions of requirements and with the high defect

---

[2] *Quality is Free*, Philip Crosby (see Bibliography).

rate that exists and is accepted today, then it is reasonable to expect that some day, as in the building industry, an outside agency will be formed to monitor and evaluate quality for us. Many computer systems have human lives dependent on them, e.g. air traffic control and medical systems, and even banking and insurance systems can put our national financial health at risk. If our profession does not take on the job of monitoring itself adequately, then this task may be performed for us.

I have lived in my house for many years now and have had virtually no maintenance costs even though I have added on to the original house significantly—the opposite of what I see for the software products from the DP industry as a whole.

We are moving towards an age of true software engineering. Software engineering by definition involves having to adjust our emphasis in the development activities of a system. In other professions, a great deal of responsibility and effort is front-end loaded (for example, in building a home, the actual building of walls is a minor undertaking compared with the job of specifying the requirements and design). So should it be in the development of a system— analysis and design should be the main considerations. As you will see in this methodology, that's where my emphasis is placed—on analysis and design deliverables or products.

I hope that the next generation of Software Engineers will read this preface and wonder just what was the problem "back then" that prompted these words.

What Is a Methodology?

I started this preface with my definition of Software Engineering. As the profession brings in new terms such as this, we need to define them before they are misinterpreted and corrupted. Let me now define what the much abused term "methodology" means when used in this book.

A methodology is:

A guideline for the total system development effort; a prototype discipline declaring a network of interdependent managerial, technical, and quality assurance activities and deliverables.

Thus it is a "system to develop systems."

In my consulting assignments with companies using the structured techniques, one question keeps arising: "How do these state-of-the-art techniques fit together?" Another typical question is "What are the managerial and quality assurance activities in a project using structured techniques and where do they fit in?" Such questions arise partly because some of the associations are not obvious, such as that of structured analysis with information/data modeling, but also because each of the structured techniques was developed separately. The methods have never been formally integrated to show how to develop a system.

Now, however, the time has come to formalize the techniques as an integrated approach: the main purpose of this book is to do just that. I have subtitled this book "A Methodology Using Structured Techniques." Many people hear the word "methodology" and immediately think of standards. Unfortunately, standards have a bad name in many organizations. In environments in which systems were produced with no documentation and were developed in an idiosyncratic manner, maintenance became a nightmare and its cost became uncontrollable. So the other extreme of rigid standards with masses of documentation was applied to solve the problem.

This solution, of course, did not solve many problems but instead became a restriction and tended to inhibit creative thinking. I believe we need to strike a balance between these two extremes, and this balance is what I call a "guideline." Therefore, this book presents a practical guideline for system development and not a rigid standard to be used zealously. I use the word "guideline" to imply that you should tailor this development methodology to your particular organization and/or project. However, such tailoring and its reasoning should be documented.

It should be noted that the methodology in this book is meant to do more than merely tie all these modern techniques into one complete guideline. It is also intended to show a practical partitioning of the complete system development process, and, in fact, it presents itself in a partitioned, readable manner.

Finally, I want this book to be a reference for system development and a document to be used to present the system development process to upper-level management, Users, auditors—all those people who are involved in or affected by system development—so they can see what is involved in the system development process. They can relate to the "system to develop systems."

Why Use a Methodology?

Utopian though it sounds, I believe we can reach the day when all computer systems are developed in a similar manner (using the same effective communication tools and techniques) with quality systems as the result. Then I should not hear such comments from my students as "I can't understand the existing documentation," "The Users don't know what they want until they see the finished system," "They kept changing the system requirement, so we froze the spec," "We're too busy keeping the old systems alive to do much new development," and worse, "This project is too big to handle."

We now have the tools and techniques available to us to cure these common data processing ills and to bring us a great deal nearer to a utopian environment. Further, I think there is a need for a methodology to unite all of these technical tools and techniques and to show how to control their managerial interfaces.

If there is no established company method—that is, if there is no standard framework to guide system development—the project manager is probably guiding the development process by using a conglomeration of methods he or she has acquired over the years or "It worked on a little payroll system I once did, so it should work for this missile tracking system." This approach is a hit-and-miss method of developing systems.

On the other hand, having a methodology can help reduce the potential for system failure by avoiding haphazard system development and by achieving consistency between projects, for example, by establishing compatible interfaces and by efficiently reassigning people so that they don't need retraining. One of the advantages in using a methodology is that it provides such standardized development techniques, therefore providing a consistent DP interface between different departments and divisions.

Many large companies already use a methodology to avoid reinventing the wheel for each new project. They either develop their own in-house approach or use one of the proprietary approaches available on the market today, unfortunately many of these classical approaches are out of date using old methods from the Sixties and Seventies. However, many small to medium-sized companies still reinvent the wheel for every new project. I hope that any company or enterprise can use this book as the basis for a consistent approach to system development, adapting it as necessary for their own organizational approach.

A methodology provides a prototype from which to fashion the appropriate set of activities and data for each development effort, thus aiding the system development process by identifying the partitioning, controlling complexity, allowing partitioning of effort, and providing a common frame of reference for activities, data, and people interfaces.

We need to partition the effort and cost of system development if for no other reason than to be able to monitor that effort and cost. To achieve such monitoring, a methodology should be used to produce plans, schedules, and estimates. Since most projects fail because of problems in planning, monitoring, and controlling, correction of these problems is probably the most important reason for having a methodology. As we all are aware, the cost of hardware in data processing is rapidly decreasing, while the cost of software, that is, the cost of personnel who develop software, is rising. Thus, we need to control software costs as the graph in Figure P-2 shows.

We need, then, to make people more efficient. This does not mean that we must train a programmer to code two programs simultaneously with a terminal at each hand. What it does mean is that we must produce quality systems that have cheaper "lifetime" costs,

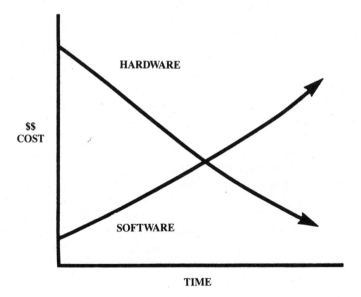

Figure P-2 Hardware/software cost ratio.

including low modification costs. Using a methodology is a way to do so.

I have found in my consulting experiences with methodology issues that many managers look on a methodology as only applicable to a large new system development project, but a methodology should be used even for significant maintenance/modification of existing systems, e.g., if a new requirement is added, then you would want to analyze its requirements in detail (i.e. identify the data needs and their required processing), design any new program modules and determine where they fit into the existing system architecture, code the modifications and test them, etc.

But also wouldn't you want to see how the modifications might affect the User manuals, operations manuals, hardware needs, training of Users staff, regression test library, etc.? In other words, everything that is addressed in this methodology, even the "cycling" concept in this methodology, may be applicable to adding just a single new field to a system. The time slice is just different. For example, on a one week modification, you may spend the first half day doing a preliminary scan of the requirements and design needs and the remainder of the time doing detailed activities from the methodology that are appropriate to your modification request.

Content of a Methodology

Methodologies drive and control projects. Because I have talked about projects, project teams, and project management, I should define "project."

A project is "the total activity of developing a system."

It begins with a formal acknowledgment of business objectives and related problems and ends with a formal acknowledgment that the solution to these objectives and problems has been implemented.

The total project activity declared in this methodology includes identifying User and data processing management approval points of resources required for further development and identifying major quality control points. These approval points help the Users gain knowledge of the system development at different stages as well as aid the communication process between system developers, Users, and data processing management.

All projects, regardless of their size, complexity, or application type, involve similar development activities. These activities and the data they use can be linked to form a standard framework that can support several types of projects (new development, rewrites, maintenance and modification, or software package selection/installation) along with several technologies (centralized or decentralized, batch or on-line systems).

Traditionally, data processing people tend to limit their view of systems to an automated environment. Let me declare here, and have it apply to the rest of the book, that a system is not just a set of automated procedures but a set of manual and/or automated activities that satisfies a business need.

Encompassing both manual and automated activities, this methodology identifies a standard framework that shows:

- Integrated structured techniques for developing a complete system
- All major deliverables, intermediate deliverables, and data flows necessary to produce a system
- All technical activities at a working level that develop and transform the data
- Major quality control points (walkthroughs/reviews)
- All managerial activities in which plans are produced
- User and data processing management approval points (e.g., feasibility approval, hardware/software approval)

It is not my intention to show extreme detail. The specifics of the technical and managerial approaches you use will depend on your organization and on what kind of system—business or scientific—you are developing. It is also not my aim to restate or discuss the ideas of structured analysis, structured design, structured programming, or database modeling, or to convince you of their value. There are many excellent books already available on these subjects (see the Bibliography). However, I will present some of the basic ideas of these techniques in the process descriptions whenever a technique is required.

Who Uses a Methodology?

Although this book is a working guide for everyone involved in the system development effort, from User to programmer, it is really aimed at the managers of this effort, from project managers to upper-level managers. Depending on your managerial level, you could approach this methodology from various perspectives.

Upper-level management should know the major activities and deliverables needed to develop a quality system and to understand the overall effort required. These senior managers most likely want an overview. Furthermore, once a project starts, managers typically get worried when there aren't lines of code to show for the first half of a structured development effort. Without knowledge of the new life cycle, they may think the project is failing and may cancel it. Therefore, upper-level managers themselves need to understand the new development process. I am not saying they need to understand every detail, but they should know what is involved. So a document is needed that allows them to see just an overview. Such a document is a high-level data flow diagram, which is a model of the entire system.

Middle-level managers probably don't want just an overview, but neither do they want to get involved in the details of system development in the way a designer or coder does. Because this methodology's set of data flow diagrams is in levels, middle-level managers can seek out the level of diagram appropriate to their area of concern.

Project managers who guide the development of a system from initiation to installation and who produce the plans and schedules have to see all of the activities and data necessary to produce a working system. Therefore, this entire methodology—data flow diagrams, process descriptions, data dictionary, and appendices—is aimed at them. This book should also be used by analysts, designers, and coders to identify their individual development activities and data and to get an overview of the other data and activities with which they interface.

It is also a good idea for Users (owners of the final system) to have an overview of the development process, so they can be aware of the costs and time involved and the quality of development. Not only do Users need to identify the effects of midstream changes to system requirements, they also need to see the resource commitments required from their area—for example, interview times and review points.

This book is not intended to be a panacea, especially for such problems as company politics, but I do believe that increased communication and better tools for communication, as presented in this methodology, will cure many data processing ills. Also, no matter how good a methodology is for a particular project, there can be no substitute for people with experience, good judgement, and motivation. If a project team has such qualities already, then this methodology should provide a perfect complement.

The Importance of Project Modeling

Over the years, I have read articles on "the User/analyst gap" and even within the DP department, "the analyst/programmer gap" and "the developer/maintainer gap." It doesn't take much investigation to see the need for good communication tools, that is, a means of documentation to aid in both development and maintenance efforts. In the past, documentation has consisted of narrative and reams of forms. I believe that in the future, documentation will consist of paper models, which will serve as replicas of a piece of the real world.

A Model facilitates conceptualization, communication, simulation, and refinement (iteration). These techniques are exactly what are needed to develop, maintain, and modify any significant product. Manual and computer systems are the products of DP projects; a project itself is the product of a management process; both the systems and the project benefit greatly from being modeled on paper before execution.

Creating a model helps us to break down the complexity (size) of any problem to aid our thought processes by allowing us to see the problem in a picture and deal with it in smaller pieces. Because separate parts of the brain deal with logic (words) and ideas (pictures), we gain extra "brainpower" by using pictures, or models, in addition to words to understand and solve a problem. Using models, we may even avoid converting from ideas into logic and back again during the problem-solving process. For example, when people give you directions for how to get to their house, isn't it always better when they give you a hand-drawn map annotated with streets and landmarks?

I am not saying that we can or should get rid of narrative completely in system development documentation, but that we should delegate whatever we can to a model. In fact, this methodology uses a model (a data flow diagram) as its presentation tool and to partition necessary narrative into single-task descriptions.

There are methodology packages on the market that are intended to guide developers of systems, but unfortunately many of them turn out to be paper generators or paint-by-number methodologies. Many classical methodologies neatly divide development into phases and some suggest bulleted tasks within them with vague deliverables but give precious little guidance concerning the technical methods for creating deliverables. They do not provide useful models.

Using such methodologies, developers attempt to create systems by filling in standard forms, and analysis, for example, is declared finished when you have completed the analysis forms. Completed forms may satisfy upper management, but they do not help the actual development effort.

Such documentation is usually solution-oriented (design) with insufficient emphasis placed on problem definition (analysis). Also, the documentation is usually not used for maintenance. Maintenance documentation is an after-the-fact issue consisting of a fresh set of forms to fill in when the system is completed. In addition to such negative aspects, classical methodologies usually also are:

- Shelf stuffers (several three-inch binders seem to be standard)
- Excessively redundant (repetition occurs throughout the methodology because narrative is difficult to partition)
- Excessively wordy (words are the main communication tool)
- Excessively physical (they consist of many forms and a sequential method of developing systems)
- Terribly tedious to read (they are wordy, too lengthy, and unpartitioned)

One of the main reasons for much of the documentation produced in classical methodologies is to protect you if you have to maintain a product or if you have to pick up and continue the development of somebody else's product. My view is that, as far as possible, documentation should be a natural by-product of the work and should be completed as soon as the comparable project stage is done, not after a complete development effort has been finished. Also, documentation should be kept to a minimum. Structured techniques help do this, as the models used in development become the maintenance documentation just as in the building industry the blueprint is a required deliverable and is used for both developing the structure and maintaining it. It's also kept on file by the local government planning department.

Some proprietary methodologies of late even have modern structured techniques included in them. Unfortunately they still suffer from the above problems, only now instead of less excess baggage, there is an extra set of deliverables to create, this time structured deliverables.

I am not saying that all existing methodologies are bad. The creators of some methodologies seem to have made a genuine effort to aid the developer. However, the methodologies can sometimes give you a false sense of security, such as leading you to think that if you've completed the forms, you've completed the system.

Most proprietary methodologies do not encourage the creation of meaningful models of the system being developed. In fact, they tend to view system development as a linear process without any emphasis on iteration, refinement, or, more importantly, asynchronous tasks. The system development activities are viewed merely as "process lumps," namely, analysis, design, programming, and installation, and are usually tracked by phases, or milestones, which are bad tracking tools. Phase deliverables are too large, have long distances between start and finish times, and are not specific in their contents. The end of a phase is usually determined by the money running out or the calendar indicating the phase has finished.

With the advent of Computer Assisted Software Engineering (CASE) tools we are starting to see the laborious aspects of model validation and updating are now easy, and with code generations these up-front models are essential inputs for automated code generation.

"Divide and Conquer" for Project Control

Projects slip gradually and noticeably; you do not suddenly wake up on the morning of the design phase review and realize you are three months late. When you notice a slippage occurring, then is the time to acknowledge and try to make up for it, not after many slippages have cost weeks or perhaps months. Therefore, if we track an individual deliverable instead of, for example, a complete analysis phase, we can make up for time slippage by taking steps such as reallocating resources or scheduling overtime, or at least we'll be able to identify that the project will be late before panic sets in.

Figure P-3 illustrates the problem of measuring by milestones. In this methodology, system development is accomplished by identifying

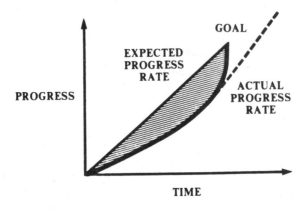

Figure P-3 Measuring by milestones.

definable intermediate deliverables. Each deliverable is defined in advance by the statement of its content, and each is small enough that a reasonable estimate may be figured for its creation. These intermediate deliverables which in total form the system documentation can be tracked. This is development by tracking the flow of data instead of development by major phases, such as analysis and design milestones. In contrast to measuring by milestones as in Figure P-3, tracking intermediate deliverables (inch-pebbles) has advantages, as shown in Figure P-4.

As Figure P-4 illustrates, identifying and tracking intermediate deliverables helps you meet one large goal by meeting many smaller

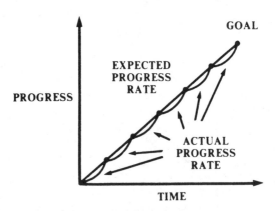

Figure P-4 Measuring by the inch-pebbles (intermediate deliverables).

goals or at least by recognizing that a final goal cannot be met. Tracking smaller deliverables and correcting their possible slippage is also desirable in case a deliverable is not approved during a quality assurance review or walkthrough in a time-critical project in which lack of time preempts correcting the slippage in a later activity. Therefore, the emphasis is on deliverables first, with activities as the way to produce these deliverables. The methodology explicitly recommends iteration and top down decomposition for producing these deliverables.

This methodology also puts the necessary emphasis on problem definition rather than mostly concentrating on the solution to poorly defined problems.

Summary

As a guideline for system development, this methodology is flexible. This flexible approach facilitates introduction of a new method of developing systems into traditional shops because it is not rigid or too detailed. As you become more familiar with this methodology and the tools and techniques it recommends, you may want to add more detail than is shown in this book.

This book, then, is for people who want a formal way of developing a system using modern tools and techniques without wading through volumes of standards and forms. It is also for those who are discontent with existing, inflexible, paint-by-number methodologies, which gather dust and fill up shelves.

Lastly, I want to state that this is a methodology "heavily disguised" as a book. But please don't let it sit on your shelf—it's a working document. If you are controlling a project, then go ahead and use this methodology fully—cut out the data flow diagrams and stick them on your wall as a project control PERT (Project Evaluation and Review Techniques) chart (data flow diagrams are far richer in content). Assign people's names or job titles/grades from your company to the processes. Also place early and late start and end dates, etc., by the processes. Use the result to make project management easier and verifiable.

As a final note, I would like to add that, at the time of going to press, the data flow diagrams, process descriptions, and data dictionary which document this methodology as a structured specification are being entered as a data file for use with a CASE (Computer

Aided Software Engineering) product. This means that the methodology can be customized interactively and quickly using a PC or terminal for any particular environment and project, the project's progress can then be monitored on-line, the project plans shared via a local area network, say, and selected parts of the plan printed out for various levels of audience. This puts a powerful tool in the hands of the project manager, one that marks the coming of age of methodologies for system development.

Introduction

Tools Used to Present the Methodology

Because a project is a system for developing systems, this methodology is presented in the form of a structured specification. It contains a leveled set of data flow diagrams—the main tool of structured analysis—backed up with a data dictionary and process descriptions. I have used the data flow diagram, which models a system by tracking the flow of data through that system, as my modeling and communication device. Because the tools present a system in a top-down, partitioned manner that shows different levels of detail, they can be used for presentation to audiences with various technical backgrounds, from managers to technicians.

I have documented what I believe to be the essential activities needed to develop a system. I have deliberately excluded physical details such as formats for deliverables, but I declare the content of those deliverables and let you format them in any way your company may require. Data flow diagrams and the data dictionary are appropriate logical tools for this methodology; I have supported them with process descriptions of activities. As many of the activities are not at the lowest level of detail (functional primitives), you may wish to develop lower-level descriptions for your particular environment and company standards.

The methodology's data flow diagrams declare the l ogical data and functions necessary to produce a system, but I also indicate some sequence and the political and managerial go/no-go points. The latter make the diagrams somewhat physical and illustrate the flexibility and adaptability of data flow diagrams.

This methodology's contents are partitioned into:

- Data flow diagrams, which compose a graphical model that declares the data and processing on that data, for a system development effort
- A data dictionary, which defines, in one place, all data used in the methodology
- Process descriptions of activities, which are concise specifications, in one place, of all transformations of data

Before we look at the actual methodology, one major concept needs explanation—that of explicit iteration or cycling through the analysis and design activities. This is a means of handling the complexity of a system in partitioned levels of detail. The methodology consists of five primary activities—initiate project, analyze, design, build, and install system—with analysis and design cycled through at different levels of decomposition. The major reason for cycling through analysis and design is to work down to the details after we understand the broad view. The process of cycling through levels of decomposition is called **explicit iteration**. Figure I-1 illustrates this.

Explicit iteration offers many advantages in medium- to large-sized projects. Project estimating, for example, is given great emphasis in projects today but generally seems poorly accomplished. It has always amazed me that we try to estimate the time or effort needed for system development at the beginning of a project, before we know any details of the system. Even a feasibility study will give only a rough idea of what to expect. We are limited to giving an estimate based on the extent of our knowledge of a system, which is

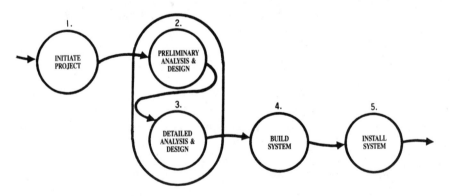

Figure I-1 Cycling through the analysis and design activities.

the Catch-22 of estimating: We can give the best estimate only after we have finished the system and our worst at the beginning. Between these two points, estimates are a shade of grey. So, I believe we should make an incremental commitment to the cost and effort of developing a system. An illustration of incremental commitment is presented in Figure I-2.

Using Figure I-1 as a guide, I believe that "Initiate Project" is where we simply scope out the gross size of the project. By the end of the preliminary study, we should have produced a feasibility report, with an estimate for the cost of the system, which could be off by as much as fifty percent. However, if the preliminary estimate is acceptable, then the detailed study can proceed. This detailed study produces a final proposal and an updated estimate which should be accurate within five percent. Of course, by this time, we should have finished the majority of the structured development effort and should be able to arrive at a precise estimate for the complete system.

I don't actually believe in "estimates" any more. We should have evolved by this point in DP to more accurate techniques such as the Survey/Probe technique described in Appendix F.

You may want to bring in another intermediate level or levels in the development life cycle as in Figure I-2.

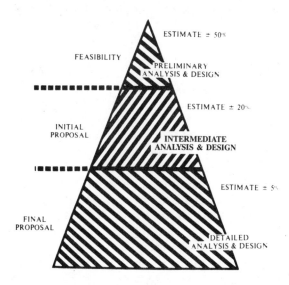

Figure I-2 Cost and effort distribution through analysis and design.

Obviously, the usefulness of cycling to produce accurate estimates will only interest those of you who make use of estimates. Many companies develop systems based on an edict from the boss, or, as a more realistic example, a system has to be built because the government states you must add some functions to your payroll system by next April. In such cases, estimates may be regarded as "funny money" figures.

Cycling through analysis and design, or explicit iteration, diverges from the process-lump idea of unmeasureable "phases" and helps us to build a product by refinement. The human mind is not able to see all the "ins and outs" of a large problem and then come up with the best solution instantaneously, but it is capable of criticizing and improving an inadequate solution. Thus, we need to iterate through a process to refine a product. In fact, refinement is one of the main reasons for cycling; producing good estimates for management and users is secondary.

Note that in practice, you will probably slip into some detailed data gathering while conducting the preliminary study—it is necessary to acknowledge the level of study being conducted in order to allocate time and other resources for accurate metrics.

As a guideline, I have observed the following percentages of effort for each major development activity (excluding system installation, which can vary greatly depending on your environment):

Initiate Project	up to 2%
Preliminary Analysis and Design	about 8%
Detailed Analysis and Design	about 65%
Build System	up to 25%

Temper the above percentages with your knowledge of your system, your staff's expertise, and the newness of hardware and support software in the organization. For example, if you are developing a straight batch system with no frills, a twenty-five percent allocation of effort to build (and test) a system may be too large; but if you are producing a distributed on-line system using a new database management system and a new programming language, you may want to allocate a higher percentage.

Of course, this two-level decomposition cycle may not be suitable for projects of all sizes. If your system is very small, you may want to compress the preliminary and detailed cycles into one. The other extreme may apply where you have a complex system and want to approach its development in many levels. (I have allowed for this customization activity in the methodology, in process reference number 1.2.1.)

The idea of cycling through part of the system development activity is not new. Various methodologies have attempted to show some type of iteration, usually limited to the design activity, and almost all projects have one kind of feasibility study or another, typically involving identifying a possible solution, unfortunately often without real problem analysis.

Cycling through both analysis and design in this top-down manner is important because they are the **paper models** of our system. Analysis consists of identifying the requirements of a system using such tools as data flow diagrams, and design involves developing a solution to those requirements using structure charts or similar documentation. "Model" is an appropriate word to use in describing the deliverables of these two activities, because both data flow diagrams and structure charts are paper models, and are therefore far easier and cheaper to iterate through than program code.

A good analogy to draw here would be that of custom home building since in data processing we are most often concerned with custom system building. The product of analysis and design would be similar to an architect's detail drawing and blueprints of the home. The equivalent of coding would be the construction. It's obviously a lot easier to move pencil walls on blueprints than it is to move constructed walls. Most companies cannot afford the luxury of building programs (or walls) and then checking to see if they accomplish what the user wants. So we must have thoroughly specified the problem and have a solid solution before we actually code programs. This, then, is the main reason for iterating through both analysis and design.

Another reason for iteration, as I have mentioned before, is achieving a more realistic estimate of a system's development time and cost. I do not believe we can give a realistic estimate or cost/benefit analysis after completing only analysis. Certainly, the cost/benefit ratio of a system will depend on the solution we propose in design. It's a poor manager or analyst who would produce a cost/benefit or feasibility study without strongly taking into account conversion, training, hardware and software installation, and system installation, all of which are governed by the design solution. In fact, realistic estimates for management are produced by quantifying sufficiently detailed technical deliverables.

I have stated one technical reason (top-down decomposition) and one managerial reason (estimating) for cycling through analysis and design, but cycling is also advantageous from the point of view of the User or client. Iteration during the development of a system increases the opportunities for communication and feedback from the User, minimizing the possibility of producing an unacceptable system, and building a system in cycles gives the customer a continuous sense of progress, rather than a long development period with no visible signs of progress followed abruptly by full implementation.

The Methodology's Deliverables

I identify two main types of deliverables: **specifications**, which describe a product (they identify what needs to be produced at each step of development); and **plans**, which identify how the development of a product is managed. There is a minimum set of addressable deliverables that applies to all projects regardless of their size, complexity, or type. The following list shows what I believe is that minimum set of addressable deliverables for a project.

Technical Deliverables	Managerial Deliverables
Project Charter	Customized Methodology
	Project Initiation Report
Current Physical Specification	Development Plans
Current Logical Specification	
New Logical Specification	
Bounded New Logical Specification	
New Physical Specification	
Hardware/Software Specification	
Data Specification	
	Implementation Plans
Operations Manual	Feasibility Report
Procedures Manual	
	Final Proposal
System Installation Specification	
Hardware/Software Installation Specification	
Conversion Specification	
Training Specification	
Test Specification	
Development Libraries	Implementation Reports
Production Libraries	Maintenance Plan
	Project Completion Report

These are defined in detail in the methodology; their composition, in the data dictionary; their purpose, in the process description that produces the deliverable. Notice that these are **addressable** deliverables; all of them may not be produced for every project, but they all should at least be addressed, that is, referenced, for their applicability (for example, the Hardware/Software Installation Specification may not be produced if an objective of the project is to use only existing hardware/software).

If you are familiar with DeMarco's book on structured analysis, you will notice that I have partitioned the analysis deliverables in a similar manner.[1] The obvious difference is what I call the Bounded New Logical Specification, which DeMarco calls the New Physical.

The order of the deliverables suggests the sequence in which they are produced. The block of technical deliverables from Current Physical Specification through Test Specification is cycled through in the methodology at preliminary and detailed levels of decomposition (with the exception of operations and procedures manuals). This means I have shown an explicit iteration in the development of these deliverables. At the completion of the detailed iteration, the system has been completely analyzed and designed.

To further clarify these analysis and design deliverables, Figure I-3 illustrates their progression in part of the system development process. (This progression is defined in more detail in the methodology contents, but let me give a brief description of their development here.)

In Figure I-3, models such as data flow diagrams are used to represent the Current Physical through the New Physical specifications of your system. If we already have documentation that shows the flow of information through the Current Manual and Automated environments and we can verify that these are up to date, then we can probably use them to derive a Current Logical Specification. In other words, we can abstract what the existing system is accomplishing from **how** it is being accomplished today. I believe that most users can validate this logical view with some training in reading the model, as it should be a model of the actual "business" environment. At worst, we may have to annotate this model with some extra

---

[1] T. DeMarco, *Structured Analysis and System Specification.*
(New York: Yourdon Press, 1979), p. 30

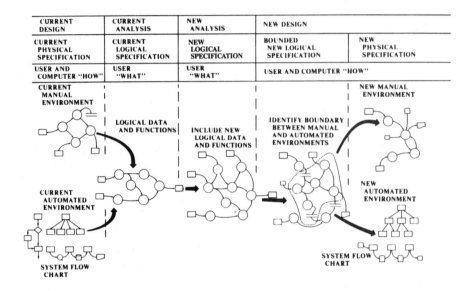

CURRENT DESIGN	CURRENT ANALYSIS	NEW ANALYSIS	NEW DESIGN	
CURRENT PHYSICAL SPECIFICATION	CURRENT LOGICAL SPECIFICATION	NEW LOGICAL SPECIFICATION	BOUNDED NEW LOGICAL SPECIFICATION	NEW PHYSICAL SPECIFICATION
USER AND COMPUTER "HOW"	USER "WHAT"	USER "WHAT"	USER AND COMPUTER "HOW"	

Figure I-3 Progression of deliverables through analysis and design.

physical characteristics to aid verification. This is what I call a "physilogical" model.

This Current Logical model then forms the foundation for incorporating any new functions and/or data to form a New Logical model. (Many of my clients find their most difficult problem to be identifying, confirming, and fitting future needs to an existing environment; yet once a readable logical model of the current environment has been developed, they are suddenly able to suggest a number of improvements.) With this New Logical model, we can now identify how we should partition the whole model of the system into New Manual and New Automated environments without being influenced by the system's current partitioning. In fact, we should identify different options of manual/automated partitioning for the new system. While identifying this partitioning, we will probably also identify the media used for the data flowing between the Manual and Automated environments. The result of this process is a Bounded New Logical Specification, a logical model with the manual/automated boundary indicated.

We are now able to concentrate on "physicalizing" the New Manual area by filling in people, roles, data forms, and other physical environmental details, and "physicalizing" the new automated area by, for example, identifying screen layouts, defining databases, and specifying the control structure for new programs. This control structure will identify "worker" processes from the New Logical Specification, "invented manager" processes to control the worker routines, and additional routines to handle data access and storage. The control structure will be used to identify the partitioning of executable programs that will form the application development libraries and will also help form the system flowchart which will become part of the operations manual. The physical specification of the New Manual area will be used to help form the procedures manual. Finally, for us to be able to produce and track these deliverables, we must have a solid definition of their contents. This is the job of the data dictionary, which is one of the tools used to present this methodology.

The Structure of the Methodology

The set of data flow diagrams contained in this book represents a graphical model of the methodology, or system development life cycle, at different levels of detail (see Figure I-4).

Each complete level of detail forms a network-oriented representation of the system and forms a system model to use in developing systems. All the levels together form a hierarchical set. This system model (i.e., leveled data flow diagram set backed up with a data dictionary and specifications for the detailed-level processes) stops at Level 2. Nothing is significant about Level 2 other than that it forms a good "guideline" for the methodology. Going into further detail would require specifying particular tools to use or types of systems, such as classing a system "scientific" or "on-line," which is too narrow an approach for this methodology.

The number of levels in any data flow diagram will depend on the complexity of the system being represented, how much detail is shown at each level, and to what degree an area needs to be studied and represented. For example, in this methodology's data flow diagram 1.1, Initiate Project, I show the lower-level process Classify Project by Gross Size and Risk. This process is at the level of a functional primitive, that is, a process I would not want to further decompose. However, the process 1.2.1, Select Customized Methodology, is not at what I would call the functional primitive level; it requires further decomposition. Since the nature of the decomposition

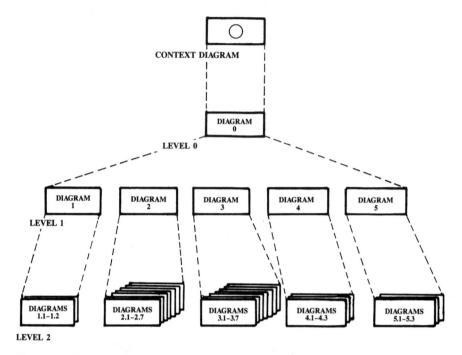

Figure I-4 The methodology's leveled set of data flow diagrams.

will depend on your environment, I have stopped at this level. This example also shows that functional primitives in a system will be reached at different levels of decomposition.

The data flow diagrams in this methodology appear in the following order:

Context diagram   Basically identifies the boundary of the methodology, that is, identifies the area to be studied by the project team as well as indicates the outside interfaces of data

Level 0 diagram   A one-diagram overview of the methodology

Level 1 diagrams   A high-level view of the methodology

Level 2 diagrams   A working-level view of the methodology

The diagrams are followed by the data dictionary, which contains the definitions of the data flows, data stores, and outside interfaces declared on the data flow diagrams. Then, finally, come the process descriptions that pertain to the Level 2 processes. The data dictionary and process descriptions can be used for presenting the detailed levels, if more than the process names on the data flow diagram are required.

While reviewing all of these diagrams, observe the following:

1. The Project Plan guides all processes, but is shown only when its data is created or used, as when the estimated and actual data are used in a progress report. This estimated and actual data should be used by the project manager to constantly monitor the project for slippage in schedules and excessive use of resources.

   I view the Project Plan as a form of agent that performs a process, and agents are not shown on a logical data flow diagram. This plan contains the identification of the estimated resources (time, money, people, and materials) and should be updated with the resources actually used after each process. The actual resources can also be updated by product; for example, the current physical data dictionary took X amount of resources to produce.

2. Only the walkthroughs on a coded program module are shown, although I recommend an informal walkthrough on each deliverable or major portion of a deliverable. Of course, the number of reviews and walkthroughs (and the degree of formality) will depend on the quality level required and on the cost-effectiveness of the system and therefore on the requirements placed on the reviews and walkthroughs themselves. For example, a project that develops a system to track the number of pencils in a company will probably have fewer quality control inspections than a project which develops an air-traffic control system.

3. The methodology's Level 1 diagrams for Activities 2 and 3 appear more cluttered than you can expect for diagrams for your systems. (Don't worry if your physical data flow diagrams are cluttered, only if your logical ones are.) Analysis and design have been deliberately joined at this level in order to em-

phasize, in graphical terms, the paper model cycling. Splitting these diagrams would create cleaner, less cluttered models.

4. The activities in this methodology concentrate on the data for one system. The exceptions to this are the information- modeling activities (producing the data specification) that review the system's data in relation to that of other systems (a data administration group might conduct this review). When reviewing these information- modeling activities, you should take a more global companywide view of the data.

5. Whenever possible, I have separated **what** needs to be accomplished (logical) from **how** it gets accomplished (physical). For example, the Conversion Specification identifies the data conversion requirements, and the Conversion Plan identifies the strategy, schedule, and resources needed to accomplish these requirements. I have carried this separation one step further and differentiated between technical processes (what is required in the development of a system), which I represent by solid circles, and managerial processes (how we control the development of a system), which I show as dashed-line circles.

6. I have tried to "starve" processes of input data flows that are not necessary to produce the output. There will be a number of instances in which extra inputs will aid in a process, such as in a review, when input data that was used to form the product under review would probably be of assistance in clarifying answers to questions. Of course, when using this methodology, you can use any additional applicable data to get the job done. On the other hand, there may be some input data flows shown in the methodology that may not be available in your environment, such as a current operations manual. In this case, the data flow is allowed to be empty, and the processes scheduled without this data.

7. I have deliberately identified very few roles, such as those of analyst, designer, or coder, in this methodology. I class such role identification as additional physical information that is determined by your particular environment. For example, the process for ordering new hardware/software may be performed by a technical support group, a special purchasing agent, or in-

dividuals responsible for each area; the operations manager orders backup equipment, the database administrator orders the database management system, and so on. These and other physical details such as methodology forms, report layouts, and special audit controls should be identified by you for your environment or project; the data dictionary in this methodology will aid you with the contents of any physical company deliverables.

8. As it is expressed by this methodology, my view of system development, presented as data and processes, with an explicit interaction between managerial and technical activities, is only one view. There are others. Depending on the nature of your environment, you may find different ways of applying this methodology that are more appropriate. Your selection or adaptation of these guidelines must be based on your environment and objectives for system development.

1

Data Flow Diagrams

Introduction

The Four Basic Data Flow Diagram Symbols

A directed line represents a flow of information or objects. The arrow indicates the direction of the data flow. The name of the data flow is written through or next to the line.

A circle represents a task or process. It identifies a transformation of input data flows into output data flows. A brief descriptive verb-object name and a reference number for the process is written inside the circle.

DATA STORE

Two parallel lines represent a store of information or objects, irrespective of the storage medium. The store identifies a time delay for its contents. The name of the store is written between the lines.

1

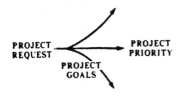

A rectangle represents an area where data originates or terminates from the point of view of the system study. It identifies a boundary of the system study; the identification of the outside interface is written inside the box.

Other Data Flow Diagram Symbols

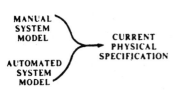

A data flow divergence indicates a distribution of the data flow with no actual transformation of data content or status. The data flow may be distributed in total, or component data flows extracted from the main data flow.

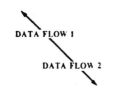

A data flow convergence indicates a collection of data flows that forms a single data flow with no actual transformation of data content or status.

A two-way data flow indicates a two-way flow of data. The data flows are separate and should be viewed as two independent flows of data. This kind of data flow is usually used to indicate that data flowing in produces the data flowing out, but I have violated this rule to reduce the visual complexity of a diagram by using it sometimes for two unrelated data flows.

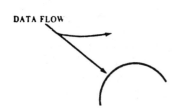

A dangling data flow indicates that a data flow is used in a subsequent process. Data flows "burn up" once they have reached their destination; that is, an item of data is no longer available in the flow once it reaches its destination. So, if it is used again in its present state and is not placed in a store, I have shown it proceeding with a dangling data flow.

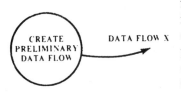

Within Activities 2 and 3 (Preliminary and Detailed cycles), I have not prefixed a data flow name with its level of detail except when it connects with another diagram, in which case I have included the level of detail in parentheses. The process that develops the data flow will contain its level of detail. (Entries in the data dictionary for such data flows are not qualified with their prefix.)

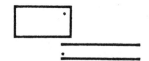

A dashed circle indicates a management process. Because the agent performing a process is never shown on a data flow diagram, I use this to distinguish the processes that are totally managerial from the technical processes. The managerial processes make the methodology diagrams more physical because they tend to be control/sequence oriented, as is the presentation of an activity report to indicate a go/no-go system approval point.

An asterisk indicates that the accompanying item is repeated elsewhere on the same diagram. Items are repeated to improve the readability of a diagram.

In this methodology's data flow diagrams, I have tried to show the actual flow of data. Therefore, where possible, I have avoided using stores because unnecessary data stores hide the true flow, and most stores are unnecessary. Therefore, the stores in the data flow diagrams are mainly used to represent multi-referenced data. For example, within a level of study, the test specification doesn't need to be shown as a store because the data is dynamic, not historical. However, showing the incremental building and use of this specification as a store aids readability.

Unlike other authors of data flow diagrams, I use crossed data flow lines. My explanation for this is that the real world is three-dimensional, but I have only a two-dimensional medium with which to represent my model of the real world.

Process Reference Number Notation

Each diagram and each process on a diagram has a reference number that can be used to navigate through the leveled data flow diagram set. The reference number of a process will point to the diagram that contains the next level of detail for that process; for example, to find the detail of process reference number 3, look at Diagram 3 (Activity 3). All processes on Diagram 3 will be prefixed with 3—3.1, 3.2, 3.3, and so on. The detailed processes of process reference number 3.2 will be numbered 3.2.1, 3.2.2, 3.2.3, and so on, until the functional primitive is reached.

How to Read Data Flow Diagrams

One of the major problems newcomers have with data flow diagrams (DFDs) is that they try to read them as flowcharts, that is, by viewing each process on a diagram as a one-time execution involving a single lump of effort and time. Another problem occurs because novices attempt to apply control and timing to the processes shown on a DFD. These problems are conceptual and are leftover habits from many years of working with flow of control instead of flow of data.

The difficulty in adapting to the iterative way of thinking used for the DFD is that the way to perform any task, even outside of the data processing field, traditionally has been sequential: working until a finished product is obtained and only then going on to the next task. Change does not come easily, but if you stick with the old way of thinking, you are liable to produce increasingly inefficient and costly systems. Analysts no longer can be reluctant to go back and rework; iteration must replace the single-step approach.

In order for newcomers to master DFDs, they must understand how they differ from flowcharts. For simplicity's sake, the distinction is that a data flow diagram shows the flow of data through a system whereas a flowchart is a model of flow of control or sequence of processing in a system. Processes form the basic components of a system, but the way you determine and segregate (or partition) the processes is the important consideration of analysis.

The DFD shows partitioning of a process from the point of view of the data rather than from the point of view of control. Hence, just as a process can be partitioned, data itself can be partitioned and processed in packets, instead of all at one time. In other words, you can perform a partial process on partial input and produce partial output. For example, a person developing a payroll report that must be completed by a deadline can cycle through the columns of a report one by one, to arrive at the finished report piece by piece. Using this partitioning approach, the developer can process an item of payroll data as he or she received it, regardless of where in the report production process the data is received.

You can infer from this that the DFD has a built-in cycling mechanism. This inherent cycling resolves another problem that some newcomers have with the DFD—how to show loops such as GET ANOTHER RECORD and how to show the reprocessing of a task if an error is found. Simple. Pick your finger up off the DFD, move it back to the process you want to reiterate, and put it back down: i.e., the data that "triggered" the system into action just comes back in revised.

You can cycle through a DFD in this way until you have a completed product or have accomplished your goal. In fact, as in our example of a payroll report development, cycling is inherent in the business problem of which the DFD is a model.

The second problem mentioned above, that of trying to apply timing to a DFD, can also be addressed with this data approach. From a logical point of view, data should drive the processes; but from a physical point of view, timing events may drive processes. This is best explained by an analogy, depicted in the figure below. Think of the DFD symbols as a real working environment. For example, a process is an individual's desk. The data flows are IN and OUT trays on the desk, and stores are file cabinets that an individual can access.

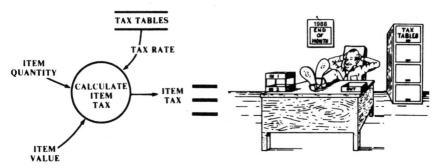

A person sits with feet up on the desk until a piece of data arrives at the IN tray. If a task can be accomplished on this piece of data by itself, then the person will perform it, place the transformed data in the OUT tray, and then put his or her feet (DFDs can be male or female) back on the desk, i.e., the process stops.

It may be that two inputs are needed before a process can take place, as for a match routine, in which case the person remains inactive until both input trays each have at least one piece of data. To extend the analogy to the timing, event-driven, or policy-driven processes mentioned above, imagine that the individual puts data in a file cabinet for later use, rather than in an OUT tray; a timing event-driven process would produce, on request or monthly, a report on this stored data. In this case, the individual may not have an IN tray but just a policy statement requesting that a certain file cabinet be reorganized and reported on at a specific point in time.

To summarize, the most common difficulties experienced by newcomers to the DFD occur because of the change from an explicitly procedural way of thinking and diagramming to a time-independent one. Do not think of the processes within a system as sequential, linked in time by order of execution, each one triggered by data from the previous process in the chain. Instead, imagine a trigger which makes a process start up, the process running until all required outputs are sent to the outside interfaces and all processed data is placed in data stores. At that point, the process can do no more until another trigger starts it up again.

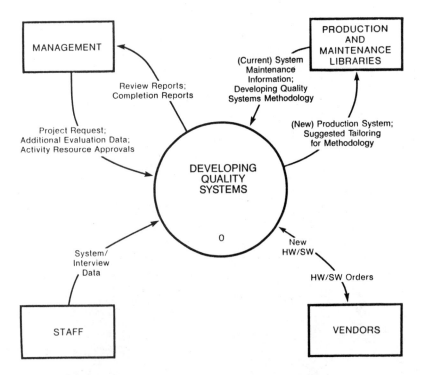

Context diagram.

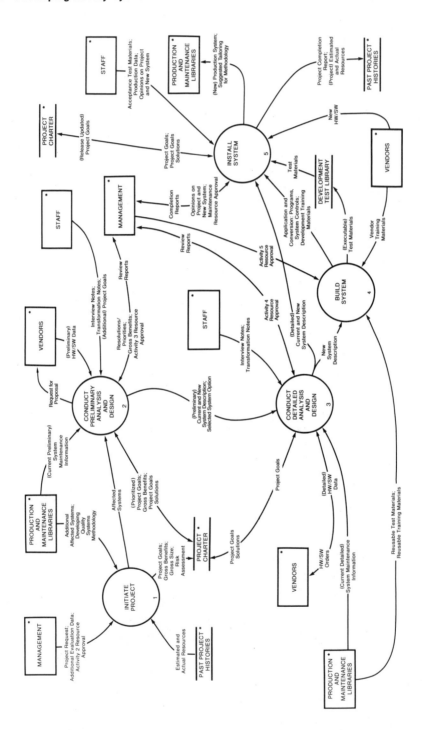

Diagram O   Developing Quality Systems.

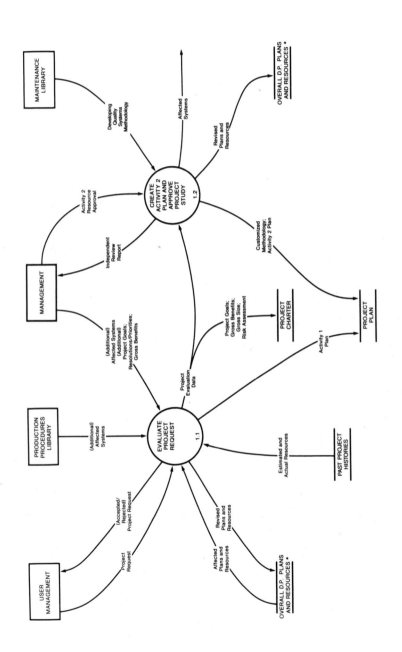

Activity 1 Initiate project.

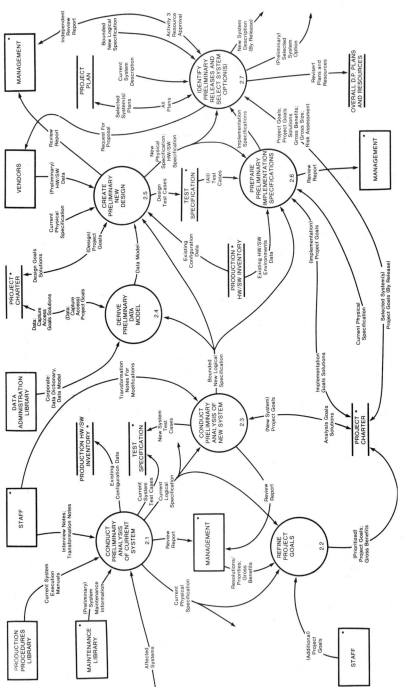

Activity 2 Conduct preliminary analysis and design.

Note: This diagram is complex in its presentation because I have combined two major activities here. The reason for this combination is to show the importance at the higher level of interated through both Analysis and Design begore building the actual coded system.

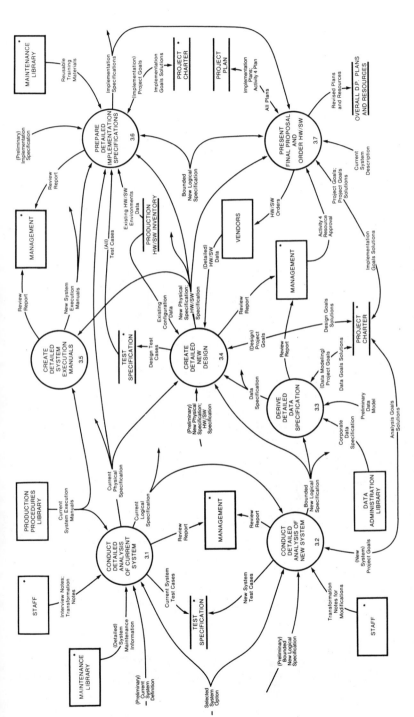

Activity 3   Conduct detailed analysis and design.

Note: This diagram is complex in its presentation because I have combined two major activities here. The reason for this combination is to show the importance at the higher level of interated through both Analysis and Design begore building the actual coded system.

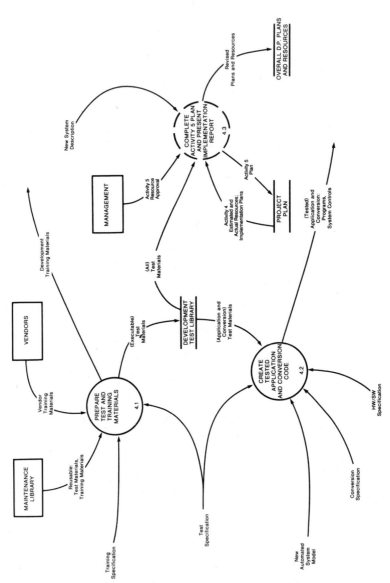

Activity 4   Build system.

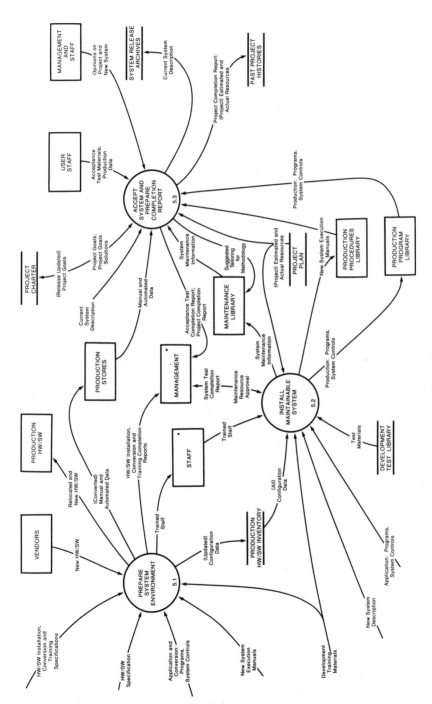

Activity 5   Install system.

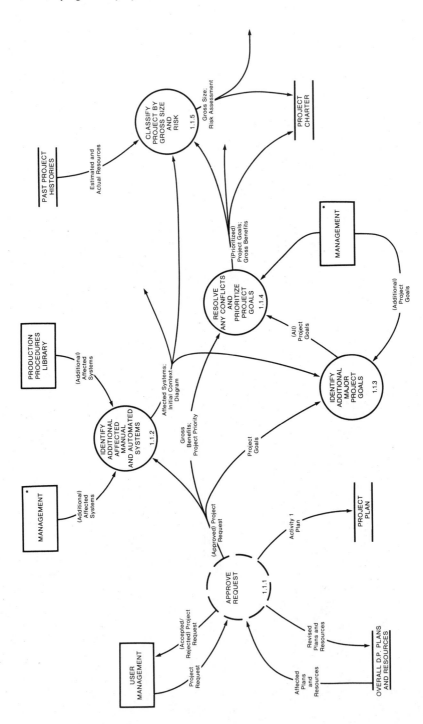

Activity 1.1 Evaluate project request.

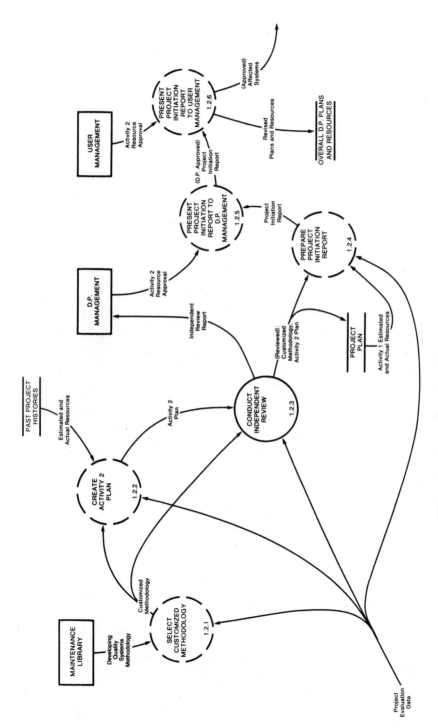

Activity 1.2   Create Activity 2 plan and approve project study.

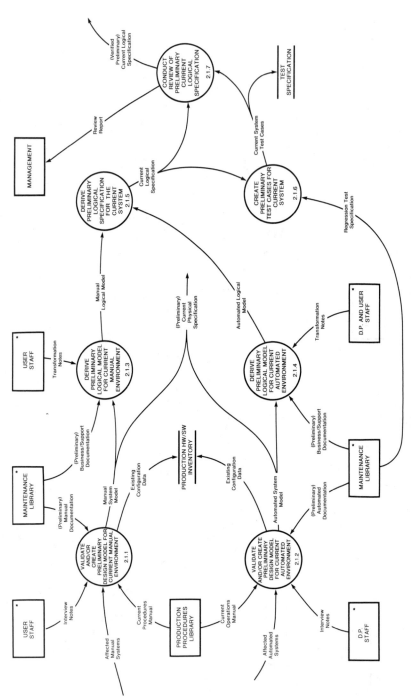

Activity 2.1 Conduct preliminary analysis of current system.

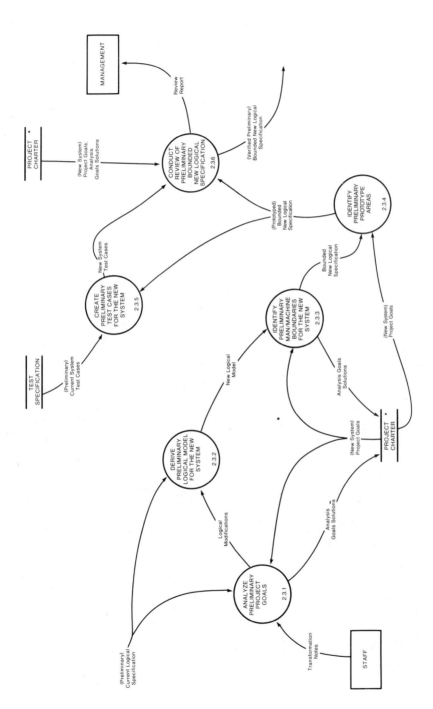

Activity 2.3 Conduct preliminary analysis of new system.

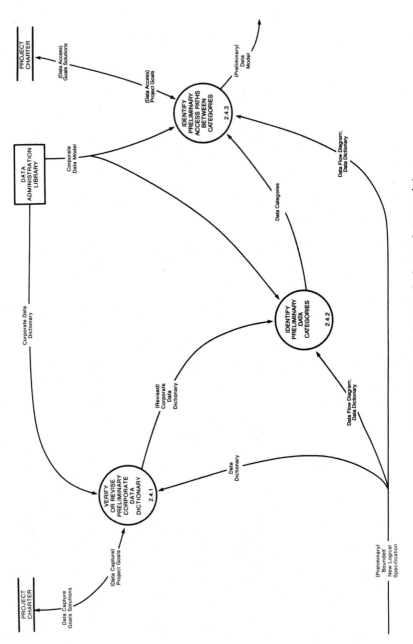

Activity 2.4   Derive preliminary data model.

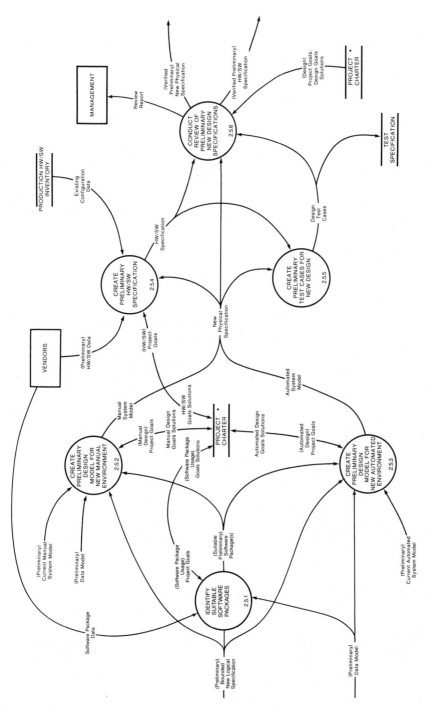

Activity 2.5 Create preliminary new design.

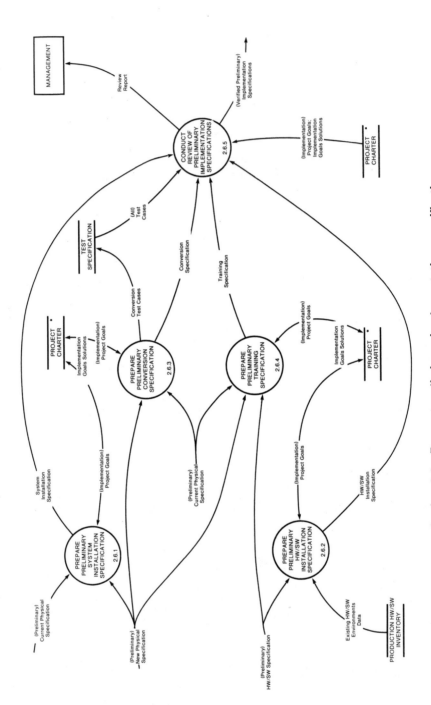

Anchor 2.6   Prepare preliminary implementation specifications.

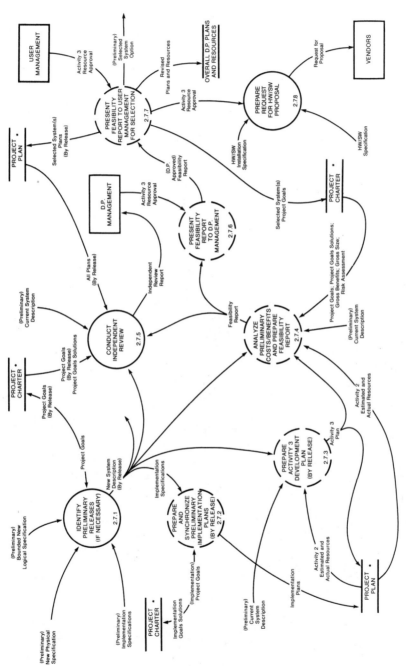

Activity 2.7   Identify preliminary releases and select system option(s).

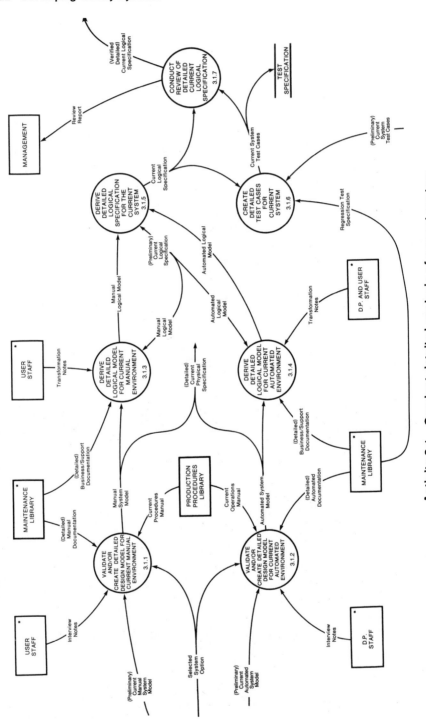

Activity 3.1 Conduct detailed analysis of current system.

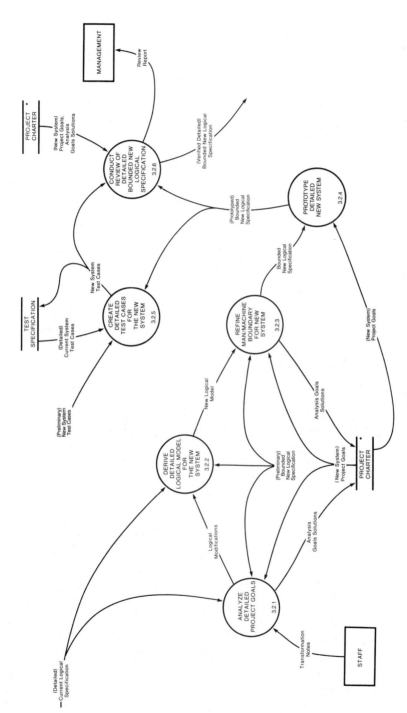

Activity 3.2   Conduct detailed analysis of new system.

Activity 3.3   Derive detailed data specification.

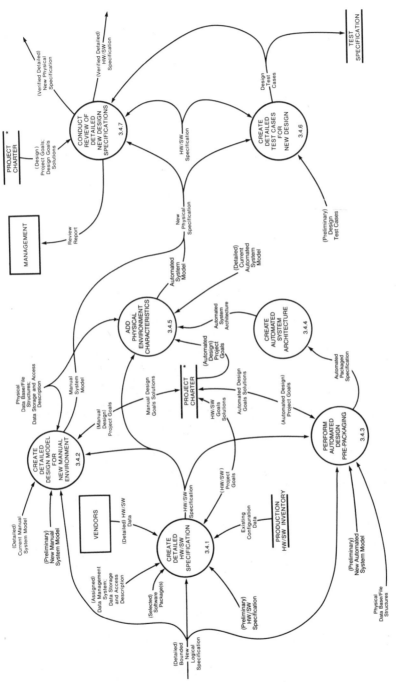

Activity 3.4 Create detailed new design.

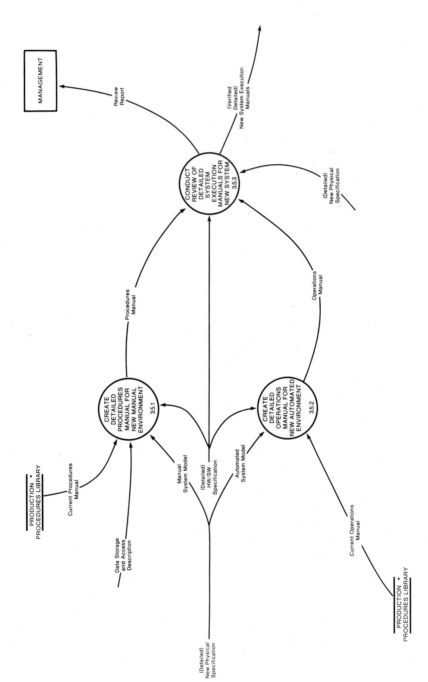

Activity 3.5 Create detailed system execution manuals.

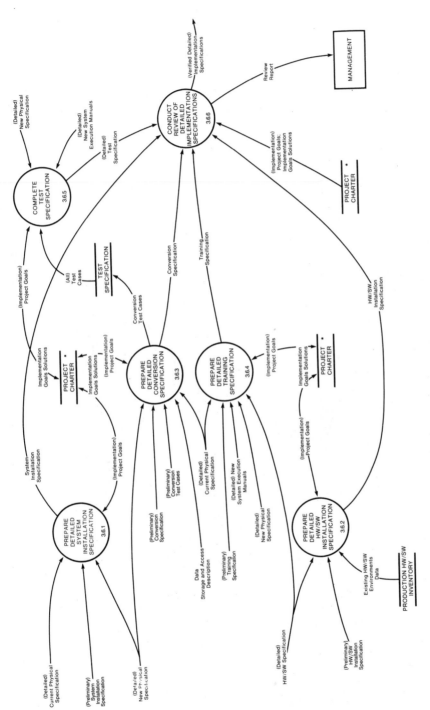

Activity 3.6 Prepare detailed implementation specifications.

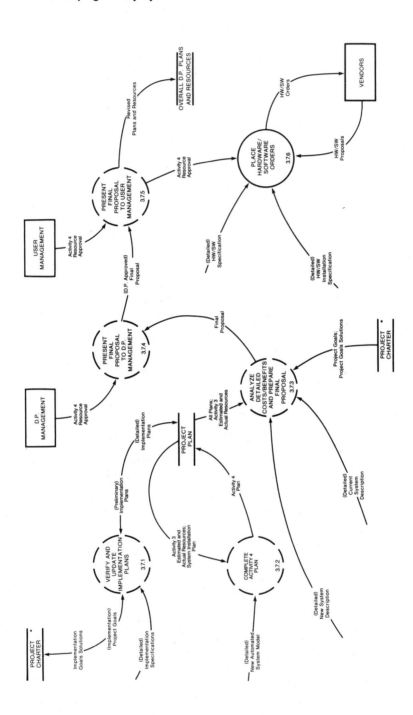

Activity 3.7 Present final proposal and order HW/SW.

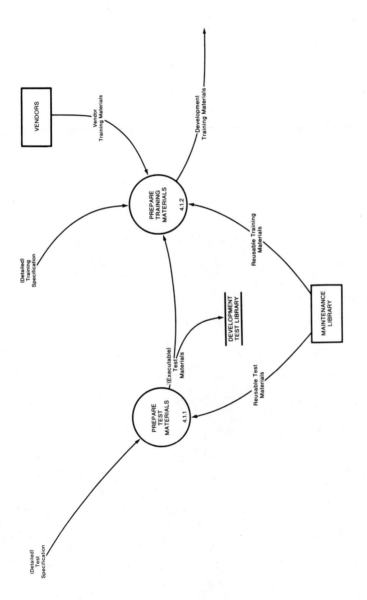

Activity 4.1 Prepare test and training materials.

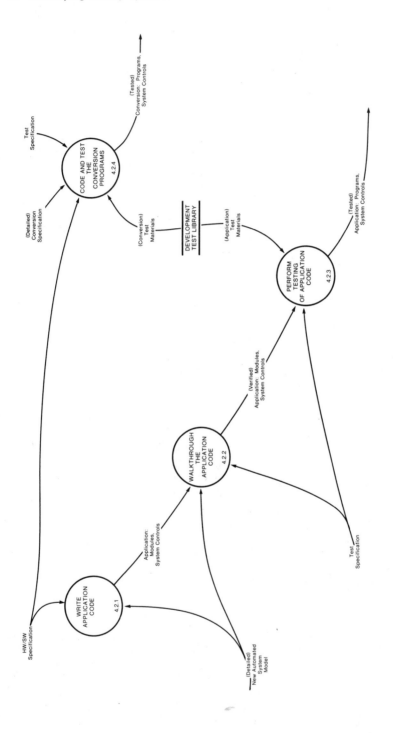

Activity 4.2 Create tested application and conversion code.

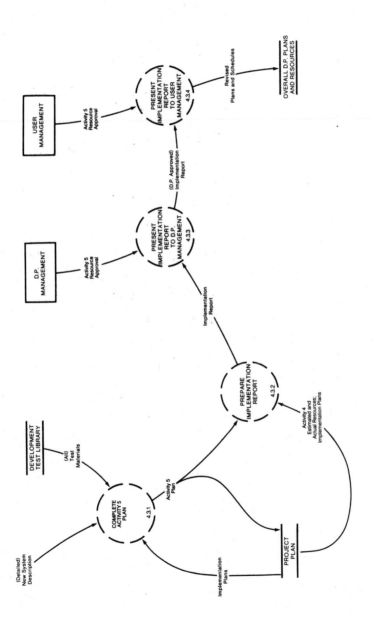

Activity 4.3 Complete Activity 5 plan and present implementation report.

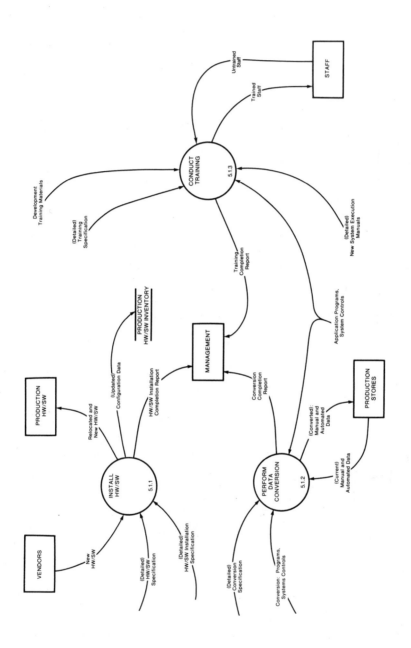

Activity 5.1 Prepare system environment.

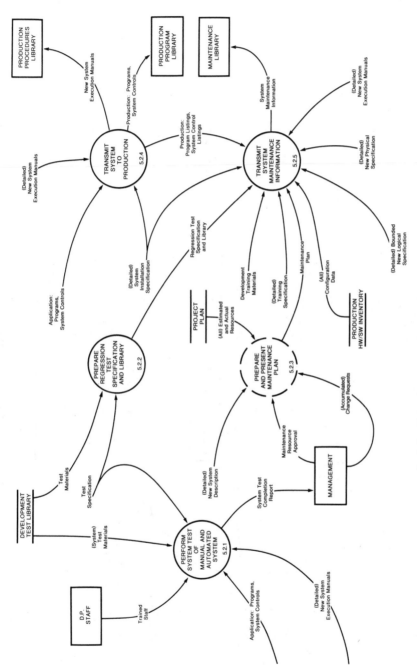

Activity 5.2 Install maintainable system.

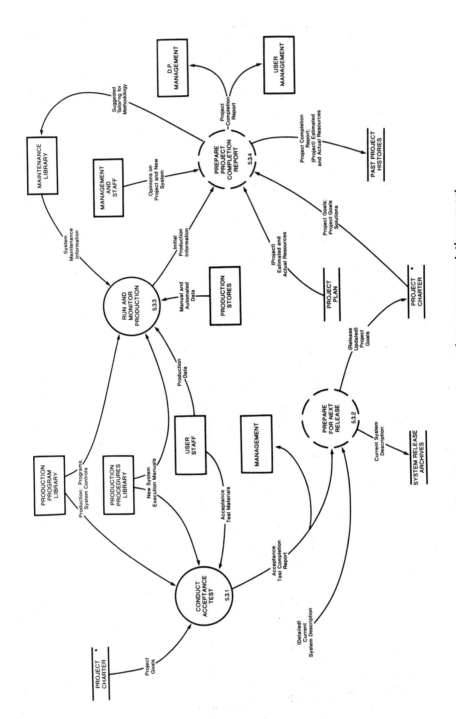

Activity 5.3   Accept system and prepare completion report.

Chapter

2

Data Dictionary

Introduction

The Analysis Data Dictionary is a set of definitions for all the data in a leveled data flow diagram set and is usually the largest part of the structured specification. The data dictionary can also be enlarged to contain definitions for data and control items on design structure charts and can be used further to include the installation's source application code.

If I had developed this methodology's data flow diagrams to a more detailed level than that in Level 2, this dictionary would have been exponentially larger. However, one of my objectives was to make this book as compact as possible, so I have omitted definitions of component data items where I felt the name sufficed, for example, **Requestor's Identification of Project Request**. In your company, the composition of this data item might consist of

Government Request Number or
Department Number or
Name and **Title** and **Department** and **Authorizing Signature**

I have also included comments, occasionally with examples, to aid data item definitions. These are needed as the methodology covers a number of classes of systems. The actual value, and even com-

35

ponents, of a data item may differ depending on the type of system being developed. Using the data dictionary content you can extend the necessary components and formats for your company environment.

When accessing a data flow declared on the data flow diagrams in the data dictionary, observe the following rules:

1. Parenthetic words are adjectives, which are not documented in the data dictionary. Therefore, look up the name without the adjective. (The adjective will be described in or be obvious from the process description that creates and/or uses the data flow.) For example:

   (Additional) Project Goals

2. A semicolon separates data flow names. Each name can be looked up individually. For example:

   Customized Methodology; Activity 2 Plan

3. A colon is used after a word that qualifies all names following it. The names themselves are separated by commas. Look up the name with the qualifying name preceding it (unless the qualifying name is in parentheses). For example:

   Conversion: Programs, System Controls

The following seven symbols are used to document entries in the data dictionary:

= An equal sign means "is defined as" or "is composed of."

+ A plus sign means "and."

[ ] Brackets mean "select one of the items enclosed."

| An "or" bar is used to separate items within brackets.

{ } Braces mean "iteration of" or "occurrences of the item or items enclosed." Where the number of occurrences, upper and lower limits, is known, it can be written next to the braces, for example,1{ITEM}5. Note that where no limits are shown, the notation means "zero to any number of."

( )   Parentheses mean "optional." If more than one item is within the parentheses, the whole set is optional. Note that (A) can also be written as 0{A}1.

* *   Asterisks are used to enclose a comment.

The data dictionary symbols can be combined, as shown in the following examples:

= ([DATA ITEM A | DATA ITEM B])

means "is composed of either DATA ITEM A or
DATA ITEM B or neither."

= DATA ITEM A + ({DATA ITEM B})

means "is composed of DATA ITEM A and
optional occurrences of DATA ITEM B."

A complex definition may employ all of the notation symbols:

SHIPPER RECEIPT =   CUSTOMER NAME +
CUSTOMER ADDRESS +
DATE RECEIVED +
1{DESTINATION NAME +
DESTINATION ADDRESS +
DECLARED VALUE +
(EXCESS VALUATION) +
[COD AMOUNT | DELIVERY FEE]} +
TOTAL CHARGES

The above example reads, "A shipper receipt is composed of a customer name, customer address and date received. Then there is one or more of the following group of data items: Destination Name, Destination Address, Declared Value, Optional Excess Valuation and either a COD Amount or Delivery Fee, and finally, Total Charges."
As you can see, the above narrative definition could be read ambiguously. The more formal version is unambiguous.

Data Dictionary Definitions

A

Acceptance Test Completion Report = * Documents the formal completion of all (or each major deliverable/ activity) of the acceptance testing for the new system.*

= Estimated Support Resources for Acceptance Testing +
Support Resources Actually Used for Acceptance Testing +
(Problems Encountered During Acceptance Testing)

Acceptance Test Material = * The User-supplied, executable information for an acceptance test unit.*

For composition, see "Test Material."

Access Description = Access Method +
Access Requirements

Access Method = * A description of a data access technique, such as sequential, direct, indexed, or a combination of these. For an automated portion of the system, additional multi- record accessing implementation may be identified, such as chains, rings, or inverted lists.*

Access Requirements = * Data usage requirements that affect accessing.*

= Security +
Frequency/Periodicity +
(Access Time Range)

Access Time Range = * The normal-to-maximum access time for a data access path to a record.*

Accessibility Times = * The times of the day that a data processing environment can be accessed, for example, special security hours.*

Activity X Estimated and Actual Resources = * The cost, time, people, and materials estimated and actually used to accomplish a particular activity.*

Activity X Resource Approval = * Approval from appropriate management to use resources for the next major activity. Approval should be in the form of a formal memo.*

Activity 1 Plan = * The plan for accomplishing the project initiation tasks.*

For composition, see "Plan."

Activity 2 Plan = * The plan for accomplishing the preliminary analysis and design tasks.*

For composition, see "Plan."

Activity 3 Plan = * The plan for accomplishing the detailed analysis and design tasks.*

For composition, see "Plan."

Activity 4 Plan = * The plan for accomplishing the tasks in Activity 4 that are not covered by an Implementation Plan.*

For composition, see "Plan."

Activity 5 Plan = * The plan for accomplishing the tasks in Activity 5 that are not covered by an Implementation Plan.*

For composition, see "Plan."

Additional Evaluation Data = Affected Systems + Project Goals + Resolutions/Priorities + Gross Benefits

Affected Automated System = * An automated area that may be affected by the project goals.*

= Affected System Identification + (Affected System Representative)

Affected Manual System = A manual area that may be affected by the project goals.*

= Affected System Identification + (Affected System Representative)

Affected Plans and Resource = * Existing data processing plans and resources that will be affected by this project, such as lower priority projects and available resources.*

Affected System = [Affected Manual System | Affected Automated System]

Analysis Goal Solution = * A project goal solution identified in analysis; that is, a project goal that can be accommodated by a new function/data content, or by a change in function/data content, or by a change to the manual/ automated environment boundary.*

= [Solution Description | Solution Reference Point]

Application Maintenance Contact = * An individual or department to contact for support or maintenance of the automated portion of the system.*

Application Module = * A unit of computer software that is developed in-house to support an application.*

Application Program = * An executable unit of computer software that is developed in-house to support an application. Programs are normally defined as consisting of many modules.

Note: The application program could also be obtained as a vendor package.*

Application System Controls = * The language used to control executable computer software that is developed in-house to support an application for example, Job Control Languages, sort/merge parameters, Program Control Blocks, etc.

Note: The application program could also be obtained as a vendor package.*

Attribute = * A named quality, characteristic or property which describes some aspect of a business entity and takes on a value when associated with a specific entity.*

Attribute Specification   =   Attribute Name +
Attribute Parent Entity +
Attribute Description/Purpose +
Attribute Range of Values +
(Rules for Creation, Deletion and Update) +
(Volume of Occurrences) +
(Attribute Integrity Rules)

Automated Data Dictionary   =   The data dictionary that defines data in the automated environment.*

For composition, see "Physilogical Data Dictionary."

Automated Design Goal Solution   =   * A solution to a project goal relating to the design of the automated environment.*

=   [Solution Description |
Solution Reference Point]

Automated Documentation   =   * The subset of the system maintenance information that applies to the automated portions of the system.*

For composition, see "System Maintenance Information," which acknowledges that what was identified as "new" becomes "current" for a system restudy.

Automated Logical Model   =   * A logical specification of the automated portions of the system.*

=   (Logical Leveled Data Flow Diagram) +
Logical Data Dictionary +
(Logical Process Description)

Automated Packaged Specification = * A specification of the automated system packaged by obvious design boundaries. Can optionally show the implementation technology used for interface data flows/stores between bounded packages.*

Automated Process Description = * The specification of a process in the automated environment.*

= (Process Identification) +
Process Name +
Process Description +
(Frequency/Periodicity of Use) +
Executing Processor Type +
(Pseudocode) +
(Source Language) +
(Process Size/Complexity) +
Cost Per Execution +
(Special Characteristics)

Automated System Architecture = * A model declaring the internal structure for the automated system in terms of modules, subordinate/superordinate relationships, and coupling (data and control). Includes supporting data dictionary and module specifications.*

Automated System Installation Procedures = * The procedures needed to support installation of the new application software.*

Automated System Installation Support = * The support needed for installation of the new system's application software, for example, development libraries, production libraries, utility programs, installation control procedures.*

Automated System Model = * A physical specification of the automated portions of the system. All or part of this information may be supplied by a vendor.*

= (Design Chart) + Automated Data Dictionary + (Automated Process Description) + System Flowchart

B

Backup Environment Description = * A description of alternative hardware and software environments that can be used in case of breakdown of regular hardware and software.*

Bounded New Logical Specification = * Basically a logical specification with an expanded data flow diagram showing the partitioning of the automation and manual areas. Optionally, there can be some physical interface characteristics shown on this man/machine boundary.*

= Logical Leveled Data Flow Diagram + Expanded Data Flow Diagram + Logical Data Dictionary + (Logical Process Descriptions)

Business Constraint = * A business-oriented limitation on the project, such as a budget or a government deadline.*

Business Documenation = * Any literature or publication, such as sales publications or presentation material, that describes the functions of the system.*

Business Objective = * A business reason for the project, i.e., something that will change the logical specification.*

Business/Support Documentation = * The maintenance and support information identifying what is accomplished by the existing system.*

= [Bounded New Logical Specification | New Logical Specification | Business Documentation] + Training Specification + Regression Test Specification

C

Change Request = * A change to the new system (or a release of the new system) that could not reasonably be accommodated during the development activities.*

= Requestor Identification + Change Requested + Reason for Change + Known Impact on Project Goals + Date Requested + Priority of Change

Change Requested = * A description of the required change, which should be in the form of a project goal.*

For composition, see "Project Goal."

Changes Since Last Presentation = * Changes made to goals, data, functions, schedules, and so on, during each major activity.*

**Company Hardware
Environments Chart** = * A diagram showing the different hardware environments (hardware groupings) at the company and how they interface with each other through channels, controllers, modems, switches, card batches, and so on. This is a high-level view of all the hardware configuration charts.*

Completion Reports = HW/SW Installation Completion Report +
Conversion Completion Report +
Training Completion Report +
System Test Completion Report +
Acceptance Test Completion Report +
Project Completion Report

Configuration Data = HW/SW Environments Data +
{HW Specification} +
{SW Specification} +
Expected Future HW/SW Updates

**Conversion
Completion Report** = * Documents the formal completion of all (or each major phase) of the data conversion for the new system.*

= Estimated Resources for Conversion +
Resources Actually Used for Conversion +
(Problems Encountered During Conversion)

**Conversion Data
Dictionary** = * The definitions of all data referenced in the conversion procedures. It is a subset of the data dictionaries of the Current Physical Specification and the New Physical Specification.*

Conversion Objective = * An aim of the data conversion effort, for example, synchronizing the payroll and personnel common data as part of the conversion task. The conversion objective can be requested by the system User or the project manager.*

Conversion Plan = * A description of how to accomplish the data conversion requirements identified in the conversion specification.*

Conversion Procedures = * The procedures required to convert data from the current to the new system, that is, from manual to manual, from manual to automated, from automated to manual, and from automated to automated. For complex or large conversion efforts, the contents of the procedure may consist of a system model (showing data flow and functions) and a design model (showing the implementation of the functions and their data coupling).*

Conversion Program = * An executable unit of computer software that is developed in-house to support the data conversion effort.*

Conversion Specification = {Conversion Objective} + {Conversion Procedures + Conversion Support} + Conversion Data Dictionary

Conversion Support = * The support (except for people support) needed to perform data conversion procedures other that those declared in the conversion data dictionary, for example, tapes, disks, folders, forms, utilities, production and development libraries, etc.*

Conversion System Controls = * The language used to control executable computer software developed in-house to support the data conversion effort.*

Conversion Test Case = * A test case for validating any part of the conversion effort.*

For composition, see "Test Case."

Corporate Data Dictionary = * The set of definitions for company data items and their relationships maintained centrally by the Data Administration group.*

= {Entity Specification} + {Relationship Specification} + {Attribute Specification}

Corporate Data Specification = Corporate Data Dictionary + Corporate Entity-Relationship Diagram + Corporate Logical Access Path Diagram + {Data Management System Option} + Corporate Data Storage and Access Description

Note: At other than the detailed level of study, the corporate data storage and access description is optional.

Corporate Data Storage and Access Description = * The storage and access descriptions for all Data Administration maintained company data.*

For composition, see "Storage Description" and "Access Description."

Corporate Entity Relationship Diagram = * A data model for the Data Administration maintained company data.*

See definition of "Entity Relationship Diagram."

Corporate Information Model = * The information model that supports the stored data needs of the whole corporation. I use the information model as a synonym for Entity-Relationship Diagram.*

See definition of "Entity Relationship Diagram."

Corporate Information Specification = * The Information Specification for the whole corporation, identifying all stored data needs.*

For composition, see "Information Specification."

Corporate Logical Access Path Diagram = * The Logical Access Path Diagram showing all entities and their access paths currently supported. This may be documented in one model or many Logical Access Path Diagrams—one for each business event currently supported.*

Cross Reference to Current Physical Definition = * A cross reference (pointer) to the original data and physical characteristics from which an item of data was derived, for example, Current Physical: data flow name(s), data store name(s).*

Cross Reference to Current Physical Process(es) = * A cross reference (pointer) to the original process or processes from which a function was derived, such as, Current Physical process reference number and/or hardware/software identification.*

Current Logical Specification = * A logical specification of the current system Specification as a whole without delineation of manual and automated areas.*

= Logical Leveled Data Flow Diagram + Logical Data Dictionary + {Logical Process Description}

Current Operations Manual = * Existing operations documentation describing how to operate the automated portions of the system.*

For expected composition, see "Operations Manual."

Current Physical Specification = * A specification of the current system (manual and automated) showing the design used to implement it.*

= Manual System Model + Automated System Model

Current Procedures Manual = * Existing User documentation describing how to use the manual and automated portions of the system.*

For expected composition, see "Procedures Manual."

Current System Description = Current Physical Specification + Current Logical Specification + Current System Execution Manuals

Current System Execution Manuals = Current Procedures Manual + Current Operations Manual

Current System Test Case = * A test case for a function or a piece of data in the Current Logical Specification.*

For composition, see "Test Case."

Customized Methodology = * This methodology, tailored to fit a particular project.*

D

Data Administration Library = * A merged, centralized source of the supported corporate data resources.*

Data Administration Management = * The head of the database group, usually known as the DBA (Data Base Administrator).*

Data Administration Staff = * The people responsible for modeling the company's data.*

Data Capture Goal Solution = * A solution to a project goal relating to the gathering of data that will be inserted into the corporate data dictionary.*

= [Solution Description | Solution Reference Point]

Data Category = * A high-level grouping of data to support a business function, for example, employee information to support the personnel functions.*

Also known as a "Candidate Object."

Data Dictionary = * A set of definitions for all data items declared on a data flow diagram. It will also contain definitions for data and control items on a structure chart and in application code.*

= {Data Flow} + {Data Element} + {Data Store} + ({Outside Interface})

Data Element = * An indivisible data flow. Also known as a "Data Primitive."

= Data Element Name + Data Element Description

Data Element Description = * Described by a comment or by the values or range of values that it takes on.*

Data Element Integrity = * A dependency placed on a data element, for example, "order total" in "order object" is equal to the sum of the "part amounts" in the "part objects".*

Data Element Physical Characteristics = (Physical Data Element Identification) +
Data Format +
Data Representation +
List/Range of Values +
(Special Characteristics)

Data Flow = * A pipeline of information between processes, data stores, or outside interfaces. A piece of information is no longer available in the pipeline once it reaches its destination.*

= Data Flow Name +
Data Flow Description

Data Flow Description = * A data flow can be made up of other data flows and/or data elements. Therefore, a description may point to these or may describe the data flow in comment form or by the values that it takes on.*

Data Flow Diagram = * A modeling tool used to represent a system (automated, manual, or mixed). Four components (data flow, process, data store, and outside interface) are represented graphically to model the system and to show its partitioning.*

Data Flow Physical Characteristics = (Physical Data Flow Identification) +
(Sample/Layout) +
Media +
Data Flow Volume +
Frequency/Periodicity of Use +
(Security) +
(Special Characteristics)

Data Format = * The makeup of a data element,
such as six characters, numeric with
two decimal places, twenty characters alphanumeric.*

Data Goal Solution = * A project goal solution identified in
data modeling.*

= [Data Capture Goal Solution |
Data Interface Goal Solution |
Data Management Goal Solution |
Data Usage Goal Solution]

Data Interface Goal = * A solution to a project goal relating
to Solutiondata interface between
systems.*

= [Solution Description |
Solution Reference Point]

Data Management Goal Solution = * A solution to a project goal relating
to the compatibility or use of data
management systems.*

= [Solution Description |
Solution Reference Point]

Data Management System = * A set of programs (manual or automated) used to store, access, and support data. For example, in an automated portion of a system, IBM's Information Management System with fast path feature using Data Language/1; in a manual portion of a system, procedures required to use an index-card system referencing tub files.*

Data Management System Options = * The existing data management systems in use at the company, or the compatible systems not currently in use at the company.*

Data Model = * A graphical model representing stored data needs. It shows simple objects as boxes and the access paths between them as directed lines.

Also known as "Data Structure/ Access Path Diagram/Schema".*

Data Organization = * A description of the physical organization of stored data, for example, consecutive, random, or parallel (consecutive and random) organization.*

Data Preparation/ Distribution Schedule = * The schedule of times for data preparation and distribution in both the manual and automated portions of the system.*

Data Representation = * The way in which the data is encoded, for example, EBCDIC, ASCII.*

Data Specification = Information Specification +
Data Management System +
(Data Storage and Access Description)

Note: At levels of study other than
detailed, the data storage and access
description is optional.

Data Storage and = * The data storage and access descrip-
Access Description tion for the system's permanent data.
It is a physical view of the data and
its support.*

= {Storage Description} +
{Access Description}

Data Store = * A resting place or reference place
for data flows. It can physically take
the form of a tape file, index-card file,
folder, database, etc.*

= Data Store Name +
Data Store Description

Data Store = * A data store described in terms of
Description the data flows/records that compose
it or by a data model.*

Data Store Physical = (Physical Store Identification) +
Characteristics Sample/Layout +
Storage Description +
Access Description +
(Special Characteristics)

Data Usage Goal = * A solution to a project goal relating
Solution to data usage, for example, a solution
to security requirements, response
time needs, or volume needs.*

= [Solution Description |
Solution Reference Point]

Dependency Network = * A schematic showing the order in which tasks must be performed based on the flow of data, for example, a data flow diagram from the customized methodology.*

Design Chart = * A model that illustrates the partitioning, architecture/structure, and communication of an automated portion of the system. It can be represented by a system flowchart (for high-level view), structure chart, Jackson, Warnier-Orr diagram, or, in the current environment, Hierarchical Input Process Output and Volume Table of Contents program hierarchy.*

Design Goal Solution = [Manual Design Goal Solution | Automated Design Goal Solution | HW/SW Goal Solution]

Design Test Case = * A test case for validating part of the system solution (design).*

For composition, see "Test Case."

Developing Quality Systems Methodology = * This book or company-tailored version of this book.*

Development Support Groups Used = * The support outside the project team available for the system, for example, the database group, technical support group, training group, etc.*

Development Support Systems = * System development aids, such as automated software tools, system support packages, etc.*

Development Test Library = * A repository of executable test material for the new system.*

= {Test Material}

Development Training Materials = * Executable materials used in the training effort for the new system. The contents of the materials will vary depending on the type of system and training effort but will consist of such things as brochures, handouts, courses, lectures, presentations, audio/visual tapes, computer-based training, test materials for testing.*

DP Management = * The managers who control and approve the data processing resources.*

= [Application Systems Management | Systems Programming Management] + Data Administration Management + (Operations Management) + (Quality Control Management) + (Data Processing Audit Management) + (Training Management)

DP Staff = * The data processing support staff for manual and/or automated systems.*

= Maintenance Staff + Data Administration Staff + Operations Staff + (Training Staff) + (Support Planning Staff)

E

Electrical Support = * A description of the electrical support for the hardware environment, (e.g. power supply, telephone circuits).*

Entity = * A significant business object such as class, employee, or customer about which the system must hold data.*

Entity-Relationship Diagram = * A normalized, decomposed model showing the entities and relationships between them that are important to the enterprise (it shows entities as boxes and relationships as directed lines or plain lines and diamonds).*

Entity Specification = Entity Name +
Entity Description/Purpose +
Entity Primary Key +
Rules for Creation, Deletion and Update +
Volume of Occurrences +
Entity Integrity Rules +
{Attribute}

Entity Business Function = * A description of why an entity exists, i.e., what the function of the entity is. For instance, for a department entity, department is a subdivision of the company that accomplishes a unit of work.*

Entity Data Integrity Rules = * Constraints placed on the data about an entity, for example, between employee and department objects, each employee is assigned to only one department.*

Entity Primary Key = * The data attribute (or combination of attributes) that is used to uniquely identify an occurrence of an entity from all others, for example, department number to identify a department.*

Entity Secondary Key = * A data attribute (other than the entity's primary key data attribute) that can be used to identify an entity occurrence, such as social security number instead of employee number to identify or retrieve the data about the employee.*

Entity Special Rules = * Any special rules governing an entity, for example, that an employee may be full or part-time but not an outside consultant.*

Environment Characteristics = * Information concerning the area in which the system study and installation were conducted.*

= Environment Type +
Extent of User Involvement +
Development Support Groups Used +
(Special Characteristics)

Environment Conditions = * A specification of the current or required environment conditions (temperature, humidity, ventilation, etc.).*

Environment Costs Per Year = * An estimate of the cost for support of a hardware/software environment (if required for a cost/benefit evaluation).*

Environment Support Staff = * A description of the support staff needed for an environment housing data processing hardware and software, such as security staff or total operations staff.*

Environment Type = * The area in which the system study and installation were conducted, such as the local main office, statewide divisions, nationwide divisions, worldwide divisions.*

Estimated and Actual Resources = * The cost, time, people, and materials estimated and actually used to accomplish each activity of system development and installation.*

Executing Processor Type = * A description of an existing configuration used to support manual and/or automated production systems.*

For composition, see "Configuration Data."

Existing HW/SW Environments Data = * Description of the environments throughout the company that house hardware/software for support of manual or automated systems.*

For composition, see "HW/SW Environments Data"

Expanded Data Flow Diagram = * A composite data flow diagram produced from a complete level of a set of diagrams. The level is one on which the man/machine boundary can be drawn without cutting through a process.*

Expected Future = * Describes the future changes to a
HW/SW Updates configuration, such as phasing out
old equipment, upgrading existing
equipment, waiting for equipment on
order, enlarging a hardware environment, etc.*

Extensibility Space = * A description of the room for expan-
sion in a data processing environ-
ment.*

Extent of User = * The level of support to which the
Involvement User commits during development
and installation of a system such as
having User staff on the project
team, allowing time for data-gathering interviews, etc.*

F

Feasibility Report = * Documented progress of the project, providing an overview of the system documentation and the resources required for the next major activity.*

= Estimated Resources for This Activity +
Actual Resources Used During This Activity +
(System Option Identification +
Summary of Project Goals +
Summary of Project Goals Solutions +
Overview of System Documentation +
Changes Since Last Presentation +
Cost/Benefit Analysis +
System Limitations +
Risk Assessment +
Estimated Resources for Next Activity +
Estimated Resources for Future Activities) +
Issues That May Affect Further Development

Final Proposal = For comments and composition, see "Feasibility Report."

Frequency/ Periodicity of Use = * A description of how often and when a piece of data or a process is used.*

G

Goal Priority = * The priority or importance placed on a project goal in relation to other goals.*

Gross Benefit = * The advantages gained by meeting a project goal; for instance, savings of up to X dollars in maintenance costs could be attained, or customer service will exceed that of the competitors, thereby attracting more customers.*

Gross Size = * The classification of the whole project by size: small, medium, or large.*

Growth Space = * A description of the stored data overflow organization: in the automated part of the system — chained overflow space, distributed free space, or cellular splitting; in the manual portion — an extra storage file, organized in sequential order.*

H

HW Compatibility = * The identification of the types of hardware that can be connected to an identified piece of hardware.*

HW Configuration Chart = * A diagram, for one environment, showing individual hardware components and how these components interface with each other using channels, controllers, modem switches, storage devices, and so on.*

HW Description   =   * A description of processors, peripherals, data preparation, and distribution equipment, teleprocessing lines as well as microfilm or microfiche equipment, measurement and communication equipment, etc.*

=   Hardware Vendor +
Hardware Model/Identification +
(HW Function) +
(Storage Capacity) +
Volume Throughput +
Data Representation Requirements +
(Hardware Connections) +
(Special Characteristics)

HW Function   =   * A description of the function that a piece of hardware performs, for example, that a communication line transmits business data between the main office and all branches. Performance can also be included, e.g., a requirement that a main processor provides a three second response time during peak periods.*

HW General Availability   =   * The number of hours or times a piece of hardware is available for general use.*

HW Specification   =   HW Description +
(HW Compatibility Requirements) +
HW Status +
HW General Availability +
Trained Operations Staff for This Hardware +
Vendor Support Availability +
(Hardware Cost) +
Hardware Support Costs Per Year

HW Status = * An indication of whether a piece of hardware is already installed and being used by other projects, already installed and being used by the current system, or is new hardware (indicate installed or on order).*

HW Support Materials = * Materials needed to support the new system hardware. This material is identified as support for installation of hardware but can be used for on-going support. Examples of hardware support materials are tapes, disks, printer ribbons, folders and cabinets, office furniture for operations, vendor support documentation, hardware cleaning equipment, moving equipment. (Support material is not already identified in the HW/SW specification.)*

HW Support Procedures = * Procedures needed to support the installation of the new system hardware, for example, arrangements for moving hardware, vendor hardware installation procedures, store and media identification, hardware testing procedures.*

HW/SW Data = *Informal documentation of hardware and software which a vendor can supply. This documentation is least specific at the preliminary level and most specific at the detailed level; for example, a range of vendor products at preliminary level versus specific documentation of a particular product at the detailed level.*

For possible composition, see "HW Specification" and "SW Specification."

HW/SW Environment Description = Environment Identification +
Site Description +
(Environment Support Staff) +
Backup Environment Description +
(Environment Costs per Year)

HW/SW Environments Data = Company Hardware Environments Chart +
{HW/SW Environment Description +
HW Configuration Chart}

HW/SW Goal Solution = * A solution to a project goal relating to the hardware and support software used for the new system.*

= [Solution Description |
Solution Reference Point]

HW/SW Installation Completion Report = * Documents the formal completion of the installation of all (or each major phase) of the hardware/ software for the new system.*

HW/SW Installation Objective = * An aim of the hardware/software installation effort requested by the system User or the project manager; for instance, that hardware/software must be installed before the training effort begins so actual hardware/software can be used for training.*

HW/SW Installation Plan = * A description of how to accomplish the hardware and software installation defined in the "HW/SW Installation Specification."*

For composition, see "Plan."

HW/SW Installation Specification = {HW/SW Installation Objective} + {HW/SW Environment Description + HW Configuration Chart} + {HW Support Procedures + HW Support Materials} + {SW Support Procedures + SW Support Materials}

HW/SW Maintenance Contact = * Name of and how to contact the representative for maintenance of the system hardware or support software.*

HW/SW Orders = * A formal request for the purchase or lease of hardware and/or software (support software or software package).*

HW/SW Proposal = * Formal proposal to supply the new system's hardware and/or software needs (support software or software package).*

HW/SW Specification = * A specification of all the hardware and support software, including software package information, needed to support the new system. This can be made up of existing or new hardware and software.*

= {HW Specification} + {SW Specification} + Hardware/Software Data from Vendors

I

Implementation Goal = * A solution to a project goal relating to conversion, training, hardware/software, and system installation or testing.*

= [Solution Description | Solution Reference Point]

Implementation Language = * The software language used to implement the system.*

Implementation Plans = System Installation Plan + HW/SW Installation Plan + Conversion Plan + Training Plan + Test Plan

Implementation Report = * Documents the progress of the project and the resources required for the next major activity.*

= Estimated Resources for Activity 4 + Resources Actually Used During Activity 4 + Changes Since Last Presentation + (Initial Test Results) + Estimated Data Processing Resources for Activity 5 + Estimated User Resources for Activity 5 + Issues That May Affect Further Development

**Implementation
Specifications** = System Installation Specifications +
HW/SW Installation Specification +
Conversion Specification +
Training Specification +
Test Specification

**Independent
Review Report** = * The documentation of the results of
an independent review.*

For composition, see "Review Report."

**Information
Specification** = Entity-Relationship Diagram +
{Entity Specification} +
{Relationship Specification} +
{Attribute Specification}

**Initial Context
Diagram** = * Basically identifies the boundary of
the system by declaring the external
areas that supply or receive system
data.*

**Initial Production
Information** = * A summary of monitored production information.*

= {Production Factor Identification + .
{Production Factor Problem} +
Production Factor Summary +
Production Factor Usage Pattern}

Interview Note = * The information-gathering documentation for the existing system. This
can be in the form of a data flow
diagram, design chart, graph,
decision table or tree, structured
English, narrative, report layout,
record layout, etc.*

J

**Job
Backup/Recovery** = * The backup procedures with supporting materials and procedures necessary to restart a job or job step from a system abend (including disaster recovery procedures).*

Job Environment = * The support environment for an executable unit in the automated system, for example, hardware needs, support software needs, backup environment options, etc.*

**Job Schedules/
Procedures** = * The run instructions for an executable unit in the automated system, for example, run times, operating instructions, system parameter updates, system action messages, etc.*

Job Security = * The security requirements for each job/job step in the automated system, for example, that special tape files should be kept in the safe when not in use or that printed output be seen only by security-cleared personnel.*

**Job/Job Step
Description** = * An overview description of an executable unit in the automated system.*

K

No Entry

L

Logical Access Path Diagram = * A graphical model showing the access paths between logical data groups *

Logical Data Dictionary = * A set of definitions for all data items declared on a logical data flow diagram.*

= {Logical Data Flow} +
{Logical Data Element} +
(Data Model) +
({Logical Data Store}) +
({Outside Interface})

Logical Data Element = * A data element with its physical characteristics removed. Also see "Attribute."*

= Data Element +
Cross Reference to Current Physical Definition

Logical Data Flow = * A data flow with physical characteristics removed.*

= Data Flow +
Cross Reference to Current Physical Definition

Logical Leveled Data Flow Diagram = * A leveled set of data flow diagrams that form a model of a system (manual, automated, or both). This model describes what the system is doing without regard to how it does it (that is, without physical characteristics or control).*

For comment, see "Data Flow Diagram."

Logical Modification = * An addition, change, or deletion of a current function and/or data content (including a complete new function and data). The modification is represented in logical form, for example, logical data flow diagram, decision table or tree, etc.*

= Identification of Modification + {Data Flow Diagram Change} + {Data Dictionary Change} + {Process Description Change}

Logical Process Description = * The specification of a process or function which is declared on a logical data flow diagram, with physical references and control removed.*

= Process Description + Cross Reference to Current Physical Process(es)

M

Maintenance Contact = * The identification of an individual or department to contact for maintaining or modifying the manual or automated portions of the system.*

Maintenance Library = * The library containing the system maintenance information for the manual and automated portions of systems.*

Maintenance Plan = * The plan for accomplishing any identified changes and for generally supporting the new system.*

For composition, see "Plan."

Maintenance Resource Approval = * The approval from appropriate management for the use of resources for maintenance. Approval should be in the form of a formal memo.*

Major HW/SW Used = * The major configuration used to support the system, for example, large-scale processor, minicomputers, microcomputers, etc. *

Management = User Management + Data Processing Management

Manual Design Goal Solution = * A solution to a project goal relating to the design of the manual environment.*

= [Solution Description | Solution Reference Point]

Manual Documentation = * The subset of the system maintenance information that applies to the manual portions of the system.*

For composition, see "System Maintenance Information," which acknowledges that what was identified as "new" becomes "current" for a system restudy.

Manual HW/SW Operating Instructions = * The operating documentation (probably supplied by the vendor) for the hardware and support software used in the manual environment.*

Manual Logical Model = * A logical specification of the manual portions of the system.*

= {Logical Leveled Data Flow Diagram} + Logical Data Dictionary + {Logical Process Description}

Manual System Installation Procedures = * The procedures needed to support the installation of the new system's manual activities.*

Manual System Installation Support = * The support needed for installation of the new system's manual procedures, for example, office layout, new office furniture and equipment (including furniture and equipment needing relocation), moving equipment, and support, etc.*

Manual System Model = * A physilogical specification of the manual portions of the system.*

= {Physilogical Leveled Data Flow Diagram} + Physilogical Data Dictionary + {Physilogical Process Description} + (Organizational Hierarchy)

Min-Max Volumes = * An estimate of the number of minimum and maximum occurrences of entities or records.*

Module Name = * A verb-object name that states a module's function.*

N

New Automated   =   * The automated system model for
System Model   the new system.*

                               For composition, see "Automated
                               System Model."

New HW/SW   =   * The actual hardware and support
                               software, e.g., computers, terminals,
                               operating systems, database systems.*

New Logical Model   =   * A logical specification of the new
                               system as a whole without delinea-
                               tion of manual and automated subsys-
                               tems.*

                          =   Logical Leveled Data Flow Diagram +
                               Logical Data Dictionary +
                               {Logical Process Description}

New Operations   =   * The operations manual supporting
Manual   the new system.*

                               For comments and composition, see
                               "Operations Manual."

New Physical   =   * A specification of the new system
Specification   (manual and automated) showing the
                               design used to implement it.*

                          =   Manual System Model +
                               Automated System Model

New Procedures   =   * The procedures manual supporting
Manual   the new system.*

                               For comments and composition, see
                               "Procedures Manual."

New System Description = Bounded New Logical Specification + New Physical Specification + New System Execution Manuals + Implementation Specifications

Note: The system execution manuals are optional at the preliminary level.

New System Execution Manuals = New Procedures Manual + New Operations Manual

New System Test Case = * A test case for a function, an item of data, or the validation of the man/machine boundary in the new system.*

For composition, see "Test Case."

Number of New System Staff/Procedures = * Indicates the effort required to prepare procedures for the new manual system. The number of new system staff/procedures can be categorized as operations staff, data preparation staff, User staff, etc.*

Number/Type of Changes During Development = * The number of changes within type that were accommodated during development of the system, for example, major project goal change, minor data format change, major hardware interface change, etc.*

O

Operations Manual = * The documentation needed for the computer operations staff to operate and control the automated portions of the system.*

= System Overview +
Operations Support +
System Flowchart +
Data Preparation/Distribution Schedule +
(Job/Job Step Description +
Job Schedules/Procedures +
Job Environment +
Job Backup/Recovery +
Job Security) +
Application Maintenance Contact +
HW/SW Maintenance Contact

Operations Staff = * The people who support/control the execution of the automated system.*

Operations Support = * The support that the operations area needs to provide for the system, for example, the number of support staff, staff skill level, staff availability, etc.*

Opinions on Project and New System = * Informal notes about the project activities and the resulting new system or about a release of the new system. The notes include all factors such as communication difficulties, disruptions, smoothness of system installation, ease of training and usability of the new system.*

Organizational Hierarchy = * The chart or charts showing the reporting relationships of the people in the manual environments that are affected by the project.*

Outside Interface = * An area where data originates or terminates from the point of view of the system study. It defines the scope of the system study.*

Outside Support Required = * The services/materials required from outside the project team and its available materials, for example, text processing, machine time, special software support.*

Overall DP Plans and Resources = * The current and long-term plans of the data processing department, showing the allocation of current data processing resources.*

= {Project Identification + Project Priority + Project Status + Project Plan Summary}

Overall Schedule = * A schematic showing the desired start and completion dates for processes and their deliverables.*

Overall Strategy = * The technique by which a goal will be accomplished, for example, that testing will be accomplished using boundary-value analysis or that all training will be performed in-house with workshop courses.*

P

Packaged Data Model = * A data model represented in a hierarchical, network or relational structure. (Although the packaged data model has some physical characteristics, it still represents a logical view of the data.)*

Past Project Histories = * Documentation of past projects for use in evaluating and planning future projects.*

= (Project Identification +
Project Characteristics +
System Characteristics +
Environment Characteristics +
Project Completion Report)

Physical Database/File Structures = * Graphical models showing the structures of databases and files needed to support the Information Specification and its processing.*

Physilogical Data Dictionary = * A set of definitions for all data items declared on a physilogical data flow diagram.*

= (Data Flow +
Data Flow Physical Characteristics) +
(Data Element +
Data Element Physical
Characteristics) +
(Data Store +
Data Store Physical Characteristics) +
(Outside Interface)

Physilogical Leveled Data Flow Diagram = * A leveled set of data flow diagrams that form a model of a physical manual environment. This model basically represents a logical view of the environment but is annotated with physical characteristics to aid verification by the User.*

For comment, see "Data Flow Diagram."

Physilogical Process Description = * The specification of a process/function declared on a physical data flow diagram.*

= Process Description + Process Physical Characteristics

Plan = * A generic definition for all plans.*

= Overall Strategy + Dependency Network + Overall Schedule + {Process Identification + Completion Criteria + Skill Level Required + (Support Material Required) + Outside Support Required + Process Actual Start Date + Process Actual End Date + Estimated Person Days + Actual Person Days + Estimated Task Cost + Actual Task Cost + Person/Group Allocated}

Problem to be Solved = * Existing system fault to be solved, for example, high system maintenance costs, unacceptable downtime.*

Procedures Manual   =   * The documentation needed to use
the manual portions of the system. It
is mostly a physical packaging of
information in the manual system
model and hardware/software
specification.*

=   Manual System Model +
Data Management System +
Data Preparation/Distribution
Schedule +
Manual HW/SW Operating
Instructions +
Maintenance Contact

Process Description   =   * The specification of a process
declared on a data flow diagram.*

=   Process Name +
[Process Notes |
Process Specification]

Process Notes   =   * Used for high-level data flow
diagram processes until lower com-
ponent processes are defined. They
are informal descriptions used when
component data flow diagrams have
not been completed.*

Process Physical   =   [Process Performed By |
Characteristics   Job Title] +
(Skill Level Required) +
(Frequency/Periodicity of Use) +
Yearly Operating Costs +
(Special Characteristics)

**Process
Specification**   =   * A formal specification of the business policy for data transformation. This can take the form of a decision table or tree, a graph, other nonlinguistic forms (such as a Nassi-Shneiderman diagram), structured English, narrative, and so on.*

Processing Mode   =   * The method of computing such as batch, on-line, or real-time.*

**Production and
Maintenance
Libraries**   =   Production Procedures Library +
                             Production Program Library +
                             Production Stores +
                             Production Hardware/Software +
                             Data Administration Library +
                             Maintenance Library

**Production Factor
Identification**   =   * The identification of a factor to monitor in production. There will be many different factors depending on the type of project and its goals. Factors include performance, maintainability, security, usability of manuals, usability of hardware, accuracy of results, and downtime.*

**Production Factor
Problem**   =   * An individual problem found for a monitored production factor.*

**Production Factor
Summary**   =   * A summary of data from a monitored production factor. Its content will vary depending on the factor. Performance factors include slowest response time, mean response time, fastest response time. Security factors include ease or difficulty of use, number of violations, type of violations.*

Production Factor = * The usage pattern for a monitored
Usage Pattern production factor. The documentation
for this usage pattern will vary
depending on the factor; for instance,
it can be formal for database usage
and number of coding errors per
program, or informal such as explaining the reluctance of Users to operate
a particular terminal.*

Production HW/SW = * The actual hardware and support
software used in the production en-
vironment.*

Production HW/SW = * A complete, up-to-date inventory of
Inventory all data processing hardware and support software (not application
software) and the support environments that are available in-house.
The inventory consists of hardware
and software to support both manual
and automated production environments.*

= {Configuration Data}

Production = * The library containing the support
Procedures Library documentation for the manual procedures of systems.*

= {System Identification +
Procedures Manual +
Operations Manual}

Production Program = * An executable unit of software
developed in-house to support an ap-
plication.*

Note: It could also be obtained as a
vendor package.

**Production
Program Library** = * The library containing executable
software.*

  = {Production Program} +
{Production System Controls}

**Production
Program Listings** = * The latest printouts or on-line
documentation of the production
programs.*

Production Stores = * The stores that contain the manual
and automated data in the produc-
tion environment, for example,
manual reports/tables, automated
stored data, transaction form layouts,
etc.*

Production System = {Production Program +
Production System Controls} +
System Maintenance Information +
Converted Manual and Automated
Data +
Relocated and New Hardware/
Software

**Production System
Controls** = * The language used to control the executable software of a system, for ex-
ample, JCL, sort/merge parameters,
control blocks, etc.*

**Production System
Controls Listings** = * The latest printouts or online
documentation of the production sys-
tem controls.*

Program Name = * A verb-object name stating a
program's function.*

**Project Actual
Resources** = * The total money, time, people, and
materials actually used for the
project.*

Project Characteristics = * Project information for a system development effort.*

= Project Type +
Gross Size +
Risk Assessment +
Project Methodology +
Structured Techniques +
Number of Walkthroughs/Reviews +
Development Support Systems +
Number of Project Team Members +
Skill Level of Project Team Members +
Estimated and Actual Resources +
(Special Characteristics)

Project Charter = * The project contract or objective, which includes the reason for doing the project.*

= {Project Goal +
Goal Priority +
{Project Goal Solution}} +
{Gross Benefit} +
Gross Size +
Risk Assessment

Project Completion Report = * The material that documents the formal completion of the new system or a release of the new system.*

= Summary of Project Goals +
Summary of Project Goals Solutions +
Initial Production Information +
Summary of Project Team
Performance +
Project Estimated Resources +
Project Actual Resources +
Project Estimated Gross Size +
Project Actual Size +
(Recommendations for Future
Projects)

Project Estimated Resources = * The total money, time, people, and materials estimated for the project.*

Project Evaluation Data = Initial Context Diagram +
{Affected System} +
{Project Goal +
{Gross Benefit}} +
Gross Size +
Risk Assessment

Project Goal = * An aim or requirement of the system.*

= (Goal Requestor) +
[Business Objective |
Business Constraint |
System Objective |
System Constraint |
Problem to be Solved]

**Project Goal
Solution**
= * A solution to a project goal, identified during system development.*

= [Analysis Goal Solution |
Data Goal Solution |
Design Goal Solution |
Implementation Goal Solution]

**Project Initiation
Report**
= * Documents the progress of the project and the resources required for the next major activity.*

= Initial Context Diagram +
(Affected System) +
Summary of Major Project Goals +
Summary of Gross Benefits +
Gross Size +
Risk Assessment +
Summary of Development Approach +
Estimated Resources for Activity 1 +
Actual Resources Used for
Activity 1 +
Estimated Resources for Activity 2 +
(Estimated Resources for Future
Activities) +
Issues That May Affect the Project

Project Plan
= Customized Methodology +
Activity 1 Plan +
Activity 2 Plan +
Activity 3 Plan +
Activity 4 Plan +
Activity 5 Plan +
Implementation Plans

**Project Plan
Summary**
= * A summary of the plans for a project, showing which, if any, activity is in progress, the resources being used, and future resources needed.*

Project Priority = * The importance of a project in relation to all data processing projects and/or in relation to other projects of a requestor.*

Project Request = * The request for system support.*

= Requestor Identification +
Date Submitted +
{Project Goal} +
{Gross Benefit} +
{Affected System} +
Project Priority +
(User Representative)

Project Status = * The state of a project, for example, deferred start date, under review, active.*

Project Type = * A project designation such as new System, Rewrite, Conversion, Modification.*

Q

No Entry

R

Recommendations for Future Projects = * Any recommendations from data processing personnel and Users that can aid future releases or entire project development, such as recommending that a User staff member be assigned to the project team for future projects.*

Regression Test Library = * The library containing the minimum executable test materials required to validate the system's data and functions.*

= {Test Material}

Regression Test Specification = * The specification of the minimum test cases required to validate the system's data and functions.*

= {Test Case}

Relationship = * An association between two or more business entities.*

Relationship Cardinality = * The number of occurrences of each entity type participating in the relationship.*

Relationship Specification = Relationship Name +
Relationship Description +
Relationship Cardinality +
Relationship Inclusion Rules +
Rules Governing Relationship

Request for Proposal = * A request for formal proposals to supply hardware and/or support software.*

= [HW Description |
SW Description] +
([HW Compatibility Requirements |
SW Compatibility Requirements]) +
Type of Contract Required +
Delivery Schedule +
Delivery Location +
Vendor Support Requirements

Resolutions/ Priorities = * Support information for conflicting or unprioritized project goals.*

Reusable Test Materials = * The executable test units that can be reused from the current regression test library.*

For composition, see "Test Material."

Reusable Training Materials = * The development training materials that can be reused from the current system or from available company training materials.*

For composition, see "Development Training Materials."

Review Report = * Documentation of the result of a review.*

= Identification of Reviewed Material + Review Data + {Review Participant} + Review Summary + {Review Recommendation}

Revised Plans and Resources = * The affected overall data processing plans and resources updated to allow for the project's next major activity.*

Risk Assessment = * A statement of the business-oriented and technical probability of meeting the project goals.*

= Overall Assessment of Risk + {High-Risk Project Goal + High-Risk Reason}

S

Safety Precautions = * A description of the safety details for an environment, for example, fire exits, smoke and water detectors, sprinkler systems, first-aid equipment, etc.*

Sample/Layout = * An example of an item of data, for instance, invoice form, report, screen or record layout, transaction form, check.*

Selected System Options = * The identification of areas for further study.*

= {Affected System} + {System Option Identification + System Option Priority}

Selected System(s) Plans = * The plans that apply only to the selected system option(s).*

Selected System(s) Project Goals = * The project goals that apply only to the selected system option(s).*

Site Description = * A description of the physical environment housing data processing hardware.*

= Site Layout + (Extensibility Space) + Electrical Support + Environment Conditions + Safety Precautions + Accessibility Times

Site Layout = * The physical layout of the hardware and the connective cables between pieces of hardware, as well as the work space needed within this location.*

Solution Description = * A brief description of a solution to a project goal.*

Solution Reference Point = * A page, diagram, or process reference number identification in a solution specification.*

Special Characteristics = * A general component in a definition used for documenting any other relevant information.*

Staff = * Staff is composed of Management, Users, and DP people. Staff can include management, but management does not include staff.*

= Management + User Staff + Data Processing Staff

Storage Description = Storage Media + Data Organization + Min-Max Volumes + (Storage Growth Space) + (Growth Space Organization)

Storage Growth Space = * The amount of storage allowed for overflow data.*

Suggested Tailoring for Methodology = * Customization of the system development methodology based on organizational characteristics and/or type and size of project. Heuristics can be included (a support group should evaluate these suggestions).*

Support Material Required = * The material needed to accomplish a process (if not already identified in a specification), for example, review facilities, presentation materials, etc.*

Support Planning Staff = * A general category of people who provide support for the data processing area, such as for hardware/software planning or technical services.*

SW Description = * A summary of the software, such as operating systems, compilers, optimizers, program generators, data management systems, report packages, software packages, utility programs, all developent libraries, etc.*

= (SW Vendor/Supplier) +
SW Identification +
{SW Function} +
Data Representation Requirements +
(SW/SW Requirements) +
(SW/HW Requirements) +
(Special Characteristics)

SW Function = * The function that the software provides, for example, packages providing the User of the system with the ability to do ad hoc inquiry. Performance can be included with the function, such as the interface software providing five second response times at any terminal.*

SW Package(s) = * A vendor-supplied complete application system that satisfies part or all of the business and system requirements.*

SW Specification = SW Description +
(SW Compatibility Requirements) +
SW Status +
SW Availability +
SW Support Staff +
(SW Cost) +
SW Support Costs per Year

SW Status = * An indication of whether the
software is already installed and
being used by other projects, is already installed and being used by the
current system, or is new software
(indicate installed or on order).*

**SW Support
Materials** = * Materials needed to back up the
new system support software. The
materials are identified as support
for installation of the software but
can be used for on-going support. Examples of software support materials
are tapes, disks, index cards, and
storage for them, vendor support
documentation, interface
hardware/software simulators, etc.
(This is material not identified in the
"HW/SW Specification.").*

**SW Support
Procedures** = * The procedure needed to support
the installation of the system
software, for example, tape/disk initialization, vendor software installation procedures including System
Generation, library creation/update,
software testing procedures.*

SW Support Staff	=	* A description of the support staff available for the software.*
	=	(Vendor-Provided Support) + In-House Support Available + Support Availability Times
SW/HW Requirements	=	* Dependencies on any hardware used to support the software, such as a maximum number of terminals that can be hooked to a package or a minimum machine capacity of one-half megabyte to support software.*
SW/SW Requirements	=	* Dependencies on any software interfacing with the software, such as Data Language/1 to interface application programs with Information Management System/Database or VSAM (Virtual Storage Access Method) in order to use the package.*

**System
Characteristics** = * System summary information,
which will vary for each type of
system.*

= System Type +
Processing Mode +
System Overview +
System Organization +
(Data Management System) +
Overall System Complexity +
Quality of Original Documentation +
Number of Affected Manual
Systems +
Extent of Effect on Manual Systems +
Number of Affected Automated
Systems +
Extent of Effect on Automated
Systems +
(Implementation Language) +
Number of New System
Programs/Modules/Lines of Code +
Number of New System
Staff/Procedures +
Major HW/SW Used +
Number/Type of Changes During
Development +
(Special Characteristics)

System Constraint = * A limitation on the system solution,
for example, that a particular piece of
hardware system software must be
used or that the system must provide
distributed, rather than centralized,
processing.*

System Controls = * The language used to control com-
puter-executable software.*

System Flowchart = * A diagram showing the control sequence for the separately executed processes in the automated environment.*

System Installation Objective = * An aim of the system installation effort, which can be requested by the system User or the project manager, such as insuring that the installation of a system does not cause an interruption in customer delivery schedules.*

System Installation Plan = * A description of how to accomplish the system installation requirements identified in the system installation specification.*

For composition, see "Plan."

System Installation Specification = {System Installation Objective} + {Automated System Installation Procedures + Automated System Installation Support} + {Manual System Installation Procedures + Manual System Installation Support} + {System Maintenance Installation Procedures + System Maintenance Information Identification}

System Limitation = * A characteristic of the system that could potentially reduce its effectiveness; for example, the upper volume of transactions before performance (response time) is degraded.*

System Maintenance Information = * The information needed to maintain the system (manual and/or automated) in production.*

= Bounded New Logical Specification + New Physical Specification + New System Execution Manuals + Production Program Listings + Production System Controls Listings + Regression Test Specification + Regression Test Library + Maintenance Plan + Training Specification + Training Materials + Production HW/SW Inventory

System Maintenance Installation Procedures = * The procedures needed to support the installation of the new system maintenance information.*

System Objective = * An objective of the system solution, i.e., something that will change the design of the system.*

System Organization = * A description of how the system processing is/will be organized, e.g., centralized, decentralized, distributed.*

System Overview = * A brief description of the system, which can be a subset of the New Physical Specification or a narrative description.*

System Release Archives = * A store for obsolete documentation.*

System Simulators   =   * Hardware and/or software that simulates the actual new system hardware and software, including simulated application software.*

System Support   =   * The identification of a portion of the actual new system, which will be used for support.*

System Test Completion Report   =   * Formal completion documentation of all (or each major phase) of the system testing for the new system.*

=   Estimated Resources for System Test +
Resources Actually Used for System Test +
Problems Encountered During System Test

System Type   =   * The type of application that the system supports, for example, stock control.*

System/Interview Data   =   {Interview Note} +
{Transformation Note} +
{Project Goal} +
Acceptance Test Materials +
Production Data +
Opinions on Project and New System

T

Test Case = * A generic definition for all types of test cases.*

= Test Identification +
Test Case Objective +
Test Input Definition +
Expected Execution +
Expected Output +
(Test Dependency) +
(Test Environment)

Test Case Objective = * An aim of an individual test, such as a customer-delete transaction that should remove customer billing and accounting information but not history information.*

Test Dependency = * A factor that a test is dependent upon, such as a cross-edit test to be executed on valid data, where normal field edits must have been applied.*

Test Environment = * An environment upon which a test is dependent, e.g., real or simulated hardware/software, stores, or support tools.*

Test Input Definition = * The definition of test input data. It should be specific enough to build executable test data from, such as a completed transaction form.*

Test Material = * The executable data for a test unit.*

= Test Set Identification +
Test Set Data +
Test Set Scaffold +
(Test Instructions)

Test Plan	=	* Description of how to accomplish the testing requirements identified in the test specification.*
		For composition, see "Plan."
Test Set Data	=	* The executable test data for a test unit. For the automated environment, it will be machine executable, such as transaction input data or test files.*
Test Set Identification	=	* The test case identification, if this is for one test case, or identification of the test cases from which it was developed.*
Test Set Instructions	=	* The instructions for executing a test unit, for example, that the User terminal must be used at noon to enter a test set ten times.*
Test Set Scaffold	=	* The executable support needed for a test unit, for example, stub modules, driver modules, JCL, dummy printed forms, etc.*
Test Specification	=	{Testing Objective} + {Current System Test Case} + {New System Test Case} + {Design Test Case} + {Conversion Test Case} + {System-Test Test Case} + Testing Support
Testing Objective	=	* An aim of the testing effort, which applies to the whole system or a major part of the system, for example, backup/recovery procedures that should return the system on-line within one hour.*

Testing Support = * The support (excluding people support) needed to perform the testing effort, for instance, tapes, disks, test data generators, test libraries, hardware/software simulators, etc.*

Training Category = * A group of people requiring training for the new system, such as employees in data preparation or operations, Users, special hardware/software operators, etc.*

Training Completion Report = * The material that documents the formal completion of all (or each major phase) of the training for the new system.*

= Estimated Resources for Training + Resources Actually Used for Training + (Problems Encountered During Training)

Training Distribution = * A description of the distribution of training for the whole training effort or for a unit of training for instance, centralized in the company's main training facility or localized at each division's training facility.*

Training Documentation = * The description of the materials needed to support a unit of training, for example, identification of execution manuals, new system overview, hardware/software manuals.*

Training Facilities = * The environment required for a unit of training, such as classroom, lecture room, dining facilities.*

Training Level = * The level of training required to support the new system, such as an overview for management, an overall familiarity for supervisors, working detail for staff, etc. It can include training an individual in totally new procedures or changing existing procedures.*

Training Number = * The number of people requiring training. It can be an overall estimate at preliminary level or a specific number in a specific course at detailed level.*

Training Objective = * An aim of the training effort, which can be requested by the system User of the project manager, for instance, that training support be provided at each major division of the company.*

Training Plan = * A description of how to accomplish the training requirements identified in the training specification.*

For composition, see "Plan."

Training Requirement = Training Category + Training Level + Training Number + (Training Distribution)

Training Specification = (Training Objective) + (Training Requirement + Training Support)

Training Support   =   * The training support to be provided for the new system, excluding people support.*

= Training Type +
Training Unit Description +
Training Documentation +
Training Facilities +
(System Support) +
(System Simulators)

Training Type   =   * The type of training provided to satisfy a training requirement, for example, lecture, workshop, audiovisual equipment, textbook, on-the-job training, training in a pilot project, etc.*

Training Unit Description   =   * A description of a unit of training, such as training objectives, the content of a course or lecture, instructor's procedures.*

Transformation Note   =   * The interview documentation that confirms and supports the transformation from a physical to a logical model. This can take the form of an updated data flow diagram, graph, decision table or tree, structured English, or narrative.*

Type of Contract Required   =   * The required terms of purchase, such as fixed-price purchase, special bulk-discount contract, long-term lease, etc.*

U

User Management = * The requestors and owners of the system and the people who control and approve the User resources. (User management may also be responsible for the approval of the total system resources.)*

User Staff = * The people who use the existing system or perform system functions or who will use or perform system functions for the new system, including data preparation and distribution staff.*

V

Vendors = * Outside suppliers of hardware, software, or training support.*

Vendor Support Requirements = * The support expected from a vendor.*

= [HW Support Materials |
SW Support Materials |
Vendor Training Materials] +
([HW Support Procedures |
SW Support Procedures]) +
Vendor Staff Availability

Vendor Training Materials = * The development training materials supplied by vendors of hardware/ software or of training support.*

For composition, see "Development Training Materials."

W, X, Y, Z

No Entry

Addendum to Data Dictionary

To avoid repetitious definitions in the data dictionary, I have identified generic definitions for some of the more complex specifications that are cycled through in this methodology and have indicated the level of detail at which each component item is identified. These generic definitions should be used in conjunction with the data dictionary. When two or more levels of detail are indicated for the same data item, refer to the appropriate detailed process description that creates that part of the specification for further clarification. Generic definitions are specified in a table of contents format for the manual system model, the automated system model, and the logical specification on the following pages. The level at which the contents are complete can be Preliminary or Detailed, indicated by a P or D respectively in the right-hand columns.

Sample Table of Contents for a MANUAL SYSTEM MODEL

	Current/New Environment[1]	
	P	D
PHYSILOGICAL LEVELED DATA FLOW DIAGRAM(S):		
* Levels developed incrementally	P	D
PHYSILOGICAL DATA DICTIONARY:		
* For each major data flow (document/transaction stream):		
- Data flow name	P	
- Data flow description (optional)	P	
- Physical data flow ID (if different from name)	P	
- Medium	P	
- Data flow volume	P	
- Frequency/periodicity of use	P	
- Security (if applicable to whole stream)	P	
- Special characteristics (optional)	P	
* For each component data flow (document/transaction):		
- Data flow name	P	
- Data flow description (optional)		D
- Physical data flow ID (if different from name)		D
- Sample/layout (optional) (Detailed in New)		D
- Medium (if different from whole stream)		D
- Data flow volume		D
- Frequency/periodicity (if different from stream)		D
- Security (optional)		D
- Special characteristics (optional)		D
* For each data element (field/attribute):		
- Data element name		D
- Data element description		D
- Physical data element ID (optional)		D
- Data format		D
- Data representation		D
- List/range of values		D
- Special characteristics (optional)		D

---

[1]P = Preliminary, D = Detailed

Sample Table of Contents for a MANUAL SYSTEM MODEL (P.2)

	Current/New Environment	

* For each major data store (file):
- Data store name · P
- Data store description · P
- Physical store ID (optional) · P
- Sample/layout (optional) (Detailed in New environment) · P
- Medium · P
- Organization · P
- Frequency/periodicity of use (if not governed by data flow · P
- Access management system (optional) · P
- Minimum/maximum store volume (estimate) · P
- Security (if applicable to whole store) · P
- Special characteristics (optional) · P

* Data model (if available in current environment) or for each record/document: (see "For each component data flow" above) · P

  * For each data field: (see "For each data element" above)

PHYSILOGICAL PROCESS DESCRIPTIONS:

* For each major process (for example, department):
- Process name · P
- Process notes (optional) · P
- Yearly operating costs (estimate) · P
- Special characteristics (optional) · P

  * For each component process (e.g. section, group):
  - Process name · P
  - Process notes (optional) · D
  - Yearly operating costs (estimate) · D
  - Special characteristics (optional) · D

    * For each individual process (procedure/task):
    - Process name · D
    - Process specification · D
    - Process agent (name or title) (optional) · D
    - Agent skill level required · D
    - Frequency/periodicity of use (if not driven by data flow) · D
    - Yearly operating cost · D
    - Special characteristics (optional) · D

ORGANIZATIONAL HIERARCHY

  (optional) (developed incrementally) · P · D

Sample Table of Contents for an AUTOMATED SYSTEM MODEL

	Current Environment		New	
DESIGN CHARTS: * Different types of design charts	P	D	P	D
AUTOMATED DATA DICTIONARY:				
* For each major data stream (transaction/report group):				
- Stream name	P		P	
- Stream description	P		P	
- Medium	P		P	
- Stream volume	P		P	
- Frequency/periodicity of use	P		P	
- Security (if applicable to whole stream)	P		P	
- Special characteristics (optional)	P		P	
* For each stream component (transaction, report):				
- Transaction ID	P		P	
- Transaction name (if different from ID)	P		P	
- Sample/layout (optional)		D		D
- Medium (if different from whole stream)		D		D
- Transaction volume		D		D
- Frequency/periodicity (if different from whole stream)		D		D
- Security (optional)		D		D
- Special characteristics (optional)		D		D
* For each data element (field, attribute):				
- Data element name		D		D
- Data element description		D		D
- Data format		D		D
- Data representation		D		D
- List/range of values		D		D
- Special characteristics (optional)		D		D
* For each data store (file and intermediate file):				
- Data store ID	P	D		
- Data store name (if different from ID)	P		P	D
- Data store description	P		P	D
- Sample/layout	P			
- Medium	P		P	D
- Organization	P			D
- Minimum/maximum store volumes	P		P	D
- Access method	P			D
- Security (if applicable to whole store)	P		P	D
- Frequency/periodicity (if applicable to whole store)	P		P	D
- Special characteristics (optional)	P		P	D

Sample Table of Contents for an AUTOMATED SYSTEM MODEL   (P.2)

* A data model (logical and/or physical if available) or for each record/document:	P		P	D
- (see "For each stream component" above, reading transactions as records)				
* For each data field:				
- (see "For each data element" above)				

AUTOMATED PROCESS DESCRIPTIONS:

* For each automated job (batch/on-line, front-end processing, etc.):				
- Job name	P		P	
- Job description	P		P	D
- Job size/complexity (estimate)	P		P	D
- Frequency/periodicity (if not governed by data)	P		P	D
- Executing processor type (if applicable to whole job)	P		P	D
- Yearly operating costs (estimate)	P		P	D
- Special characteristics (optional)	P		P	D
* For each program:				
- Program ID	P			D
- Program name	P			D
- Program description (optional for new)		D		
- Frequency/periodicity (if not governed by data)		D		D
- Executing processor type (if different from whole job)		D		D
- Source language		D		D
- Program size/complexity		D		D
- Cost per execution		D		D
- Special characteristics (optional)		D		D
* For each module (routine):				
- Module ID		D		D
- Module name		D		D
- Module description		D		D
- Frequency of use(if not governed by data)		D		D
- Pseudocode (for current environment, use actual code listing)		D		D
- Source language (if not same for whole program)		D		D
- Special characteristics (optional)		D		D

SYSTEM FLOWCHART: P   D

Sample Table of Contents for a LOGICAL SPECIFICATION

Current/New
Environment

LOGICAL LEVELED DATA FLOW DIAGRAM(S):

* Levels developed incrementally   P   D

LOGICAL DATA DICTIONARY:

* For each major data flow (originally documents, trans-
  actions, and report streams or time-delayed stores):
  - Data flow name   P
  - Data flow description (optional)   P
  - Cross reference to current physical description P

  * For each component data flow (originally documents,
    transactions, reports or records):
    - Data flow name   P
    - Data flow description (optional)   D
    - Cross reference to current physical definition D

    * For each data element:
      - Data element name   D
      - Data element description   D
      - Cross reference to current physical definition D

DATA MODEL (optional in manual and automated logical
    models):

  - Data categories   P
  - Informal data model/access diagram   D
  - Formal data model/access diagram   D

  * For each entity (originally records/documents):
    - Entity name   P
    - Entity description   D
    - Cross reference to current physical definition D

    * For each data attribute (originally field/element):
    (see "For each data elements" above)

LOGICAL DATA STORE (for manual and automated logical
                models):
* For each (necessary) data store:
  - Data store name   P
  - Data store description   P
  - Cross reference to current physical definition P

  * For each data store component (originally record,
      document):
    (see "For each component data flow" above)

    * For each data element (originally field):
      (see "For each data element" above)

Sample Table of Contents for a LOGICAL SPECIFICATION (P. 2)

LOGICAL PROCESS DESCRIPTIONS:

* For each major function (originally department or
  automated job):
  - Process name
  - Process notes (optional)
  - Cross reference to current physical process(es)

  * For each component function (originally section,
    group or program):
    - Process name
    - Process notes (optional)
    - Cross reference to current physical process(es)

    * For each functional primitive (originally
      procedure/task or module/routine):
      - Process name
      - Process specification)
      - Cross reference to current physical process(es)

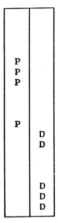

Second Addendum to Data Dictionary

If you have a project that is quite large you may want to bring in another level of cycling through analysis and design. I have removed this intermediate level (general) from the data flow diagrams but have been requested to leave this extra level breakdown in this addendum. On the following pages is the partitioning of major deliverables through three levels of decomposition and study—preliminary, general and detailed.

Sample Table of Contents for a MANUAL SYSTEM MODEL

*Current/New Environment**

■ **Physicalized Leveled Data Flow Diagram(s):**

Levels developed incrementally	P	G	D

■ **Physicalized Data Dictionary:**

☐ For each major data flow (documents/transaction streams):

○ Data flow name	P		
○ Data flow description (optional)	P		
○ Physical data flow ID (if different from name)	P		
○ Media	P		
○ Data flow volume	P		
○ Frequency/periodicity of use	P		
○ Security (if applicable to whole stream)	P		
○ Special characteristics (optional)	P		

☐ For each component data flow (documents/transactions):

○ Data flow name	P		
○ Data flow description (optional)		G	
○ Physical data flow ID (if different from name)		G	
○ Sample/layout (optional) (at detailed level in new environment)		G	
○ Media (if different from whole stream)		G	
○ Data flow volume		G	
○ Frequency/periodicity (if different from whole stream)		G	
○ Security (optional)		G	
○ Special characteristics (optional)		G	

☐ For each data element (fields/attributes):

○ Data element name		G	
○ Data element description			D
○ Physical data element ID (optional)			D
○ Data format			D
○ Data representation			D
○ List/range of values			D
○ Special characteristics (optional)			D

☐ For each major data store (files):

○ Data store name	P		
○ Data store description	P		
○ Physical store ID (optional)	P		
○ Sample/layout (optional) (at detailed level in new environment)	P		
○ Media	P		
○ Organization	P		
○ Frequency/periodicity of use (if not governed by data flow)	P		
○ Access management system (optional)	P		
○ Min-max store volume (estimate)	P		
○ Security (if applicable to whole store)	P		
○ Special characteristics (optional)	P		

---

*P = Preliminary, G = General, D = Detailed

Sample Table of Contents for a MANUAL SYSTEM MODEL (P.2)

	Current/New *Environment*		

☐ A data model (data structure diagram) (if available
in current environment) or for each record/document:
(See "For each component data flow," above) — P

☐ For each data field:
(See "For each data element," above)

■ Physicalized Process Descriptions:

☐ For each major process (for example, departments):
- ○ Process name — P
- ○ Process notes (optional) — P
- ○ Yearly operating costs (estimate) — P
- ○ Special characteristics (optional) — P

☐ For each component process (for example, sections/groups):
- ○ Process name — P
- ○ Process notes (optional) — G
- ○ Yearly operating costs (estimate) — G
- ○ Special characteristics (optional) — G

☐ For each individual process (procedures/tasks):
- ○ Process name — G
- ○ Process specification — D
- ○ Doer of the process (his/her name or a title) (optional) — D
- ○ Skill level required — D
- ○ Frequency/periodicity of use (if not driven by data flow) — D
- ○ Yearly operating cost — D
- ○ Special characteristics (optional) — D

■ Organizational Hierarchy

(optional) developed incrementally — P G D

Sample Table of Contents for an AUTOMATED SYSTEM MODEL

	Current Environment*			New Environment*		
■ **Design Charts:**						
□ Different types of design charts	P	G	D	P	G	D
■ **Automated Data Dictionary:**						
□ For each major data stream (transaction/report groups):						
○ Stream name	P			P		
○ Stream description (optional)	P			P		
○ Media	P			P		
○ Stream volume	P			P		
○ Frequency/periodicity of use	P			P		
○ Security (if applicable to whole stream)	P			P		
○ Special characteristics (optional)	P			P		
□ For each stream component (transactions/reports):						
○ Transaction ID	P				G	
○ Transaction name (if different from ID)	P			P		
○ Sample/layout (optional)		G				D
○ Media (if different from whole stream)		G			G	
○ Transaction volume		G			G	
○ Frequency/periodicity (if different from whole stream)		G			G	
○ Security (optional)		G			G	
○ Special characteristics (optional)		G			G	
□ For each data element (fields/attributes):						
○ Data element name		G			G	
○ Data element description			D			D
○ Data format			D			D
○ Data representation			D			D
○ List/range of values			D			D
○ Special characteristics (optional)			D			D
□ For each data store (files and intermediate files):						
○ Data store ID	P		D			
○ Data store name (if different from ID)	P			P	G	D
○ Data store description	P			P	G	D
○ Sample/layout	P					
○ Media	P			P	G	D
○ Organization	P					D
○ Min-max store volume	P			P	G	D
○ Access method	P				G	D
○ Security (if applicable to whole store)	P			P	G	D
○ Frequency/periodicity (if applicable to whole store)	P			P	G	D
○ Special characteristics (optional)	P			P	G	D

---

* P = Preliminary, G = General, D = Detailed

Sample Table of Contents for an AUTOMATED SYSTEM MODEL (P.2)

	Current Environment			New Environment		
☐ A data model (logical and/or physical, if available) or for each record/document: ◯ (See "For each stream component," above, reading transactions as records)	P			P	G	D
☐ For each data field: ◯ (See "For each data element," above)						
■ Automated Process Descriptions:						
☐ For each automated job (batch/on-line, front-end processing, and so on):						
◯ Job name	P			P		
◯ Job description	P			P	G	
◯ Job size/complexity (estimate)	P			P	G	
◯ Frequency/periodicity (if not governed by data)	P			P	G	
◯ Executing processor type (if applicable to whole job)	P			P	G	
◯ Yearly operating costs (estimate)	P			P	G	
◯ Special characteristics (optional)	P			P	G	
☐ For each program:						
◯ Program ID	P					D
◯ Program name	P					D
◯ Program description (optional in new environment)		G				
◯ Frequency/periodicity of use (if not governed by data)		G				D
◯ Executing processor type (if different from whole job)		G				D
◯ Source language		G				D
◯ Program size/complexity		G				D
◯ Cost per execution		G				D
◯ Special characteristics (optional)		G				D
☐ For each module (routines):						
◯ Module ID		G				D
◯ Module name		G			G	D
◯ Module description			D		G	D
◯ Frequency of use (if not governed by data)			D			D
◯ Pseudocode (for current environment − actual code listing)			D			D
◯ Source language (if not same) for whole program			D		G	D
◯ Special characteristics (optional)				D		D
■ System flowchart	P					D

Sample Table of Contents for a LOGICAL SPECIFICATION

*Current/New
Environment**

■ **Logical Leveled Data Flow Diagram(s):**
☐ Levels developed incrementally   P   G   D

■ **Logical Data Dictionary:**
☐ For each major data flow (originally documents, transactions,
and report streams or time-delayed stores):
  ○ Data flow name   P
  ○ Data flow description (optional)   P
  ○ Cross reference to current physical definition   P

  ☐ For each component data flow (originally documents,
  transactions, reports, or records):
    ○ Data flow name   P
    ○ Data flow description (optional)   G
    ○ Cross reference to current physical definition   G

    ☐ For each data element:
      ○ Data element name   G
      ○ Data element description   D
      ○ Cross reference to current physical definition   D

■ **Data Model** (optional in manual and automated logical models):
  ○ Data categories   P
  ○ Informal data structure/access diagram   G
  ○ Formal data structure/access diagram   D

  ☐ For each data object (or group) (originally records/documents):
    ○ Data object name   P
    ○ Data object description   G
    ○ Cross reference to current physical definition   G

    ☐ For each data attribute (originally fields or elements)
    (See "For each data element," above)

■ **Logical Data Store** (for manual and automated logical models):
☐ For each (necessary) data store:
  ○ Data store name   P
  ○ Data store description   P
  ○ Cross reference to current physical definition   P

  ☐ For each data store component (originally records/documents):
  (See "For each component data flow," above)

    ☐ For each data element (originally fields):
    (See "For each data element," above)

---

* **P** = Preliminary, G = General, D = Detailed

Sample Table of Contents for a LOGICAL SPECIFICATION (P. 2)

Current/New
Environment

■ **Logical Process Descriptions:**

□ For each major function (originally departments or automated jobs):
  ○ Process name   P
  ○ Process notes (optional)   P
  ○ Cross reference to current physical process(es)   P

  □ For each component function (originally sections/groups or programs):
    ○ Process name   P
    ○ Process notes (optional)   G
    ○ Cross reference to current physical process(es)   G

    □ For each functional primitive (originally procedures/tasks
      or modules/routines):
      ○ Process name   G
      ○ Process specification   D
      ○ Cross reference to current physical process(es)   D

Chapter

3

Process Descriptions

To ensure that this methodology can be applied to a variety of environments, the Level 2, or detailed, activities in this methodology's data flow diagrams are not all "functional primitives," the detailed specification level of a requirements model. Because this methodology can be applied to a variety of environments, I have chosen to support the diagrams with process notes instead of the detailed policy descriptions usually required in a structured specification. If your environment requires that you use unique processing and data to produce a particular deliverable, you should further decompose these Level 2 processes. You can then describe your company's methods for carrying out these tasks. Also any processes that relate to specific techniques can be further supported by technical reference material such as the books recommended in my bibliography.

Process name: APPROVE REQUEST
Process reference number: 1.1.1
Process guided by: General department plan/corporate strategic plan.

Process notes: Examine the request in the light of your overall plans and resources and assess its clarity as a working statement of intent.

Verify the project request, especially if it comes directly from a User without being reviewed by data processing management.

- Is your department the appropriate one to act on this request?
- Is the requestor authorized to initiate a project?
- Are the contents of the request clear and complete? (see "Project Request" in the data dictionary)

The most common problem with Project Requests is that the need for the project is stated as a solution, e.g., to improve data turnaround. "I want an on-line system with a terminal on everyone's desk," instead of as a business objective, "Improve customer relations with regard to accurate return of data on payment inquiries within the same day."

In analysis, you may find the turnaround problems were not due to storage and retrieval speed but due to unreadable reports. If the requirements definition was skipped, the on-line solution may just give faster unreadable reports. Analysis should identify the problem. Solving it should be left until after analysis.

You may have to assist the User if business requirements are stated in terms of system solutions or system objectives. By the way, if all the objectives relate to correcting existing design and implementation characteristics, this just means that the old design (manual and/or automated) was a poor one, and the reason for the project is simply to replace the old design without any business policy changes. Actually this is quite common in the DP environment where we find ourselves legitimately rewriting the nightmare systems of the past.

After verifying the request, review the following:

- Does the request conflict with or duplicate an existing request, or conflict with any restrictions, such as Federal regulations or company policy?

- Should the request be deferred? For example, is the product or service in the request likely to be phased out, or does the project extend an existing system that is going to be rewritten or is in the process of development? (In the latter case, the request can be accommodated in the next release.)

If the request is not rejected or deferred and if you have the resources available for an initial study, update the overall data processing plans and resources accordingly and develop a project plan. This plan need only identify the scheduling of resources for the initial project evaluation. Inform the project requestor (User management) of the outcome of this process.

Process name: IDENTIFY ADDITIONAL AFFECTED MANUAL AND AUTOMATED SYSTEMS
Process reference number: 1.1.2
Process guided by: Activity 1 Plan

Process notes: Examine the environment surrounding the subject area and assess any impact of the request on it.

Often, more than one User and/or automated system will be affected by a Project Request, and the initial requestor may not have identified all of the affected systems in the request. So, using the contents of the project request as a guide, extract additional affected systems from the productions procedure library.

The procedures manual or operations manual should identify departments that give or receive information which may be affected by, as well as affect, interfacing systems. Supplement these with any departments identified by management, and identify possible User representatives for affected departments and automated systems.

Then develop an initial Context Diagram for the system by looking for an area of study for the project that will completely bound the functions and data that will be affected. The Context Diagram will help you understand where input data is produced and where output data is directed. The areas that bound the system should be identified as external interfaces (data originators and terminators) on the Context Diagram. These indicate the project scope (i.e., the points where you begin and stop studying the system's data).

Do not assume that output from an existing computer system is the point where you should lose interest in the data. (A User on one project said to me "This is a good computer report, we can type directly from it!" Clearly, the output was not the product the User needed if it was necessary to reformat or recalculate any data on it into a retyped report.)

You may want to produce a "business event" Context Diagram which shows the system as a single process with business triggers (or data flows) entering its perimeter and their associated responses leaving. The data flows and business time triggers represent the occurrences of events outside the context of the system study—events to which the systems must respond (for example, a customer wants to order goods from you; this results in a purchase order triggering your system into producing an invoice and ordered goods as outputs from the system). This business event Context Diagram will aid significantly in producing a logical model of business requirements for the system.

Process name: IDENTIFY ADDITIONAL MAJOR PROJECT GOALS
Process reference number: 1.1.3
Process guided by: Activity 1 Plan

Process notes: To maximize the benefits from a project, you should identify any other major goals associated with the affected systems.

These project goals should relate either to the original project request or to some function or data that would be affected by the request. However, some goals may come from areas that are not obviously related, such as database administration management or operations management. The database group might request: "Because most of the affected interface systems utilize our centralized database, we would like any new data to be on our database or at least to be stored and accessed with a compatible database management system."

Operations management may also identify problems with the original or affected system: "Try to reduce the time-consuming operating and set-up procedures for this system." Such requests may be easily incorporated into the system solution.

Inform the Users/clients that the earlier an essential project goal is requested, the easier it is to absorb it into the system study. The cost of a new or changed goal escalates more rapidly the later in the project life cycle it is introduced.

Process name: RESOLVE ANY CONFLICTS AND PRIORITIZE
PROJECT GOALS
Process reference number: 1.1.4
Process guided by: Activity 1 Plan

Process notes: Identify any conflicts between project goals. Conflicts are likely to arise if more goals have been added to the ones indicated in the original request.

Compare the objectives and constraints of all the project goals, and, if any conflicts are discovered, aid management in resolving them. To resolve conflicts, identify the gross benefits and assign priorities to the various goals, which may result in some goals being modified or even deleted. If you end up cancelling or deferring the original request, this means that this project brought to light more important business objectives.

Some examples of goals or objectives and constraints follow.

Business objectives:

1. Reduce operating costs of Department X by forty percent in the first year of production.
2. Eliminate inaccuracies in summaries of company revenues and payments.

Business constraints:

1. The project costs must not exceed $200,000.
2. The project must be completed by the end of the fiscal year (six months hence).

System objectives

1. The on-line portion of the system must have ninety-nine percent availability.
2. Response time must be three seconds or less ninety percent of the time and must not exceed five seconds.
3. The system must minimize data redundancy.

System constraints

1. DB2 must be used as the database management system (DBMS).
2. COBOL must be used as the programming language.
3. The FRAMMIS Mark II must be used as the controller.
4. The system must provide centralized, not distributed, processing.

Given the above goals and constraints, there are a number of apparent conflicts:

1. Business objective versus business objective. Accounting inaccuracies may be due to lack of resources and may require adding additional personnel, thereby increasing operating costs.

2. Business objective versus business constraint. A cost reduction as large as forty percent may not be possible to achieve with a system to be built in six months.

3. Business objective versus system objective. A system with ninety-nine percent availability could cost two or three times as much as one with ninety-five percent availability. The increased expense could offset the forty percent cost reduction.

4. Business objective versus system constraint. Centralized processing could increase the cost of data communications and therefore affect the forty percent cost-reduction goal.

5. Business constraint versus business constraint. During the planning of a project, time optimization usually requires more people and therefore added costs, thus conflicting with the cost limitation.

6. Business constraint versus system objective. A system with ninety-nine percent availability is fairly sophisticated and requires thorough design and testing. This would probably conflict with the six-month time constraint.

7. Business constraint versus system constraint. If this is the group's first database project, then you must expect a steep learning curve, which could cause the project to exceed both the time and cost limitations.

8. System objective versus system objective. A database system that tries to minimize data redundancy may require significant processing overhead, making a three-second response time impossible.

9. System objective versus system constraint. Using COBOL as the programming language may slow down the response time from time critical program modules and therefore may not permit an overall three-second response time objective to be met.

10. System constraint versus system constraint. The FRAMMIS Mark II does not support COBOL.

The most important point to make here is that the objectives must be measurable. Avoid any vague objectives like "Provide better service to the customer." Determine what's wrong with customer service currently. Is it response time to specific requests for information, or inaccurate data, or unreadable output? You run a serious risk of implementing the wrong system solution if the project starts off with poorly stated goals.

Avoid suggesting any solutions to the User at this point; wait until the requirements have been studied and analyzed.

Process name: CLASSIFY PROJECT BY GROSS SIZE AND RISK
Process reference number: 1.1.5
Process guided by: Activity 1 Plan

Process notes: Estimate the project's size and determine the probability of meeting the project goals.

Consider such factors as the number of affected systems, project goals and gross benefits. (Remember you're just evaluating the project request here, not trying to do a full feasibility study—that's the task of the preliminary level study, Activity 2.)

The best estimate that you can give at this point is to classify the project as either Small, Medium, or Large because no analysis or identification of a solution has been done yet. "Small," "Medium" and "Large" are relative terms and vary in meaning at each company. For example, Small may be less than six months elapsed time and fewer than two person-years; Medium, six months to one year elapsed time and two to ten person-years; Large, greater than one year elapsed time and greater than ten person-years.

Of course, to evaluate gross size and risk, you must make some assumptions about the classes of possible solutions (on-line/batch, distributed, totally automated, etc.) that are most appropriate for this problem but without committing to any solution yet.

Then, compare this project with similar projects documented in Past Project Histories (if you have any in your environment) to find and use their cost, time, and size data (estimated and actual). If your department doesn't have a Project Histories File, start one today. This is especially valuable if the projects used a consistent project methodology.

Assess risk based on your experience and knowledge of the environment and on the clarity of the project goals as well as on possible solutions. For example, if the existing system is undocumented and totally automated and requires rewriting, and nobody wants to represent this maintenance nightmare, then the risk involved in producing a satisfactory new system is going to be high. On the other hand, if the existing system is mainly manual, the User is friendly, knowledgeable, and truly wants the new system, and if project staff with appropriate skills are available, the risk is lower.

Other major risk factors include the requested delivery date for the completed system and the complexity level of the environments being studied. Again, the best you can do is to classify the project and each project goal as having low, medium, or high risk. Use any available resources to help with this process. If the request is for a database environment, a representative from the database support group or anyone in the system department who has worked on a similar project would be helpful. These two items of evaluation data (gross size and risk) should be recorded in the Project Charter, which constitutes the project contract with the User.

Note: Depending on how much time and resources you have available for the Project Evaluation activity you may want to use the Survey/Probe technique or a portion of it for this evaluation (see Appendix F), or build it into the preliminary study as mentioned in "Create Activity 2 Plan" process reference number 1.2.2.

Process name: SELECT CUSTOMIZED METHODOLOGY
Process reference number: 1.2.1
Process guided by: Activity 1 Plan

Process notes: Using the evaluation data gathered so far, customize the selected methodology. (I shall assume that if you've read this far, you have elected to customize this methodology.)

As mentioned in the introduction, this book presents a standard framework for developing systems, but you may need to tailor the deliverables and activities of the methodology to fit your particular project. However, I recommend that you employ all activities and deliverables if you are a first-time User of this methodology on a full project. Then, for future projects, customize where you see fit, documenting the reason for customizing.

1. **Identify the number of cycles of decomposition necessary.** If a particular project is very small, then you can compress Activities 2 and 3 into one activity (in fact, for a very small project, this methodology may be used just as a checklist). At the other extreme for a large, critical project, you may identify three or more analysis and design levels or cycles.

2. **Identify unnecessary deliverables and processes.** In many cases, not all deliverables are needed. For example, the Hardware/Software Installation Specification is not needed if a system objective is to use existing equipment. If a project objective is to use a software package, most of the design and coding deliverables and activities may be omitted from the methodology.

3. **Allocate roles for project members.** For example, designate that all data modeling will be performed by the database group or that an analyst will be responsible for designing data stores; that the project leader will be a member of the development team or will additionally act as an interface between data processing and the User area. (It may also be helpful to identify User roles and the participation expected from them.) Allocate project team members' names to individual processes on the data flow diagrams in this methodology and use them as a project plan in the next process.

4. **State the quality assurance approach and how deliverables will be reviewed.** Identify people not on the development team who can act as independent reviewers. They should have been involved in similar projects and may be outside consultants.

5. **Identify the approach to system development.** Should we use a conservative, linear approach or a higher-risk, fast-track approach. In the extremely conservative approach, the activities of analysis, design, and implementation are conducted sequentially (e.g., design not beginning until all of the analysis is complete). In the fast-track extreme, the activities are overlapped (e.g., design for a functional unit beginning before analysis is complete). This would introduce a two-dimensional view to project planning—cycling and overlapping analysis and design.

6. **You could select prototyping as a viable approach if:**

   - There is no current system in place (manual and/or automated) to act as a point of reference for making changes.
   - The User wants to see a sample of the proposed system before committing to a set of requirements.
   - The User wants answers to hypothetical "what if" questions.

   In these situations, prototyping will provide a point of reference for a good set of requirements.

7. **Determine the change-management (or change-control) procedure.** Your decision, if incorrect, can jeopardize project success. If you decide to manage change by freezing a specification as soon as possible, then you run the risk of producing a system that doesn't satisfy the User's needs. On the other hand, if you allow changes without any control, the project may never reach completion. The latter is a case of the project deadline being moved constantly, a common complaint of many system developers (and Users).

   Even though this methodology uses development tools that accommodate change easily, you must still have realistic change-management procedures. (For further discussion, see "Refine Project Goals" —Activity 2.2.)

8. **Specify standards for the project development effort based on the project goals.** For example, if a quality, defect-free system is the most important goal, then a project standard could be to hold formal walkthroughs and reviews on all deliverables; use total logic-coverage testing and use boundary-value analysis with separate Quality Assurance testing teams. (Note that standards effectively become additional project goals.)

Document each of the above decisions you make in the Project Plan, especially the deletions in Item 2. This will help future project teams in their customization. Some of the customizing resulting from this activity may be modified after preliminary analysis and design as you gain additional knowledge of the system.

Process name: CREATE ACTIVITY 2 PLAN
Process reference number: 1.2.2
Process guided by: Activity 1 Plan

Process notes: Plan for the Preliminary Analysis and Design phase, Activity 2. The Activity 2 Plan is the most difficult one to prepare, because there is yet no knowledge of the complexity of the system. However, you are not trying to plan for the whole development effort, just for preliminary analysis and design (feasibility level).

The Activity 2 deliverables and their associated tasks are defined in the methodology, so you know that you are allocating resources to a definable product.
The evaluation data created so far will aid planning:

- Affected Systems identifies the area of study, and possible representatives who may help the planning effort.
- Project Goals and Gross Benefits identify the main reasons for the study of an area (that is, key areas of study that deserve allocation of major resources).
- Gross Size aids in determining the amount of resources needed overall.
- Risk Assessment identifies areas of business and technical difficulty and aids in identifying the individual skills needed.
- The estimated and actual resources used in a similar past project can help us ensure success instead of repeat failure.

I have starved this process from one input it may need: the overall data processing plans and resources identifying available resources. It is probably better to identify the resources you realistically need to accomplish Activity 2 on time (although yourer request for them may be rejected), as opposed to altering the project figures to fit the available resources (wishful thinking). Of course, if the project resources have already been dictated, then derive the realistic completion date using these resources.
In doing this or any planning activity, you may uncover additional risks, such as lacking staff with needed skills for the development activities, a situation that will probably necessitate an update to the risk assessment for presentation to management.

Note: It is probably a good idea to allocate extra time during preliminary analysis and design for a projection procedure I call Survey/Probe. This procedure guards against making any assumptions about the project and produces accurate predictions of project costs and schedules. Please see Appendix F for a description of this procedure.

Process name: CONDUCT INDEPENDENT REVIEW
Process reference number: 1.2.3
Process guided by: Activity 1 Plan

Process notes: Conduct an independent review of the approach for the project as specified in the Activity 2 Plan and more generally of your customization of the methodology.

You can avoid compounding any errors by holding an independent review. The people conducting this review should be independent of the project because the test is to determine if the project is on the correct path; therefore, objective observers are the best reviewers. Use reviewers who have worked on similar projects, who understand project plans, and who have a knowledge of the concepts of this methodology. The reviewers should verify the customizing of the methodology and the project plan for reasonableness against the evaluation data gathered so far. (For further description of reviews in general, see Appendix E.)

Process name: PREPARE PROJECT INITIATION REPORT
Process reference number: 1.2.4
Process guided by: Activity 1 Plan

Process notes: Produce a Project Initiation Report containing sufficient information to enable management to decide whether to approve the resources necessary for continuing the project.

The report's importance, of course, depends on whether the project is mandatory or optional. A project based on externally mandated government requirements probably has to be approved, whereas another project, not high on a company priority list, may not need to be approved. In either case, management will need a summary of resources actually spent compared with what was projected and will require a projection (or an estimate) of future resources, at least through Activity 2.

Remember there is not enough information gathered so far about the system to produce a cost/benefit report. So this task is to prepare presentation material about the project to enable management to decide on granting enough resources to do the preliminary system analysis and design.

Process name: PRESENT PROJECT INITIATION REPORT TO
D.P. MANAGEMENT
Process reference number: 1.2.5
Process guided by: Activity 1 Plan

Process notes: Present the Project Initiation Report to D.P. management who have authority to approve or disapprove the next major project activity.

In addition to providing management information for approval of resources for the project (if DP management rather than the User is responsible for approval of resources), the initiation report also gives an overview of the information gathered to date and a gross size and risk assessment to help management evaluate whether to continue the project.

The formality of the presentation will depend on the environment. In some companies, this initial project approval is so informal that no formal document is produced from this process. But, more and more, I am beginning to think that these go/no-go presentation points should be formal; at least there should be documented project information given to DP management. If the project is approved, you should get a commitment for all resources needed to complete Activity 2.

Process name: PRESENT PROJECT INITIATION REPORT TO USER MANAGEMENT
Process reference number: 1.2.6
Process guided by: Activity 1 Plan

Process notes: This presentation makes User management aware of your progress and seeks commitment for the resources needed for Activity 2 (if the User is responsible for approval of resources).

The User, as the receiver and owner of the new system, should be kept informed of the project's progress, especially in environments in which system development costs are paid for by the User. This presentation keeps communication lines open with User management and can be formal or informal (although you may care to make User presentations more formal). In either case, all the information in the Project Initiation Report should be presented.

If resource approval is given, the overall data processing plans and resource projections (estimates) need to be revised to reflect the real location of resources now dedicated to this project.

"(Approved) Affected Systems" is shown as an output from this process. This implies that you might reduce the area of study (i.e., reduce the number of project goals) to gain approval for continuation of the project. If this reduction takes place, you must realize that you cannot reduce your area of study without affecting the Project Plan, and you may affect project deliverables as well. So, in this case, you must cycle back and do a quick review of Activity 1 to ensure that Activity 1 deliverables and the Project Plan/schedules are still accurate.

Note:

1. The Project Initiation Report has served its purpose as of this process, but it can be kept for reference and used as documentation for Project Histories, if you think it helpful.
2. If the User managers will not ultimately own and/or pay for the development, you may wish to distinguish between User and client and conduct differently oriented presentations for each group.

Process name: VALIDATE AND/OR CREATE PRELIMINARY
DESIGN MODEL FOR CURRENT MANUAL
ENVIRONMENT
Process reference number: 2.1.1
Process guided by: Activity 2 Plan

Process notes: Produce a high-level data flow diagram of the current manual portion of the system.

The main deliverable from this task is a model of the manual portions of the existing system, showing major data streams, files, and the activities that act on this data. I have called this deliverable a design model, because it is physical and shows **how** things are being accomplished; that is, it depicts the existing design.

If you can get User approval on a logical model, annotated with physical characteristics such as department names or numbers, file IDs, and form numbers, then this model can be the deliverable from this task (as well as an aid in the logicalization process later). I call the result of this task a "physilogical" model.

Important note: I recommend you do the minimum "physical" modeling of the manual environment needed to understand it and gain the support and confidence of the Users. Of course, if you have a project objective to fully describe the current physical environment (e.g., because of a lack of any documentation), then you should allocate enough time in the project plan to do just that. If you don't have this specific objective, then try to merge this task with the logicalization of the manual environment—process reference number 2.1.3.

Your aims in this task are to:

• Produce a high-level communication model (a data flow diagram and supporting data dictionary) of the User area that may be affected by the project goals, so the User can verify the model as correct.
• Familiarize yourself with the User environment, establish credibility, develop a working relationship and understand the areas into which the new system must fit.
• Gather cost/benefit information and performance data to be used in future development tasks.

- Familiarize yourself and your User with the use of the system modeling tools.

You will use data collected during this task for other activities. For example, current frequency and volume of use of the data shown in your data flow diagram feed such managerial and technical tasks as cost/benefit analysis and conversion. Also, an organizational hierarchy chart will be useful in identifying where and from whom to gather information. Therefore, the task involves gathering information that makes up the manual system model for this level of study. (To identify preliminary-level data, see the "Sample Table of Contents for a Manual System Model" in Addendum to Data Dictionary.)

If you have an existing data flow model for any area you have to study, then simply validate that model at a preliminary level.

Material for this level of the manual system model comes from several sources:

- At this preliminary level of study, interviews should be held with managers or key staff members responsible for departments, sections, and major business functions. The interview notes should consist of first cut data flow diagrams supported by a preliminary data dictionary.
- Acquire any available maintenance documentation (for example, training materials for new employees).
- Copy actual production procedures and information from procedures manuals.

Note:

1. An unusual output at this level of detail is the Production HW/SW Inventory. Along with equivalent data gathered about the automated system in process reference number 2.1.2, this output specifies all manual system equipment (e.g., typewriters, personal computers, data preparation hardware, and support software) available in the company (not just that being used by the affected systems). This is the most practical process in which to gather this information, but only if it is available in a complete, detailed state (that is, documented in a support library or purchasing area); otherwise, do not spend time gathering the detailed-level information. This data can be gathered when needed as input to a task.

The data in the Production HW/SW Inventory will probably not be the responsibility of the project manager or team, but each must be aware of it because it can greatly affect the cost/benefit analysis. For instance, the cost/benefit study will be affected if the new data preparation facility needed for your system requires constructing a new building.

2. Because this is only a preliminary study, you may represent an automated system with which the manual system currently interfaces as a single process on one complete high-level data flow diagram (or show separate high-level data flow diagrams derived from different affected manual systems). In creating the high-level data flow diagrams and data dictionary, you may encounter different names for the same data item, but it is sufficient at the preliminary level of study merely to document this by the use of aliases.

3. An overview description or a meaningful process name will suffice for a process description at this level. You will later describe the preliminary-level processes you identify in this task by means of lower-level diagrams.

4. If you have difficulty in identifying exactly when you have sufficiently studied the preliminary model for a particular project, the Survey/Probe model, discussed in Appendix F, can help you assess the level of detail appropriate for this portion of the project.

Process name: VALIDATE AND/OR CREATE PRELIMINARY DESIGN MODEL FOR CURRENT AUTOMATED ENVIRONMENT

Process reference number: 2.1.2

Process guided by: Activity 2 Plan

Process notes: Produce a verified high-level model showing the data and associated processes in the automated portions of the system, and how they are controlled today.

The model provides a physical representation, perhaps system flowcharts with supporting information such as input and output documents and control parameters, showing how the automated functions are implemented.

The aims of this process are to:

• Produce an overview model for communication about the automated systems affected by the project goals (you can use the model for initial communication with maintenance and data processing staff members who are familiar with the current computer system).
• Gather cost/benefit information and performance data to aid future tasks.
• Begin to familiarize yourself and the User (in this case it will probably be DP support staff) with the use of the system modeling tools.

To accomplish these aims, complete the information that makes up the automated system model for this level of detail. (To identify preliminary-level data, see the "Sample Table of Contents for an Automated System Model" in Addendum to the Data Dictionary.)

Validate, at a preliminary level, any design charts available in the automated system's maintenance documentation for the system or the part that must be studied. The type of design chart that is appropriate at this level will be similar to a system flowchart; that is, it will be a diagram that shows the major jobs with their programs in the system, and the files and data records they use. You should also document the streams of data, i.e., transactions and reports.

Important note: If there is no one to validate this automated design model, for example, if the User doesn't relate to the existing computer system, then the only reason to produce the current physical design model is to guide producing a current logical model of the business. If this is so, I recommend that you attempt to go straight to the logical modeling task, skipping the physical model (if you are familiar with the current automated design). You will have to rely on the User relating to the logical model for business requirements validation.

Complete this level of the automated system model by using the affected systems to:

- Point to any maintenance documentation available (possibly a hierarchical input, process, and output chart or high-level program flowchart).
- Identify maintenance and operations personnel and even the programmers of the original code for data-gathering interviews.

The current operations manual (if available) should contain information for a system overview. If all else fails, you may have to gather a list of all programs and job/system control language and produce a system overview from the affected programs.

Note:

1. An unusual output at this level of detail is the Production HW/SW Inventory. Along with equivalent data gathered about the manual system in process reference number 2.1.1, this output specifies all DP hardware and support software available in the company— not just that being used by the affected systems. This is the most practical process in which to gather this information, but only if it is available in a complete, detailed state (that is, documented in a support library or purchasing area); otherwise, do not spend time gathering the detailed-level information. This data can be gathered when needed as input to a task.

The data in the Production HW/SW Inventory will probably not be the responsibility of the project manager or team, but each must be aware of it because it can greatly affect the cost/benefit analysis. For instance, the cost/benefit study will be affected if the extra equipment needed for your system requires constructing another computer room.

2. In an automated environment, you may have difficulty deciding when you have studied the current systems enough to satisfy the preliminary model for a project, especially if the systems being studied consist of classical programs of 5,000 lines or more. Therefore, you may want to do a Survey/Probe of one of your typical automated subsystems to identify the level of detail expected in this portion of the system. (See Appendix F.)

Process name: DERIVE PRELIMINARY LOGICAL MODEL FOR
CURRENT MANUAL ENVIRONMENT
Process reference number: 2.1.3
Process guided by: Activity 2 Plan

Process notes: Derive the logical equivalent of the physical manual system model; that is, extract the essential business data and functions that the manual system model portrays without reference to how the data and functions are performed.

The more you can divorce yourself from the physical characteristics and control of the current manual system, the better chance you have of understanding the essential (business view) system, and of developing a good solution for the new system. We accomplish this separation by the process of logicalization. If a logical model already exists in the maintenance library for any areas to be studied, then validate that model. If we have a business event Context Diagram from process reference number 1.1.2, the task at this level will be even easier because we can concentrate on just the data and functions for each business event individually.

At this preliminary level, logicalization is not easy and we do not obtain most of the benefits until the detailed level.

If the current manual system is partitioned only into great huge chunks, then this task may only help you scope out the number of job titles, manual procedures, files, departments, etc., for cost/benefits analysis. However, if the current manual system is reasonably partitioned, then given a valid manual system model, turn it into a high-level logical data flow diagram by tracking the major flows of data and identifying the major manual system functions that act on that data.

The greatest help here will come from a technique called Business Event Partitioning, which partitions together all data and processing associated with each business event data trigger (data flow containing data about the occurrence of an external business event), business time trigger, or control prompt entering the manual portion of the system. Use the Context Diagram and the manual system model to produce a data flow diagram partitioned by business events (data flows and triggers), showing their associated manual processing and intermediate data summed up in one process bubble, plus outgoing and other incoming data flows. (See Appendix D for a discussion of business event partitioning.)

At the same time, remove from this model all physical characteristics (other than those that are essential to the business) such as:

- References to document numbers, colors, or media
- Sequencing or control procedures
- Departments that perform the procedures
- Media used for major filing systems

(To identify preliminary-level data, see the "Sample Table of Contents for a Logical Specification" in the Addendum to Data Dictionary.)

Note:

1. Even at this level, you may find processes that seemingly do not need to be represented on a logical model (for example, backup or data preparation/distribution processes). Therefore, some repartitioning or regrouping of nonfunctional areas may be necessary.

    If you are in doubt about whether to repartition, postpone repartitioning until you derive the logical model for the whole system (manual and automated) in the detailed level of study. Logicalizing interfaces to and from automated systems can also be delayed until you logicalize the whole system.

    Use any existing business and support documentation to assist in deriving and validating the logical model. As this model is a business view, Users should be able to validate this logical model for the manual portions of the system.

2. In this process you are deriving a separate model, not modifying the manual system model. The manual system model will be needed for reference in future processes.

3. See Business Event Partitioning—Appendix G, for how to partition the logical model.

Process name: DERIVE PRELIMINARY LOGICAL MODEL FOR
CURRENT AUTOMATED ENVIRONMENT
Process reference number: 2.1.4
Process guided by: Activity 2 Plan

Process notes: Using the Automated System Model, derive the equivalent logical model to isolate the essential business functions that the automated system currently performs.

As stated in the equivalent manual task (process reference number 2.1.3), the more you can divorce yourself from the current automated system design, the better chance you have of understanding the essential system (the business view) and therefore of being able to develop a the new system which truly meets business requirements. I see too many computer system partitioned along "Edit-Update-Print" or "Input-Process-Output" lines. These are awful partitions for systems, and you should remove them during logicalization.

The complexity of this task will depend on the input (the Automated System Model) and how knowledgeable the Users or DP maintenance staff is about the data and functions performed by the automated system. At this preliminary level, the difficulty arises if program boundaries are purely arbitrary (such as the previously mentioned "Edit-Update-Print" boundaries) and the major logical functions are obscured by data processing technology.

If the current automated system design is partitioned only into great huge chunks, then this task may only help you scope out the number of programs, files, lines of code, etc., for cost/benefit analysis. If the current automated system is reasonably partitioned by business needs, then given a valid automated system model, convert it into a high-level logical data flow diagram by tracking the major flows of data and identifying the major automated system functions that act on that data.

The greatest help here will come from a technique called Business Event Partitioning, which partitions together all data and processing associated with each business event trigger (data flow containing data about the occurrence of an external business event), business time trigger, or control prompt entering the automated portion of the system. Use the Context Diagram and the automated system model to produce a data flow diagram partitioned by business events (data flows or triggers), showing their associated automated processing and intermediate data summed up in one process bubble, plus outgoing and other incoming data flows.

At the same time, remove from this model all physical characteristics, other than those that are essential to the business. Nonessential characteristics include references to transaction numbers or media, to sequencing or control issues, to program numbers, to file identities, etc. Remove these physical references. (To identify preliminary-level data, see the "Sample Table of Contents for a Logical Specification" in the Addendum to Data Dictionary.)

Note:

1. Even at this level, you may find processes, such as housekeeping and backup/recovery jobs, that do not need to appear on a logical model. Some repartitioning (regrouping) of nonfunctional systems may be accomplished here. If you are in doubt about whether to repartition, wait until you derive the logical model for the whole system (manual and automated) in the detailed level of study. Also, you can defer logicalizing the interfaces from and to manual systems until you logicalize the whole system.

   This logical model is your communication tool with the User because computer system design charts are not as readily understood by the User. Use any business and support documentation from the maintenance library (e.g., system purpose or business need statement in system documentation) when deriving and validating this logical model.

2. In this process you are deriving a separate model, not modifying the Automated System Model. The Automated System Model will be needed for reference in the future processes.

3. See Business Event Partitioning—Appendix G, for how to partition the logical model.

Process name: DERIVE PRELIMINARY LOGICAL SPECIFICA-
TION FOR THE CURRENT SYSTEM
Process reference number: 2.1.5
Process guided by: Activity 2 Plan

Process notes: Produce a logical model for the whole system
(manual and automated systems combined).

In effect, this task will consist of merging the models of major
tasks that were physically split between portions of the old design,
i.e., data flows partly processed in the Current Manual system and
partly processed in the Current Automated system.

The reason for producing a complete logical model is similar to the
reason for performing previous logicalization tasks—if you can
remove these last physical remnants of how manual and automated
processes are partitioned in the existing system, you will probably
develop a more cost-effective and maintainable partitioning for the
new system.

This process involves combining two high-level logical models into
one; it shouldn't be too difficult because now the physical characteristics will occur only at the interfaces between the manual and
automated components. Match the major interfaces and remove their
physical characteristics (e.g., equipment used, timing features). This
should be easy to accomplish at the preliminary level, because you
are mainly dealing with streams of data and their components, and
the major overall processes that transform this data.

As with other logicalization tasks, a business event partitioned
context diagram, if available from the Project Initiation activity,
should greatly help. Business event partitioning brings together all
data and processing associated with each single stimulus to the system. This will be either a data flow (containing data about the occurrence of an external business event) or a business time or control
prompt entering the system.

If an interface in the manual model does not correspond to one in
the automated model (allowing for aliases), you must investigate the
missing interface by cycling back to the original manual or
automated design models. Any interfaces that were missed will require the same development effort as used to derive other interfaces,
such as looking for repartitioning.

In this process, you should apply the same principles as in the
other logicalization tasks:

- Remove physical characteristics from the interfaces (other than those that are essential to the business) and develop logical (non-computer) names for those remaining business-related characteristics.
- Identify interface stores that are really data flows, such as those that are used just for time delays (e.g., batch to on-line, manual to automated, Friday extract files) and that can be turned into data flows because they only held onto data until the computer system was invoked.
- Look for partitioning problems; for example, functions that are performed partly in the manual system and partly in the automated system and join together business event–related data and functions.

This process should give a reasonably useful overview of the Current Logical system even though it is performed at a high level of detail. This system model should show the major essential processes and their data.

To confirm the data required for this level of study, see the "Sample Table of Contents for a Logical Specification" in the Addendum to Data Dictionary.

The only parts of the model that may still retain physical characteristics are the stores, which you should now investigate to see if they are "kitchen sink" stores (stores that can be broken down into more functional simple stores). Split these stores and regroup them into high-level categories (for example, from Master File into employee data, client data, and project data), and reincorporate them into the logical system model, with the correct data flows connected to them.

You may also discover stores that are duplicated in both the manual and automated environments. Remove any duplicated store. Cleaning up the stores should improve the readability of the model and should also remove any final high-level physical characteristics remaining from the current design.

Process name: CREATE PRELIMINARY TEST CASES FOR
CURRENT SYSTEM
Process reference number: 2.1.6
Process guided by: Activity 2 Plan

Process notes: Identify the test cases needed to validate the Current Logical Specification at a preliminary level.

Because the logical system should stay relatively intact, these test cases will probably be used in total for the new system. If you are lucky enough to have a Regression Test Specification in the maintenance library for any of the automated or manual systems being studied, use it to help create the preliminary test cases.

For systems that don't have a Regression Test Specification, review the Current Logical Specification and develop test cases that will validate the information contained in the specification, such as major streams of data, stores, and functions.

Of course, the best source to use for identifying and defining test cases is the Data Dictionary in the Current Logical Specification, with the data flow diagram serving as a guide to identify the flow of all boundary (context) data from input to output.

The test cases at this level of detail will probably be specified informally in narrative scenario form, as in the following example:

Test objective: to ensure that there are no defects in applying payroll exception monies to the general ledger

Test input: all payroll update transactions

Expected execution: valid payroll update transactions logged for audit; general ledger updated with revised payroll amount

Expected output: payroll exception check and equivalent amount on general ledger update report

Since the User is obviously a good source of information, the User or User representative can help to create test cases to validate the current system and can be particularly helpful in identifying invalid (negative) tests.

Note:

Not only can you use these test case scenarios to verify the completeness and correctness of the current specification (and, therefore, the current analysis effort itself); you can make them the basis for new system test cases.

Process name: CONDUCT REVIEW OF PRELIMINARY
CURRENT LOGICAL SPECIFICATION
Process reference number: 2.1.7
Process guided by: Activity 2 Plan

Process notes: This review identifies any problems, inaccuracies, ambiguities, and omissions in the Current Logical Specification at the preliminary level of detail.

Since the specification will be used as the basis for the new system, it must be correct. A walkthrough should have been conducted for each intermediate deliverable (e.g., the data dictionary) up to this point. Since the system can now be viewed in total (with manual and automated portions combined), a formal quality control inspection may take place. This review should include the project manager or User and project analysts. The current system test cases can be used in the validation of the Current Logical Specification.
(See Appendix E for rules for standard reviews.)

Process name: REFINE PROJECT GOALS
Process reference number: 2.2
Process guided by: Activity 2 Plan

Process notes: Assemble known project goals and identify any new project goals, prioritize them, and resolve any conflicts.

With the User, compare the logical model for the whole system with the current physical system to identify any additional project goals at this point. Goals that may already have been identified during preliminary system study should also be included here. Removing physical characteristics from the current system model may reveal new goals or modifications to existing goals. For example, new hardware/software goals may be revealed when you eliminate physical interfaces between manual and automated systems.

You may identify additional goals at this point because this is still only a preliminary study and if the new goals can be accommodated in the project, including them at this stage will not cause serious rework. However, you must be realistic; any new major project goals may affect your area of study, so don't add them unless they are essential to the success of the project.

Any new project goals requested at this stage should be compared with existing goals to ensure that they are not duplicates or already encompassed within existing goals. If not, highlight the new goals so they can be identified as having been introduced after approval of the project initiation report.

Next, prioritize the new project goals and resolve any conflicts that may arise. (This task is similar to "Resolve Any Conflicts and Prioritize Project Goals," process reference number 1.1.4 in Activity 1. You may need to cycle back to this process if the new goals affect the area of study and must be included in this development effort.)

This is a good time to identify goals that cannot be satisfied completely by this system, as well as to inform the User of them so he or she can modify expectations. Your knowledge of the system to date will allow you to help management reorder the priority of the goals and discuss the repercussions of any conflicts. As with the original project goals, any additional goals should be measurable.

Note:

No doubt, additional project goals will be uncovered as the project continues to unfold. If a new goal simply refines an existing goal and has little or no impact on the project, then it can probably be accommodated directly. But if the goal is completely new or is a major change to an existing goal, then it may affect your area of study or conflict with an existing goal. If this is the case, the new goal may be processed by the project change management mechanism and documented during process reference number 5.2.3 as a change request to be included in the next release.

If an essential project goal is discovered in a later activity, you must cycle back to repeat this process, even returning to Activity 1 if our area of study is affected. If so, you must consider the new goal's impact on every deliverable and process performed so far.

(This process is the only one that I have not decomposed to Level 2. This is a significant task that is already a primitive task at Level 1 in my diagrams.)

Process name: ANALYZE PRELIMINARY PROJECT GOALS
Process reference number: 2.3.1
Process guided by: Activity 2 Plan

Process notes: Analyze and derive the logical modifications needed to accommodate any business and project goals in the new system at this level of detail.

If business goals are specified, they will be of two types: those modifying data and/or functions in the Current Logical Specification, and those requiring completely new data and/or functions. Such goals will be documented as business objectives and constraints in the Project Charter.

This process will require little effort if all goals relate to the design and implementation of the new system, for example, changing the current system from batch to on-line or from manual to automated. In fact, don't be surprised if there are no logical modifications for the new system (i.e., the Current Logical Specification *is* the New Logical Specification; just design changes are needed).

On the other hand, this process can require much effort if the current study identified only interface systems to a new business function and new data. In such a case, analyzing some of the preliminary project goals can be equivalent to doing just about all the tasks so far performed in this methodology, only now you are working with the new data and functions. The amount of work depends on how the new data and functions are identified; for example, there will be significant work if knowledge about the necessary data and functions can be obtained only at another company.

Also note that project goals may identify changes or deletions to data and functions, which may require validating the physical-to-logical transformations of the new data and functions, and producing minimodels to be included in or used to update the Current Logical Model to form the New Logical Model. At this level of detail, however, the task will probably be relatively easy, as you are identifying only major streams of data and their major functions.

For those project goals that can be completely or partly analyzed in this process, document the solutions to analysis goals in the Project Charter.

To identify preliminary level data, see the "Sample Table of Contents for a Logical Specification" in the Addendum to Data Dictionary. If there are only changes and deletions to data and functions, this process involves documenting that fact in your project log.

Process name: DERIVE PRELIMINARY LOGICAL MODEL FOR
THE NEW SYSTEM
Process reference number: 2.3.2
Process guided by: Activity 2 Plan

Process notes: Produce the New Logical model by applying the logical modifications to the Current Logical Specification.

This process simply involves adding, updating, and deleting portions of the data flow diagrams and data dictionary that make up the Current Logical Specification. In fact, there may be nothing to do in this task if there are no logical modifications (actually, you are developing a separate model here, not modifying the Current Logical Specification, which will be needed for reference in future processing).

The greatest help here will come from a technique called Business Event Partitioning, where we partition together all data and processing associated with each single stimulus to the system. A stimulus here will be a single data flow or business time or control prompt entering the automated portion of our system.

If any high-level partitioning problems result from new data and functions being added, you can probably take care of them in the next process, when you repartition the model into manual and automated functions. If new stores were introduced into the model, investigate to see if they satisfy many functions (they are a group store) or contain data that is redundant with the contents of an already existing store. This process may involve regrouping and/or splitting stores (in combination with existing stores) into changed high-level groupings.

One of the aims of studying the current system is to ensure that all modifications fit inside the current model and are completely bounded by the area of study. If not, the study is not complete. This process should be relatively easy at the preliminary level because you are dealing mainly with streams of data and their components and with the major processes that transform this data. In fact, the modification may not be completely identifiable in the model at this level of detail, making it necessary for you to give an estimate of the percentage of change to functions and data. It is useful to highlight the modifications in the new system model so that you can identify them easily in the future.

Process name: IDENTIFY PRELIMINARY MAN/MACHINE
BOUNDARIES FOR THE NEW SYSTEM
Process reference number: 2.3.3
Process guided by: Activity 2 Plan

Process notes: Identify the portions of the logical model that are to be implemented manually and those that are to be automated. This process can be viewed as one of physical change (design), whereas the previous two processes were involved with logical change (business requirements).

In the case where the major project goal is to convert a manual system to an automated system, this task focuses on the most significant change to the system—the difference between old and new automation boundaries. Because the New Logical model shows no old design partitioning, you have the advantage here of being able to identify the best automated/manual partitioning for the new system without being influenced by the old design. Even if there are constraints on what you are allowed to automate, you still should identify the most cost-effective automation boundary as one of a number of options and let the client or User select the partitioning.

Draw a bounded area or areas on the logical model that will encompass the automated functions and data and therefore leave unbounded the area of the model to be manually implemented. Develop various other automation boundary options guided by the project goals in the Project Charter, and identify the overall costs and schedules associated with each option.

Look for project goals that state requirements for the physical environment. For example, "Department X must not be affected by automation." In this example, refer back to the Current Physical Specification (although not shown on the methodology's DFD) to identify which parts of the logical model represent Department X. (This is why I've put a cross-reference to Current Physical Definition/Processes as a data item in the logical Data Dictionary in this book.)

Again, you may want to use the Current Physical DFD model to help identify the current physical areas that will be affected by the new manual/automation boundary. The current physical characteristics of a data flow may help you select an automation boundary. For instance, frequency of use may be a significant factor because you may not want to automate a function that is performed only once a year if the benefits are trivial. (The use of the Current Physical Specification in this instance will depend on the project goals; therefore, this process has been starved of the Current Physical Specification so that the current design will not negatively influence the new design.)

At this high level of detail you may not be able to clearly describe the automation boundaries. Therefore, you may have to estimate the percentage of automation of each major function and its data and show the automation boundary line cutting through functions on the DFD. For clearly defined boundaries, you can repartition the DFD, i.e., group automated functions and data together and manual functions and data together and redraft the DFD to clearly show this partitioning.

You may find it helpful to identify some physical characteristics of the interfaces between the manual and automated portions of the system such as the media used for interface data flows or for interface stores. This will probably allow you to review the diagrams more easily with the Users from the viewpoint of the new system issues. Also, you may introduce interface stores (i.e., stores that hold data over a period of time between the manual and automated systems) because of the new boundary definition.

If the physical characteristics are introduced during this process, note that the Bounded New Logical Specification becomes somewhat physical. Also note that the automation boundary itself is a physical characteristic. Physicalizing the interfaces will be one of the first tasks in design, if it is not done in this task.

For any project goals that can be completely or partly satisfied in this process, document the solutions in the Project Charter.

Note:

Remember that the different automation boundaries defined in this process represent the system options for later presentation and you should perform all processes until the end of Activity 2 for each option. This is necessary to identify an honest cost/benefit analysis and feasibility report. The amount of work involved may seem considerable, but realize that there will be overlap between tasks (in fact, one option may be completely encompassed within another), and that you are working at only a preliminary level of detail.

Process name: IDENTIFY PRELIMINARY PROTOTYPE AREAS
Process reference number: 2.3.4
Process guided by: Activity 2 Plan

Process notes: Use the New System Project Goals and the Bounded New Logical Specification to identify the part(s) of the new system which will be studied in the future at the detailed level using prototyping methods.

Prototyping may be used on the new parts of the system in order to gain User approval of these new areas. Often logical system components are difficult to specify because neither the DP staff nor the User has a frame of reference from which to operate. In other words, the new requirements have never been implemented in the company either in a manual or automated environment. Prototyping helps here by simulating the boundary results of the system because there are no existing environments that you can study to develop a current requirements model. Use the Bounded New Logical DFD to identify potential areas of uncertainty and mark them and their inputs and outputs to be prototyped on the Bounded New Logical DFD. Use prototyping principles to gather the new "nonestablished" data and functions from the Users requesting these new data and functions. The prototyping results will then be used to supplement the existing requirements model.

Alternatively, if none of the Bounded New Logical Specification are available because the entire system will consist of completely new business data and functions, you could use prototyping methods to develop a rudimentary New Physical system (i.e., a prototype).

At this point, not much work has yet been done on anticipating the new physical system. If you adopt prototyping methods in order establish technical feasibility for the new system, you may need to get into more detail here.

Once the User approves the resulting prototyped new system (or parts of it), you should back up to process reference numbers 2.3.1 to 2.3.3 to use the prototype to define essential preliminary business data and functions, to develop a New Logical Specification and to identify a Preliminary Man/Machine Boundary.

Process name: CREATE PRELIMINARY TEST CASES FOR
THE NEW SYSTEM
Process reference number: 2.3.5
Process guided by: Activity 2 Plan

Process notes: Develop test cases for the new system.

If you already developed test cases for the current system, use them to help develop the new system test cases. How much they will help depends on how much modification you made to the Current Logical Specification. If there were no modifications, all of the current system test cases can be used. If modifications were made, the test cases will need additions and/or changes depending on the modifications.

You can think of these tests as logical tests, which do not pertain to the design or implementation of the system, but which verify whether the system accomplishes the business functions and data. These test cases will be employed later to develop system and acceptance test cases.

Note:

Select test cases carefully as they are candidates for further decomposition and will be used finally for development of executable tests.

As with preliminary current system test cases, new system test cases will probably be specified informally in narrative form (see process reference number 2.1.6).

Process name: CONDUCT REVIEW OF PRELIMINARY
BOUNDED NEW LOGICAL SPECIFICATION
Process reference number: 2.3.6
Process guided by: Activity 2 Plan

Process notes: Identify any problems, inaccuracies, ambiguities, and omissions in the Bounded New Logical Specification.

This is the final deliverable from the analysis activities at the preliminary level. Since this specification is going to be used to develop the preliminary new design, it has to be complete and correct. You should have conducted walkthroughs on the intermediate deliverables up to this review. Therefore, this task involves a formal review of the Bounded New Logical Specification as a whole.

The agents reviewing the specification should be the project manager, User or User representative, project analysts, and, optionally, the designer. You should use the new system project goals and their solutions as well as the new system test cases to help validate the Bounded New Logical Specification.

(For standard review rules and procedures, see Appendix E.)

Process name: VERIFY OR REVISE PRELIMINARY
CORPORATE DATA DICTIONARY
Process reference number: 2.4.1
Process guided by: Activity 2 Plan

Process notes: Validate the data from the preliminary system model (which consists at this level of files and records) by comparing it with the corporate data dictionary of stored data.

Most large companies have a corporate data administrator; but even if you are not using a central data administration group to coordinate data, you should compare the data needs for your project with those in other systems within the corporation and attempt to synchronize all of the data and reduce redundancy.

Identify any project goals that relate to data capture (e.g., centralizing data or sharing data). Using these goals, identify and incorporate any system data declared in the preliminary data dictionary which is not already in the corporate data dictionary. (A companywide data dictionary and common database(s) reduce (if not eliminate) data redundancy, multiple updating, and inconsistency of common data between systems.)

For any project goals that can be completely or partially satisfied in this process, document the data capture goals solutions in the Project Charter.

Note:

1. This task, the others in Activity 2.4, and the equivalent detailed tasks, take a companywide view whereas all the other tasks concentrate on only your project's area of study. Data should not be looked upon as just the property of one application because most data tends to span many systems.

2. I have shown this process and the other data specification processes being fed by Structured Analysis. The Structured Specification presents what is known as a "User View" for Information Modeling. Another view is that Information Modeling can be the initial activity of a project, delivering an Entity-Relationship model as input to the structured analysis process. I have shown the former case in this methodology as the book takes a single project view and I believe the product of each

structured analysis effort should feed the information modeling effort. (An Entity-Relationship Diagram is a view of a system or enterprise from a **static** data perspective, whereas a Structured Specification is a view of a system from an **active** data perspective.)

3. This process may be performed by an agent outside the project team, such as data administration personnel.

Process name: IDENTIFY PRELIMINARY DATA CATEGORIES
Process reference number: 2.4.2
Process guided by: Activity 2 Plan

Process notes: Identify the system groupings of data (data categories or entities, e.g., Employee data, Project data, Customer Account data) using the corporate data model (showing data objects/entities, and relationships) and the corporate data dictionary.

In this process, we are identifying the best functional data groupings possible at this preliminary level of detail. These functional groupings are called "candidate objects" or "entities," and they represent "things" that are verifiable and recognizable within the company. Such groupings are not confirmed until you have studied their attributes in more detail.

Candidate objects are suggested/identified from things (actual essential objects in the business), people, roles, events, contracts, in fact, at this level of study, anything about which you wish/need to retain information or history within your area of system study. Of course, at this point don't usurp the Structured Specification; that is, don't redocument the information already gathered and recorded from an active view of the data, in the flows and processes on the data flow diagrams. For instance, the system DFD shows a flow of information through the system and the transformation policy on that data; therefore, information flow and transformation policy don't need to be documented here.

Check to see if your system candidate objects match with any entities in the corporate data model. In the case where the same data item or entity has one name in the corporate dictionary and another name in your dictionary, use the corporate name. Use the system data flow diagram to show the functional reasons for why you created these objects/entities.

The new or modified data categories should be noted, especially those that require significant change to the corporate data dictionary, as they will affect the cost/benefit analysis for the new system.

Note:

This process may be performed by an agent outside the project team, such as data administration personnel.

Process name: IDENTIFY PRELIMINARY ACCESS PATHS
BETWEEN CATEGORIES
Process reference number: 2.4.3
Process guided by: Activity 2 Plan

Process notes: Identify the relationships that exist between the data categories for the system. Investigate the corporate data model for access paths that exist between any data categories that are in your system. Check for usable access paths for your system.

Using the DFD and Data Dictionary for the Bounded New Logical Specification, identify the access paths that are not already supported and that you need for your system's view of the data and indicate them on the data model. For example, a report (data flow) output from the system may be formed from the data accessed from many data stores.

Even with your limited knowledge to date of the system, you should be able to identify many necessary access paths between data categories, if only by looking at the access flow(s) among the categories necessary to form the output report. The report may need Employee data within Project data and also show all completed deliverables for the project. Identify the accesses between Project and Employee objects and between Project and Project Deliverable objects needed to produce this output.

For any project goals that can be completely or partly satisfied in this process or the previous process, document the data model goals solutions in the Project Charter.

Note:

1. An agent outside the project team such as data administration personnel may perform this process.

2. If you are not performing the Information Modeling activities at the same time as the Structured Analysis data modeling, use the data model resulting from this Information Modeling process to cycle back and amend the stores in the New Logical model. Replace any complex data stores on the New Logical DFD with their simpler components (i.e., data categories). This should make the New Logical model easier to read from a business point of view.

3. I am advocating "access paths" at this level of study rather than "relationships." In a top-down approach to system development it may be difficult to assess the actual relationships to specific entities at this level of detail; therefore a simpler model of data categories and their access paths may suffice for our information needs here.

Process name: IDENTIFY SUITABLE SOFTWARE PACKAGES
Process reference number: 2.5.1
Process guided by: Activity 2 Plan

Process notes: Determine whether any or all of the business requirements for the new system can be satisfied by one or more software packages.

The Bounded New Logical Specification and Data Model should contain enough high-level requirements information to determine whether all or part of the business requirements could be satisfied by a software package. If so, contact vendors of suitable packages for their documentation. The vendors will probably supply this package documentation in detail form, but at this stage, you should really only compare your high-level requirements with an overview of the package. The detailed portion of the package documentation will be of use to you in the detailed level process "Evaluate/ Select Software Package(s)" (process reference number 3.3.5).

If a package or packages are identified in this process as potentially suitable, then include their documentation as input to all processes from here on via the Automated System Model and New Physical Specification.

For any project goal that can be completely or partially satisfied in this process, document the Software Package Goal Solution in the Project Charter along with purchase and ongoing costs.

Note:

If there is a special project goal to implement the new system in a software package, then you will not perform the tasks in this methodology relating to new design and code. The software package's design and code will replace these. Of course, where customized portions of the system need to be added to any sofware package then that's where the design and code task of this methodology come in to play. You should evaluate all other tasks, however, for inclusion in your customized project methodology, e.g., hardware selection, conversion, training, installation.

Process name: CREATE PRELIMINARY DESIGN MODEL FOR
NEW MANUAL ENVIRONMENT
Process reference number: 2.5.2
Process guided by: Activity 2 Plan

Process notes: Identify the high-level design for the manual portion
of the Bounded New Logical Specification.

The manual system design process is normally given little attention in data processing, even though the manual system is just as
important as the automated system for accomplishing business functions. The data flow diagram is an excellent tool for modeling the
new manual environment, the design of which will be governed by
the project goals. For example, the existing manual environment
could be significantly affected by an objective that states, "automate
as much of the manual system as is cost-effective."

If a software package(s) was identified earlier as potentially able to
satisfy some or all business requirements, introduce it into your
design model to show the interfaces with the manual portion of the
new system.

Designing the manual environment at this level consists of identifying any new boundaries for departments, sections or groups
within the manual portion of the system, and then identifying overall
physical interface characteristics between these boundaries, as well
as the physical characteristics of major streams of data within them.

Changes to data stored in the manual environment could be significant. Data spans both the manual and automated portions of a
system. Therefore, some regrouping (repartitioning) of existing
manual files may synchronize and reduce data redundancy.

The New Logical high-level DFD (after its data stores have been
modified as a result of Information Modeling) will declare the more
functional major stores to be shared among major functions of the
system. The Data Dictionary will point to the original physical
store(s) used to derive a logical data store. We can use the cross
reference (declared in your system Data Dictionary) to identify the
level of change for stored data.

To create a preliminary design model for a new manual environment, first identify any support characteristics (e.g. input/output
media, physical storage requirements, operations support) associated
with the automation boundary that separates the new manual and

automated systems. (This may have been done when the automation boundary was identified.)

Look for environment modifications on the DFD by comparing the current with the new manual system boundaries. These modifications to the environment will be the key areas of change on which to concentrate. In addition, concentrate on any project goals that can be satisfied at this point.

At this preliminary level, you can do little more than identify the major high-level design and major boundary choices. (These may change greatly in the detailed-level study.) This will assist in the cost/benefit analysis and feasibility study of the new system. Even at this high level, you may identify support functions that need to be inserted in the model, such as a new data preparation section, operations support, and the areas where Users will perform data entry to the new system.

You are starting to introduce physical characteristics to the Bounded New Logical Specification here, so this process is basically the reverse of logicalization. (To identify preliminary-level physical data, see the "Sample Table of Contents for a Manual System Model" in the Addendum to Data Dictionary.)

For any project goals that can be completely or partly satisfied in this process, document the manual design goal solutions in the Project Charter. It is useful to highlight the areas of change in the new design model so that you can identify them easily in the future.

Note:

In this process you are developing a separate model, not modifying the Bounded New Logical Specification. The Bounded New Logical Specification will be needed for reference in future processes.

Process name: CREATE PRELIMINARY DESIGN MODEL FOR
NEW AUTOMATED ENVIRONMENT
Process reference number: 2.5.3
Process guided by: Activity 2 Plan

Process notes: Design, at the preliminary level, the automated portion of the Bounded New Logical Specification.

Use Business Event Partitioning (already used in deriving the New Logical model) to partition together all data and processing associated with each stimulus to the system. These will be either single data flows containing data about an external business event, business time triggers, or control prompts entering the automated portion of our system. (At this point the model will already have been event-partitioned, but a business event may be split between the automated and manual parts of our system.)

Later, in detailed design, you will make the response to each partitioned business event into a complete structure chart (a hierarchical design tool which shows the partitioning and control structure of a computer system). Just how much of the computer system internal architecture you can design now depends on the level of detail you studied in analysis.

If you have just a "Figure 0" DFD, then the design will reflect only the major events (different partitions of the design based on major data streams) that appear in the system requirements definition. If you have more detail from analysis, you can start to identify the specifics of event partitions that will become structure charts, and which in turn may become programs or jobs in the new system.

If you earlier identified one or more software packages which could potentially satisfy business requirements, introduce it into your design for the automated part of the new system. In fact, simply substitute the software package design documentation. The package documentation becomes the Automated System Model or part of it.

You will not perform the tasks in this methodology relating to new design and code for the part(s) of the system which will use the software package. The software package's design and code will replace these. You should evaluate all other tasks, however, for inclusion in your customized project methodology, e.g., hardware selection, conversion, training, installation.

Next, identify any User-defined goals or constraints that dictate the prepackaging for the automated system. Review the project goals here. There may be an objective to partition the automated system between batch and on-line boundaries (based on time constraints or business cycles), or to use software packages. Such a goal/constraint will make you package parts of the system together for reasons other than business events. Represent these prepackage boundaries on the DFD by drawing boundary lines encompassing groups of functions, and at this high level even cutting through functions.

Next identify the high-level physical support characteristics such as terminals, transaction stream/report media and file storage needs on the data flows crossing the automation boundary (assuming they were not already identified during the establishment of the automation boundary or manual system design.

To identify preliminary level physical data, see the "Sample Table of Contents for an Automated System Model" in the Addendum to Data Dictionary.

For any project goals that can be completely or partly satisfied in this process, document the automated design goals solutions in the Project Charter.

Highlight the areas of change in the new design model so that you can identify them easily in the future.

Note:

1. To avoid creating the next generation of maintenance nightmares, do not partition the automated system into "Edit-Update-Print" or "Input-Process-Output" partitions here.

2. Also, avoid setting program boundaries at this point; the detailed level study is the best place for that. The number of business event partitions and whether the automated system is mostly transaction-oriented or transform-oriented will serve better than a vague program count for cost/benefit and feasibility studies of the new system.

Process name: CREATE PRELIMINARY HW/SW
SPECIFICATION
Process reference number: 2.5.4
Process guided by: Activity 2 Plan

Process notes: Identify the major hardware and software needed to support the manual and automated portions of the new system.

The best you can do at the preliminary level is to identify the classes of equipment and support software needed to support the preliminary design. In order to support a true cost/benefit analysis, it is necessary to identify hardware and support software for both the automated and manual environment; for example, you may identify not only the need for minicomputers for each division but also for typewriters with by-product optical character recognition output to support the manual environment.

If using a software package was identified as a possible system solution, then this will already be documented in the New Physical Specification. If so, incorporate the software package documentation as part of the Hardware/Software Specification.

A project goal may state that you must use the existing system hardware/software or other company hardware/software that is not being used to capacity. Such a goal will make this process very simple (it will involve just preliminary allocations of this hardware/software) as the design boundaries will have had to accommodate this goal. Otherwise, use the New Physical Specification along with any hardware/software goals (e.g., the new hardware/software must be compatible with that of a central division) to identify your hardware/software needs.

The Production HW/SW Inventory identifies all company hardware and software, the current system hardware/software being a subset of this information. If you do not have project goals that dictate hardware and software requirements, proceed as follows:

- Identify possible reusable portions of existing system hardware/software.
- Identify possible reusable portions of the company hardware/software.
- For those requirements not satisfied as a result of the previous two steps, research the purchase of new hardware/software. To aid in cost/benefit analysis, you could also obtain hardware/software data

from applicable vendors, especially as in this process we are dealing with major needs. This data should be stored in the Hardware/Software Specification.

Use the manual and automated system data flow diagrams to aid in this task if the automation boundary was annotated with physical characteristics.

For any project goals that can be completely or partly satisfied in this process, document the hardware/software goals solutions in the Project Charter.

Indicate in this specification whether the hardware/software will be new, or already exists in the company.

Process name: CREATE PRELIMINARY TEST CASES FOR
NEW DESIGN
Process reference number: 2.5.5
Process guided by: Activity 2 Plan

Process notes: Begin to add physical tests cases to those already in the Test Specification.

These physical test cases are those needed to validate, at a preliminary level, the New Physical Specification (e.g., the partitioning of the manual and automated systems) and the Hardware/Software Specification for the new system.

The new system test cases already created from the Bounded New Logical Specification are the logical tests. You can build upon these to form physical tests. You can have two objectives for a test case: to test a business function and data, and to test the implementation of that function and data. Use the data dictionary of the New Physical Specification and the data flows declared on the physical DFDs to identify and define test cases at this stage.

The physical partitioning between and within the manual and automated systems and its physical characteristics such as record types and files will aid in identifying physical tests. Specify the test cases at this level of detail informally in narrative form.

Note:

Have someone other than the designer(s) create these test cases, especially negative test cases, to insure the objectivity of the tests.

Process name: CONDUCT REVIEW OF PRELIMINARY NEW
DESIGN SPECIFICATIONS
Process reference number: 2.5.6
Process guided by: Activity 2 Plan

Process notes: Identify any problems, inaccuracies, ambiguities, and omissions in the New Physical Specification and the Hardware/Software Specification for this level of detail.

These specifications are the final design deliverables at this level of study. You will use them to develop the Implementation Specification and, when completed at the detailed level, to build the system code and User procedures; therefore, they have to be complete and correct. This should not be a lengthy review because intermediate walkthroughs should already have been conducted on the individual deliverables after their development.

Because this is an internal DP review, the review body should include the project team, the project manager, and optionally a hardware/software planner. You should try to keep the User or User representatives involved, especially as this is the first major review showing the partitioning of the User's area and the physical interface to the automated system.

The design project goals, their solutions, and the design test cases will help to validate the design specifications in this review.

(For standard review rules and procedures, see Appendix E.)

Process name: PREPARE PRELIMINARY SYSTEM
INSTALLATION SPECIFICATION
Process reference number: 2.6.1
Process guided by: Activity 2 Plan

Process notes: Identify procedures and support requirements needed for installing the new system's application software and manual procedures, at a preliminary level.

First, identify the area of change between the current and new systems. The area of change should already be indicated in the New Physical Specification, but if it isn't, the Current Physical Specification can be used for comparison. At this level of detail, you probably can only estimate the extent of change within the area of study and therefore can only estimate the procedures and support needed for installation of the new system. For example, on the automated portion of the system, a complete transfer of software and operations procedures might be called for; on the manual side, a relocation of the data preparation department to a new environment may be required. These are the types of things to note in the preliminary System Installation Specification. (Don't get over-detailed in this preliminary level with assumptions—I think of these implementation specifications as "one-pagers.")

If the project is a rewrite of an existing system (that is, with no change to the manual environment and possible little change to the operations procedures), then the installation can be identified easily .

You should identify any project goals that can be completely or partly satisfied in this process (for example, an objective might be to ensure no loss of customer data during the installation period of the new system). For this example objective, you might document a solution, in the Project Charter, that a three-cycle backup history will be kept during installation to preserve customer data.

To do this task, you will have to rely on the conceptual design in the New Physical Specification and estimate the volume of User procedures and systems operations tasks that will change. You may even know, for example, that the new system will be implemented as a transaction-oriented on-line system. This knowledge will help you identify system support needs from a technical service group and an associated hardware/support software group. Document these needs here.

You will probably find some overlap between this and the other implementation specifications, but try to keep it to a minimum.

Process name: PREPARE PRELIMINARY HW/SW
INSTALLATION SPECIFICATION
Process reference number: 2.6.2
Process guided by: Activity 2 Plan

Process notes: Identify preliminary environment and support requirements needed to install the new system's hardware and support software.

The Hardware/Software Specification describes the major hardware and support software needed for the new system and also identifies the portions that are new. Focus attention on the new hardware/software as well as on existing environments that require modification.

If there are no new purchases or modifications of hardware and support software, then this process will just involve predicting whether the existing environment can accommodate the new system's needs as well as identifying any support requirements, such as a need for extra operations staff for an increased workload on existing hardware/software.

If there are new hardware and support software needs, then you should identify any project goals applying to its installation that can be wholly or partly satisfied in this process. For example, there might be an objective to use existing computer room space for significant new hardware purchases; you should document the implementation goals solutions to this (e.g., the space needed for the new equipment in the existing computer room) in the Project Charter.

Next review the hardware/software environment's data in the Production HW/SW Inventory store and determine if an existing environment can be used as a base or a model for any new hardware/software. If so, this environment's documentation should be used as part of the Hardware/Soft- ware Installation Specification and should indicate the extent of change.

For the hardware/software that doesn't fit in an existing environment, identify the necessary preliminary new environment description and first-cut configuration chart. Whether an existing environment can or cannot be used, you should predict the hardware/software installation support requirements. You will only be able to give approximations of installation needs because you have identified only major hardware/software in the Hardware/ Software Specification at this point of the project. (Don't get overly detailed in these preliminary level specifications—I think of these implementation specifications as "one-pagers.")

Note:

1. The agent performing this process may be outside the project team, such as a support planning group.

2. You will probably find some overlap between this and the other implementation specifications, but try to keep it to a minimum.

Process name: PREPARE PRELIMINARY CONVERSION
SPECIFICATION
Process reference number: 2.6.3
Process guided by: Activity 2 Plan

Process notes: Identify the procedures and support requirements needed in the conversion of data for the new system, at a preliminary level.

The first task in this process is to identify the area of change between the current and new systems, as this is the focal point in this process (specifically, the change of stored data and input/output composition). The area should be indicated already in the New Physical Specification (in the data dictionary); if it isn't, the Current Physical Specification can be used for comparison.

You should look for files containing data that will probably change or for new files that need to be created, in addition to files that will need a change of sequence, access, or media. At this level of detail, you have only identified the major stores with their records and the transaction streams with their transactions, but you may have already identified considerable changes after having derived more business-oriented data categories (for stores, during information modeling) and a new automation boundary during design.

You should identify any project goals that can be totally or partly satisfied in this process; for example, an objective might state that all records in the personnel file that are not in the payroll file should be identified and deleted. For this project goal, you would document the implementation goal (e.g., one centralized payroll/personnel file will be produced with an error file for nonmatched records) in the Project Charter.

Note:

The conversion effort can be a system in itself if the data conversion is large and complex. If this is the case, create a preliminary system model (perhaps in the form of a small Structured Specification) showing existing data and the data transformations necessary to produce the new data, and a design model showing the implementation of these functions and their data coupling. Also, you should develop a conversion data dictionary so the conversion effort can be independent. You can identify preliminary test cases to validate the conversion procedures and results.

For this preliminary level of detail, the specification will identify and predict the data to be converted and the degree and complexity of the conversion effort. (Don't get overly detailed in these preliminary-level specifications—I think of these implementation specifications as "one-pagers.")

You will probably find some overlap between this and the other Implementation Specification, but try to keep this to a minimum.

Process name: PREPARE PRELIMINARY TRAINING
SPECIFICATION
Process reference number: 2.6.4
Process guided by: Activity 2 Plan

Process notes: Identify the requirements and support needed for training the Users and the operations staff so that they can make the new system run effectively.

First, identify the area of change between the current and new system, as this is the area on which you will concentrate. You can treat the prepackaged automated portions of the system as "black-boxes" (i.e., you know what they accomplish by reference to their inputs and outputs, without knowing the details of how they accomplish it). Your areas of concern are the new processes and the partitioning of the manual system and the interfaces to the automated system.

For operations training, you also concentrate on the new partitioning and pre-packaging of the automated system and the interfaces to operations. The area of change should be indicated already in the New Physical Specification; if not, the Current Physical Specification can be used for comparison. Any new hardware/software will also require that training requirements be identified in the Training Specification. (At this level of detail, you may have to document a percentage of change for some areas and predict the volume and frequency of training to support the new system.)

Identify any project goals that can be totally or partly satisfied in this process; for example, there might be an objective to ensure that all people using and controlling the new system have the level of skills necessary to operate it. (For this project goal you could document an implementation goal solution in the Project Charter as follows—high-level overview training for the new system will be provided for management as well as detailed seminars for "hands-on" Users.)

Vendors of hardware/software or external trainer may provide some of the training support, but you should still identify the requirements and support needs in your Training Specification.

Note:

1. Don't get overly detailed in these preliminary-level specifications—I think of these implementation specifications as "one-pagers.")

2. You will probably find some overlap between this and the other implementation specifications, but try to keep it to a minimum.

Process name: CONDUCT REVIEW OF PRELIMINARY
IMPLEMENTATION SPECIFICATIONS
Process reference number: 2.6.5
Process guided by: Activity 2 Plan

Process notes: Identify any problems, inaccuracies, ambiguities, and omissions in the Implementation Specifications for this level of detail.

These specifications document what is required to support the implementation of the new system, so they must be complete and correct for this level of study. This should not be a lengthy review because you should have been conducting walkthroughs after development of each specification, and these are only "one-page" specifications.

This review can involve a number of groups; for example, a planning group for hardware/software installation, the Users and operations staff for training, the database group for conversion, and the project members for installation. Each group, as well as the developers of the specifications and the project manager, should be represented. Each specification can be reviewed individually with the agents concerned, but note that there will be overlap in these specifications, as stated in the process notes (for example, the training support may include part of the new system hardware/software and the some actual system documentation).

Use the project goals applicable to implementation and their solutions to validate these specifications.

(For standard review rules and procedures, see Appendix E.)

Process name: IDENTIFY PRELIMINARY RELEASES
(IF NECESSARY)
Process reference number: 2.7.1
Process guided by: Activity 2 Plan

Process notes: Determine whether there is a need to deliver the new system in releases and if so, identify the release boundaries. (Releases are implementable, stand-alone, working parts of the new system that support significant parts of the business but are not the complete system. The complete final system can consist of many releases.)

Remember that you should have already identified more than one preliminary automation (man/machine) boundary for the new system. These automation options may already correspond to acceptable releases, or you may identify releases within these options. You can think of releases as equivalent to subset automation boundary options, especially as you will probably be delineating the system into releases using the same factors, such as business cycles, functions, and products, etc.

You have little detail available at this level of study; but, even so, you should know the scope and complexity of the system, since you now have performed all the preliminary analysis, design, and support implementation activities. With such knowledge and the preliminary documentation, you should make an overall prediction of the amount of time needed for the project.

If for any automation option you predict that it will take more than one to one-and-a-half years to deliver a product to the User, you should seriously consider splitting the option into releases. Beyond this one-and-a-half year time period, either the User loses interest, the original request's priority changes, or even the business need/requirements may have changed. (Software metrics show that long-term projects have a significantly larger risk of failure than short-term projects.)

If releases are necessary, use the Bounded New Logical Specification, with its cross reference in the data dictionary to original physical details, to aid in identifying releases by replacing current physical areas or functions. Again, at this level of study, these will be rough partitions of releases.

A release strategy may identify the least disruptive installation method or an incremental implementation that requires the least support effort. For example, you may have to develop extra interface functions to accommodate each release's physical boundaries, such as in converting old data to new data and back to old again.

It may be wise to identify releases based on the areas of the old system that cause the User the most problems or even based on one of the implementation needs (conversion, training, hardware/ software, or system installation).

Note:

1. If you identify releases, you will need to review the implementation specifications and possibly partition them by the releases in order to give a correct cost/benefit presentation to management at the end of our work in Activity 2. Annotate the new system documentation and the Project Charter to reflect these releases.

2. After approval of releases, you will then focus on just the first release in the detailed study.

3. The output data flow of this task is shown driving the development of the plans. This is where we need an internal iteration in the development process; these two processes in the methodology will probably rely on each other. The reverse view could be that releases are identified based on project planning considerations, e.g., given existing project staffing levels, the new system can only be delivered with the identified releases by the next yearly business cycle.

Process name: PREPARE AND SYNCHRONIZE PRELIMINARY IMPLEMENTATION PLANS (BY RELEASE)
Process reference number: 2.7.2
Process guided by: Activity 2 Plan

Process notes: Prepare the implementation plans to show how the implementation will be conducted. Base this on the specifications that you have derived containing implementation requirements and identified releases.

Then synchronize each plan with all others for this preliminary level of study, i.e., identify and allow for the dependencies between the different implementation plans. An example of synchronizing plans at this level might be documenting the fact that the hardware must be installed prior to running the conversion effort and training the Users. This should not be a large managerial task at this level of system detail.

Identify any project goals in the Project Charter that are concerned with implementing the new system and which can be partly or completely satisfied in this process. Document their solutions.

Your plans themselves can be a solution to a project goal; for example, a goal might be to insure that the purchasing department staff are the first ones to be trained and have new system hardware installed. Your solution to this goal is your Implementation Plan showing the schedule of implementation sequence.

At this level of detail, you can only roughly synchronize these specifications, for example, "Install new data entry hardware/software early in order to aid training," or "Convert all data before beginning to install the system in any of the branches of the company." Along with such scheduling activities, confirm the availability of any outside support such as a database group or vendor training.

Note:

This task is identified as a managerial task because the agents performing it are typically the project manager and higher management, but the members of the project team should help with the implementation plans because they are familiar with the effort involved, based on their work with the preliminary system models.

Process name: PREPARE ACTIVITY 3 DEVELOPMENT PLAN
(BY RELEASE)
Process reference number: 2.7.3
Process guided by: Activity 2 Plan

Process notes: Prepare the development plan for the detailed-level study (Activity 3) based on the products of the development activities for analysis and design at a preliminary level and the identified releases for the new system.

We have a problem here. The Users and DP management must make a decision on whether to proceed with the project beyond feasibility level, and need information on the resources needed for the rest of the project. You must decide whether the detailed-level study should include just the first release or the complete system. Therefore, you may wish to develop a plan for each automation option and even each release within each option for presentation to management.

The extent of this planning task will probably depend on how critical the project is to the business. If the decision to proceed is already predetermined, then produce and present high-level plans for each option and release. Alternatively, if the project is fighting for resources to proceed, then you will probably need to develop a more detailed presentation of the resources for each option/release.

Having completed the preliminary study, you have five factors to help you develop the Activity 3 plan:

- Familiarity with the system to date
- Declarations and definitions in the methodology for those deliverables and processes that you are planning
- The preliminary Current System Description and the preliminary New System Description, with initial automation boundary options and possible releases defined
- Figures for estimated and actual resources used in Activity 2
- Results from any Survey/Probe, conducted during the preliminary study, that can be used to identify detailed-level resource requirements

Using these five factors, prepare the development plan for Activity 3. Include all tasks, resources, dependencies, and information about schedules needed to conduct the detailed-level analysis and design.

The plan should be as detailed as possible for Activity 3, but for cost/benefit analysis and feasibility presentation purposes, you should project as best as you can the resources needed for Activities 4 and 5. For an accurate presentation, the plans should include the use of resources beyond the project team, such as a database group, the User, and the operations staff (confirm their availability from management).

Note:

Even though this is a management task typically assigned to the project manager, the best source for identifying resources for Activity 3 will be the project team members who have already performed the equivalent preliminary tasks.

Process name: ANALYZE PRELIMINARY COSTS/BENEFITS AND PREPARE FEASIBILITY REPORT
Process reference number: 2.7.4
Process guided by: Activity 2 Plan

Process notes: Produce a feasibility report containing sufficient information to allow management to decide whether to approve the resources for further study. Producing this Feasibility Report was one of the main reasons for doing the preliminary study.

This report should provide:

- A summary of estimated and actual resources used in the preliminary study drawn from the Project Plan.
- An overview of the system documentation developed so far, with automation options and releases identified for the new system based on the preliminary current and new system descriptions.
- A list of the project goals and preliminary solutions identified in the preliminary study, and recorded in the Project Charter, noting any goals that have been added since project initiation.
- A cost/benefit analysis for the new system, by automation option and release, along with a summary of any limitations and risks for each option, produced from the cost data in the specifications of the current and new system descriptions and from cost/benefit information in the Project Charter. You should add any benefits and risks that you have identified yourself, such as improved documentation or a more maintainable system. (If the new system description shows a software package solution(s), then the Project Charter will contain information about the package solution. Extract any pricing information required for costing comparisons against the current system and any solution involving in-house development.)
- A detailed presentation of plans and the resources needed for Activity 3 and an overall projection for Activities 4 and 5, produced in process reference number 2.7.3.

In this process, you will be working with information gathered during the preliminary study. Therefore, the degree of accuracy in the cost/benefit analysis and plans is not very high. State this in the feasibility report, along with the notation that all estimates may be off by as much as fifty percent with the exception of any information gathered and projected from a Survey/Probe activity.

Process name: CONDUCT INDEPENDENT REVIEW
Process reference number: 2.7.5
Process guided by: Activity 2 Plan

Process notes: Confirm that you are taking the correct approach to the project and that you are using the development tools correctly. (This is a timely review because you have completed only the preliminary study and are not too far into the project.)

You can avoid compounding any errors made up to this point further into the project by holding an independent review. The review body should not be the project members because you want objective observers to verify that the project team is on the correct path. You should enlist reviewers who have worked on similar projects, who are familiar with the method of documentation, and who have a knowledge of the methodology being followed.

(For standard review rules and procedures, see Appendix E.)

Process name: PRESENT FEASIBILITY REPORT TO DP
MANAGEMENT
Process reference number: 2.7.6
Process guided by: Activity 2 Plan

Process notes: This formal presentation informs Data Processing management of:

- Progress of the project to date
- Resources used to date
- Feasibility of the new system
- Risks associated with the project

If the project is approved, management should approve data processing resources for further system study.

Keep DP management informed of project progress as this is one way of avoiding cancellation of resources if a schedule slippage is necessary. In this presentation, you may be requesting additional data processing staff to be hired or brought in on contract for the detailed-level study.

Process name: PRESENT FEASIBILITY REPORT TO USER
MANAGEMENT FOR SELECTION
Process reference number: 2.7.7
Process guided by: Activity 2 Plan

Process notes: This formal presentation is intended to:

- Inform User management of the resources used so far
- Give an overview of the preliminary system documentation showing the options for the new system with any necessary releases
- State why the options were identified
- Present the feasibility and cost/benefit of each option
- Obtain approval and commitment for resources for the detailed study of the selected new system option

The last item is included if User management is also responsible for the overall resource cost. There is, of course, the possibility of the project being cancelled at this stage, but you are presenting options (different areas of change—automation boundaries), so it is likely that the User will accept one of them.

The data flow diagrams and data dictionary developed during preliminary study are flexible enough to allow you to easily adapt your new system options, even during this presentation, to accommodate different suggestions from the User. Therefore, you can accommodate almost any restriction in resources for the rest of the project by agreeing on a smaller/less complex new system option.

As you have completed only a preliminary study so far, you should inform the User that further study will help refine the accuracy of all information in the feasibility report.

The client/User should select *one* of the new system options (an automation boundary and its implementation) as it is expensive to proceed into detailed study with multiple options.

After User selection, update the Project Charter and Project Plan to reflect the option selected, and revise the overall data processing plans and resources for reallocation of resources, including new hiring and contracting needs. (Now that it has served its purpose, the feasibility report can be kept as reference and used as documentation for project histories.)

Process name: PREPARE REQUEST FOR HW/SW PROPOSAL
Process reference number: 2.7.8
Process guided by: Activity 2 Plan and Hardware/Software
Installation Plan

Process notes: Prepare any necessary Requests for Proposal for hardware or software that could potentially be supplied by vendors.

After you have obtained management's approval of resources, prepare any necessary Requests for Proposal (RFPs) for hardware and support software that cannot be obtained in-house or for suitable application software packages. Prepare a list of qualified vendors for each item of hardware and/or software (identified as unavailable in-house) in the Hardware/Software Specification.

Also take into account the information in the Hardware/Software Installation Specification, the schedule requirements in the Hardware/Software Installation Plan, and the software package information in the Hardware/ Software Specification in order to complete the formal RFP. Note that at this level of system study, these RFPs will be for major hardware and/or software needs. Include requests for vendor proposals for customizing the package if necessary.

For hardware and/or software that requires a long lead time, you could send out actual orders at this point, having already sent the RFPs when the preliminary Hardware/Software Specification was created. (If time allows, you should wait until the detailed Hardware/Software Specification has been prepared before placing any orders.)

At this point, you may want to initiate the building of new hardware and/or software environments identified in the Hardware/Software Installation Specification.

This process may be performed by an agent outside of the project team, such as a planning support group.

Process name: VALIDATE AND/OR CREATE DETAILED
DESIGN MODEL FOR CURRENT MANUAL
ENVIRONMENT
Process reference number: 3.1.1
Process guided by: Activity 3 Plan

Process notes: Use the selected system option approved by management to identify which portions, if not all, of the preliminary manual system model will require further study and decomposition. (Allow for studying the areas that immediately bound the selected option.)

Your aims in this task are the same as the equivalent task in the preliminary study (see process reference number 2.1.1), but now you will validate the existing model (if one is available in the current detailed manual system documentation or procedures manual) or decompose the preliminary model by producing low-level detailed data flow diagrams and supporting documentation that show specific individual flows of data and the processes that act on this data.

Decomposing and validating the model involves creating Data Dictionary definitions for all the fields within current documents and transactions, all the fields within current records and documents in files, and, probably the most time-consuming job, developing process specifications (minispecs) for the lowest-level processes on the data flow diagram. (These processes are called Functional Primitives.)

See the "Sample Table of Contents for a Manual System Model" in the Addendum to Data Dictionary for detailed data required at this level.

If acceptable to the User, use graphical representations for process specifications (such as a decision table or graph for decision logic, or a Nassi-Shneiderman diagram for both decision and nondecision logic). This will reduce ambiguity and increase quality.

If a graphical means is not acceptable, as a last resort, use Structured English to represent process policy. (You can find a good discussion of Structured English in DeMarco's book—*Structured Analysis and System Specification*—see Bibliography for reference; also see Appendix C of this book for an example of Structured English and a Nassi-Shneiderman diagram.) Of course, if a current procedures manual is available for any portion of the system, extract portions of it as process descriptions, after User validation that it is still current.

Conduct the data gathering at this level of detail in the same manner as in the preliminary study, except that you now interview mainly "hands-on" User staff and place greater emphasis on validating detail process specifications. If the User cannot validate your documentation and detailed requirements while you are actually gathering data, I recommend a maximum User validation turnaround of twenty-four hours for a process specification.

Immediate validation may be obtained by using good communication tools; for example, while defining a process with a User, you could take the interview notes in the form of data flow diagrams and document the lowest-level detail processes with a decision tree for detailed logic to ensure on-going small validations of data and processing.

Obviously this task is going to require much more effort than the equivalent preliminary level study.

As I mentioned in my discussion of the processes of preliminary study, a logical model annotated with physical characteristics can serve this task's purpose if your Users know or can understand **what** they are accomplishing in their manual activities instead of just **how** they perform these activities. So, in developing process specifications, you may have to embellish the logical (essential) process descriptions somewhat with some physical characteristics to obtain validation. For example, in a manual banking system, the User may more readily understand and verify physical description such as: "The loan officer verifies sufficient funds on Blue Form No. 986 by checking the bad customer list in the Red Book; if the customer has insufficient funds, then the loan officer rejects the customer request using Form 12."

During full logicalization of the model, processes that are purely data transporters and do not transform data status or content (e.g., data preparation/distribution processes) will disappear completely. Therefore, you do not want to produce process descriptions using such tools as detailed Structured English for these. A process note will suffice as long as you are sure no business (essential) processing is being performed.

Because this is the most detailed level, you should have already resolved most alias names for data; otherwise, the full logicalization task in 3.1.5 is the last chance to resolve these names.

During this detailed study, you will probably discover additional specific project goals and important input/output data flows and their associated processing that were missed at preliminary level.

Note and communicate these omissions to management for a decision on whether to include them in the project at this stage (and, therefore, modify the budget and schedule for this project) or to defer them for inclusion in a future release via change management. (See process reference number 2.2 for processing these omissions.)

Important note: I recommend you do only as much "physical" modeling of the current manual environment as you need in order to understand the current manual system and gain support and confidence of the Users. Of course, if you have a project objective to fully describe the current physical environment (e.g., because of a lack of any available documentation), then enough time should have been allocated in the project plan. If you don't have this specific objective, then try to merge this task with logicalizing the manual environment—Activity 3.1.3.

If you can get User approval on a logical model annotated with physical characteristics such as people names or titles, file names, and report numbers, then this can serve the purpose of this task as well as aid in the logicalization process later. I call the result of this task a "physilogical" model.

Process name: VALIDATE AND/OR CREATE DETAILED DESIGN MODEL FOR CURRENT AUTOMATED ENVIRONMENT
Process reference number: 3.1.2
Process guided by: Activity 3 Plan

Process notes: Use the selected system option approved by management to identify which portions, if not all, of the preliminary automated system model will require further study and decomposition. (Allow for the study of areas that immediately bound the selected option.)

The aims of this task are the same as those in the preliminary study (see process reference number 2.1.2), but now you validate in detail the existing documentation or decompose the preliminary model until all modules (individual routines) and the data they use (coupling parameters) have been specified.

An additional aim, via a project goal, at this level may be to identify reusable resources from the existing automated environment, for example, reusable code if the current system has good partitioning and is not "spaghetti" code.

Important note: If the current automated system is going to be totally replaced and there is no specific project objective to produce a Current Physical model of the existing automated system, then I recommend you skip this process and use the Current Logical Specification, produced in process reference number 3.1.4, for your system specification of requirements for the current automated system. I see little reason for producing a Current Physical Specification showing the old design of the automated system, especially as this old design will probably be replaced and it may get in the way of gathering essential business requirements from the User. The logical specification will be a better analysis User communication and validation tool here.

If you do produce a Current Physical Specification of the automated environment, then data gathering at this level of detail will be conducted in the same manner as in the preliminary study but will be concentrated on individual modules and their data. You should study and define all fields within transactions/reports in major data streams, all fields within records in data stores, and all modules (routines) within programs in major jobs. You should also identify any significant internal program stores, such as working-store tables and data parameters between modules. (To identify detailed data, see the "Sample Table of Contents for an Automated System Model in the Addendum to Data Dictionary.)

The current automated system module descriptions can be actual portions of program code if they are written in a high-level language; otherwise, you may want to use pseudocode (English-like, readable logic) or a decision table or tree as documentation. The clearer you make the module descriptions, the easier the upcoming logicalization task will be. Knowledge-able maintenance programmers may be the only people who can validate the Current Physical design.

I have found that most old programs seem to have no sensible structure but are just big monolithic process "lumps" with bad cohesion. However, you may find typical modular programs with a "flat" structure (one boss module with one level of subordinate worker modules), you can use the modules in the structure to show the partitioning of the detail design of the current system. If there are no "partitionable" modules in the existing programs, it is worth-less trying to develop a detailed design chart of partitions of programs. Therefore, you may have to rely on more effort in the logicalization task, working from the program listings (performing code analysis) to identify the business data and functions.

During this process, you may discover additional specific project goals and important input/output data flows and their associated processing that were missed at preliminary level. These omissions may affect the cost/benefit and feasibility analyses. They should be noted and communicated to management for a decision on whether to include them in the project at this stage (and, therefore, modify the budget and schedule for this project) or defer them for inclusion in a future release via change management. (See process reference number 2.2 for advice on how to process these omissions.)

Process name: DERIVE DETAILED LOGICAL MODEL FOR
CURRENT MANUAL ENVIRONMENT
Process reference number: 3.1.3
Process guided by: Activity 3 Plan

Process notes: Using the preliminary model as a guide, derive the detailed logical model of the current manual system from the detailed physical design model for the manual system.

As at the preliminary level, this task derives the necessary business data and functions that the manual system model contains, without reference to how those data and functions are currently designed and partitioned. (The more you can divorce yourself from the physical characteristics of the current system, the better chance you have of understanding the essential business system, and, therefore, of being able to develop a good solution for the new system.) We accomplish this process of separation of the old design from the underlying business system by performing logicalization.

The detailed logical model is derived by removing all physical characteristics, i.e., those not essential to the business, that are documented in the detailed manual system model. Such physical characteristics to be removed would include:

• References to documents and field numbers or physical format, to the sequencing or control (and to the section, title or person who performs them) of processes, and to the media used for stores or input/output
• Processes that only change data from one medium to another, that collect or distribute data, or that copy, back up, or restore data

The last item includes processes that do no data transformation (that is, they do not change the status or composition of data and therefore are only there to support the old design). (See the sample case study in Appendix C for additional physical/logical issues.)

To identify detailed logical data, see the "Sample Table of Contents for a Logical Specification" in the Addendum to Data Dictionary.

I feel the most important part of this task is to produce a logical model partitioned by business events. In my technical seminars, I advise my students to perform an analysis process I call "Interviewing The Data" to accomplish this partitioning. (See Appendix G: "Business Event Partitioning."

Performing business event partitioning at this level of detail will help you spot current system partitioning problems; that is, processes with poor cohesiveness which may not have been noticed at the preliminary higher level. (If you produced a business event–partitioned Context Diagram, as recommended in the Project Initiation task, you probably will already have a well-partitioned higher-level model.)

This repartitioning task should aid the readability of the resultant current logical model. In fact, this repartitioning should remove the most corruptive influence of the old design—an influence which may have led to an unmaintainable/inflexible new system design.

During business event partitioning you should also have replaced, with data flows, any stores that were only needed to support the old design (e.g., a "pending/in-basket" store that only held onto data until a person from the accounting staff removed it). Physical stores and data flows that interface with automated functions can be left on the model for matching-up purposes, until the logical system model is derived in process reference number 3.1.5. At this point in development, you can clean up most aliases and idiosyncratic User names and replace them with business names.

Producing the process specifications (minispecs) of business policy is the largest effort in this task, but you will be aided in this effort if you have a "physilogical" model as input to this task.

You may have a smaller area of study now, based on resource approval for Activity 3 from management; this may cause the upper-level functions on the preliminary model to be only partially valid. You may have to go back and repartition the higher-level diagrams. However, I recommend you hold off any upper-level repartitioning or formal redrafting of the model until the automated and manual logical models are combined into a logical system model in process reference number 3.1.5.

You may gain some help in deriving and validating the logical model by referring to any business and support documentation in the User procedures library. After some User overview training in the analysis process, they should be able to validate the logical transformation of data because the logical model is a business view of the system.

Note:

You are developing a separate model in this process, not modifying the manual system model. The latter will be needed for reference in future processes.

Process name: DERIVE DETAILED LOGICAL MODEL FOR
CURRENT AUTOMATED ENVIRONMENT
Process reference number: 3.1.4
Process guided by: Activity 3 Plan

Process notes: Derive the detailed logical model of the current automated system from the detailed automated system model or from the actual current automated system (if you decided not to document the current physical system). Use the preliminary model as a guide.

This task, as with the equivalent preliminary task, derives the necessary business data and functions that the automated system model contains without reference to how those data and functions have been currently designed and partitioned. (The more you can divorce yourself from the physical characteristics of the current system, the better you can understand the essential business system and, therefore, develop a good design solution for the new system.) We accomplish this process of separation of the old design from the underlying business system by performing logicalization.

Data-gathering and User verification task for the automated system in this process is a little harder to perform than the equivalent task for the manual system. The detailed policy is usually buried in the program code, and you can't validate code too easily with the Users. If the User is unable to validate the detailed business policy contained in the computer code (this can happen if the computer system has been in place for so long, the original Users who dictated the policy have left the company, and the computer system is the only place where the detailed business policy is documented), you may have to use code analysis to capture the essential business policy for the Current Logical Specification and not throw it out with the old physical (design) details. Therefore, the amount of effort required to complete this task will depend on the level of detail and complexity of the automated system model input and/or the knowledge the User or data processing maintenance staff regarding the detailed functions that the automated system performs.

Derive the detailed logical model by removing all physical characteristics, other than those essential to the business, that are documented in the detailed automated system model (or, if this model was not produced, from the actual automated system). Such physical characteristics to be removed would include:

- Design flags and switches (e.g., End of File, Not Found)
- References to transaction, report, and field numbers/acronyms or physical formats
- References to the sequencing or control of processes and removal of any pure nonbusiness coordination routines
- References to the media used for stores, their access method and their sequencing
- Initialization and termination processes
- Processes that only change data from one medium to another, that read, write, collect or distribute data, or that copy, sort/merge, back up, or restore data

The last item contains processes that do not transform data status or composition and are therefore only there to support the old design. (See the sample case study in Appendix C for additional physical/logical issues.)

To identify detailed data, see the "Sample Table of Contents for a Logical Specification" in the Addendum to Data Dictionary.

As I stated in the previous logicalization task, process reference number 3.1.3, I feel the most important part of this task is to produce a logical model partitioned by business events. In my technical seminars I advise my students to perform an analysis process I call "Interviewing The Data" to accomplish this partitioning. (See Appendix G: "Business Event Partitioning.")

Performing business event partitioning at this level of detail will help you spot current system partitioning problems; that is, processes with poor cohesiveness which may not have been noticed at the preliminary higher level. (If you produced a business event-partitioned Context Diagram, as recommended in the Project Initiation task, you probably will already have a well-partitioned higher level model.) This repartitioning task should aid the readability of the resultant current logical model. In fact, this repartitioning should remove the most corruptive influence of the old design—an influence which may have led to an unmaintainable/inflexible new system design.

During business event partitioning you should also have replaced any stores that were only needed to support the old design with data flows (e.g., an "input transaction" store that only held onto data between the front-end on-line and nightly batch systems). Physical stores and data flows that interface with manual functions can be left on the model for matching-up purposes, until the logical system model is derived in the next task. At this point in development, you can clean up most aliases and physical data processing names and replace them with business names.

You will probably find that a large portion of the effort in this task is devoted to documenting detailed process specifications. This effort will be reduced if the existing computer code was written clearly in a high-level computer language. The code can be extracted and repartitioned to form minispecifications to support the logical (functional) partitioning in the logical model.

Note:

You are developing a separate model, not modifying the automated system model. The automated model will be needed for reference in future processing.

Process name: DERIVE DETAILED LOGICAL SPECIFICATION
FOR THE CURRENT SYSTEM
Process reference number: 3.1.5
Process guided by: Activity 3 Plan

Process notes: Produce a detailed logical system model to get the business picture of the whole system (manual and automated systems combined).

This task, as with the equivalent preliminary process (process reference number 2.1.5), removes the physical view of how processes and their data are partitioned (manual and automated partitioning) in the existing system. Having done this, you can develop the best, most cost-effective, and most maintainable partitioning for the new system, without being influenced by the existing partitioning.

This process involves combining the logical models of the current manual and automated systems. This shouldn't be too difficult because it involves only matching up and logicalizing the physical characteristics at the interfaces between these two models.

As this is a task similar to the logicalizing within the manual and automated system partitions, see the lists of physical characteristics to be removed in processes 3.1.3 and 3.1.4 and apply them to this process.

If an existing automated system has been in place for many years, you may find "dead fields" in the interface data flows between the manual and automated boundaries. Most typically these dead fields will be found in the physical fixed form layouts and large record stores. The "hands-on" Users of the system should verify these fields as no longer required; then you should check to see if any associated processing descriptions and/or data dictionary entries need to be amended. (Most of the dead-field problems should have been taken care of by good analysis techniques prior to this point in the project.)

Any interfaces that do not match need to be investigated by cycling back to the design models. Determine whether they were:

- Aliases for other interfaces
- Missed in the other portion of the system during the design study
- Documented as supported in the manual system but not in the automated system (which rarely happens)

- Phased out of the manual system but still supported in the automated system (which often happens)
- Components of another interface (this can happen when different partitions of the model are developed to different levels of detail)

If an interface data flow is completely missing from one of the models, you will have to cycle back in the methodology and perform all the tasks for that data flow up to this point.

Look for:

- Interface stores that are only there to support the old automation boundary—for example, stores that are created by data entry staff, to be fed into the computer system run at some (old design) scheduled time, or transaction message queues created to support the current system terminals—and replace them with data flows.
- Partitioning problems, such as detailed functions that are performed partly in the manual system and partly in the automated system. These should be combined if they make a more cohesive function together.
- Duplicate functions, i.e., those performed in both the old manual and automated environments.
- Processes that were split by the previous designer into partly manual and partly automated processes. These should now be merged to show a true business flow of data through the total system.

Important note: Business event partitioning is again going to be of great help in this task. If a business event Context Diagram was produced in process reference number 1.1.2, then this diagram can be used to trace all detailed data and functions that were fragmented in the current environment.

The only parts of the model that may still reflect the current design are the stores (i.e., their partitioning). These will be cleaned up and repartitioned in the data modeling tasks (Activity 3.3) and will be reinserted, if necessary, into the logical model of the system. (If a data model is not being produced at the same time as the function model, then the stores can be cleaned up after the detailed data specification tasks are completed in Activity 3.3.)

In developing the data, or after incorporating the stores into the model, you may find problems such as data (attributes) in stores that are supported but never used, or data that is retrieved but not entered. They will require investigation by cycling back to the design models, since they may be signs of uncollected data, uncompleted analysis, or genuine faults of the current system. Replacing physical stores with logical stores in the model (as well as removing all final physical characteristics of the current design, except those that are essential to the business) is the final step in producing a totally logical view of the current system. The resultant model should be a true representation of the current system's business requirements.

To confirm the data requirements for this detailed level of study, see the "Sample Table of Contents for a Logical Specification" in the Addendum to Data Dictionary.

Note:

You can now see that another way to perform the requirements definition activity of systems development would have been to take each business event data flow (or control stimulus) at the boundary of your system and model its intermediate data and processing needs through the total system, ignoring any and all current partitioning. After doing this on all stimuli for your system boundary, you would arrive at the same model that this task produces.

Process name: CREATE DETAILED TEST CASES FOR
CURRENT SYSTEM
Process reference number: 3.1.6
Process guide by: Activity 3 Plan

Process notes: If you don't want to delay starting testing, then now identify all test cases needed to validate the completeness and correctness of the Current Logical Specification at a detailed level. Because this logical model should not change much (if at all), the test cases you create here should be usable, as is, as test cases for the new system.

If you have a regression test specification in the maintenance library for any of the affected automated and manual systems, use it to help form these test cases. If you do not have a regression test specification, you will need to review the Current Logical Specification and develop test cases that will validate the completeness and correctness of the affected portions of the system, as well as the complete system. The test cases will be developed in detail and may form one of the sources for the machine-executable Development Test Library produced in Activity 4.

Use the preliminary test cases created in Activity 2 as a guide, but you may have a smaller area of study at this level, so you may not develop all the preliminary test cases.

Note that the test cases being developed are individual tests to validate the Current Logical Specification. Other types of tests, including tests for the complete range and boundary values for the new system, will be generated from the New Physical Specification in a later process. (A good reference for testing issues is Glenford Myers' book *The Art of Software Testing*; see Bibliography.)

Using the stimulus and response data flows declared on the data flow diagram at the edge of your system, you can build test cases from the "data content" definitions in the Data Dictionary of the Current Logical Specification. As you have not yet identified the physical content of the new system fields, the test case definitions here will consist of identifying all the possible combinations of fields within each stimulus and response data flow of your complete system. An example of a detailed test case might be:

Test objective: Validate that order status and discount are correctly updated on a late delivery order input to the system.

Test input: Late Delivery Purchase Order with Express Delivery Date and regular values for all other fields (see Data Dictionary definition).

Expected execution: Normal validation processes are successful; order scheduling processing with late delivery processing performed.

Expected output: Product Invoice with Late Delivery Notice showing Discount Rate applied; Customer Order store updated with late Order Status (see Data Dictionary definition)

Test environment: Customer Order store available indicating this customer as Active and Order Status as Normal.

The Users will be ideal participants in creating test cases, especially to help identify invalid (negative) tests, because of the Users' knowledge of the current system.

Process name: CONDUCT REVIEW OF DETAILED CURRENT
LOGICAL SPECIFICATION
Process reference number: 3.1.7
Process guided by: Activity 3 Plan

Process notes: This review identifies any problems, inaccuracies, ambiguities, and omissions in the Current Logical Specification at the detailed level.

Since the specification will be used as the basis for the new system, it must be correct. A walkthrough should have been conducted for each intermediate deliverable (e.g., the data dictionary) up to this point. Now, since the system can be viewed in total (with manual and automated portions combined), a formal quality control inspection should take place. This review should include the project manager, User or User representative, and project analysts. The current system test cases can be used in the validation of the Current Logical Specification.

(See Appendix E for rules for standard reviews.)

Process name: ANALYZE DETAILED PROJECT GOALS
Process reference number: 3.2.1
Process guided by: Activity 3 Plan

Process notes: Now that you have a specification model showing the true requirements of the current business system, concentrate on project goals that can be satisfied in detailed analysis and that concern both data and functions in the Current Logical Specification and any completely new data and functions. Your task is to identify the logical modifications necessary to meet these goals.

You need to ensure that all project goals relating to the analysis effort have had their data and functions modeled in the requirements definition model (the New Logical Specification). The modifications identified in the preliminary-level study will help here as a guide to the decomposition of new data and/or functions.

This task may be considerable if the project involves adding any major data and/or functions. You may have to perform a physical design study and perform logicalization for these new data and functions. Adding any new data and functions potentially involves cycling back through all of the methodology tasks to this point.

Other logical modifications consist of changes to and deletions from data and functions in the existing system. For any changes, you may have to validate with the User any physical-to-logical transformations of those data and functions. Probably the most difficult task at this level of detail is developing or modifying process specifications. If there really are new data and functions within your business, then it may be difficult to obtain a definite approval of the new data items and their values, and of the actual policy logic for transformations of the data. You could use prototyping to identify and define the "nonestablished" data and functions from the Users requesting these new data and functions. The prototyping results will then be used to supplement the existing requirements model. (See process reference number 3.2.4.)

On the other hand, there may be no logical modifications if the project is concerned only with design and implementation goals, i.e., if there are to be no changes to business data or functions. The Current Logical Specification is the total definition of the requirements for the new system. (To identify detailed data, see the "Sample Table of Contents for a Logical Specification" in the Addendum to Data Dictionary.)

For those project goals that can be completely or partly satisfied in this process, you should document the analysis goals solutions in the Project Charter, e.g. highlight the data flow diagrams that show the new area of study identified by the new goals.

Note:

If there are only minor changes, then this task can be merged with the next task, otherwise you will be creating "mini-models" here that will be used in the next task.

Process name: DERIVE DETAILED LOGICAL MODEL FOR
THE NEW SYSTEM
Process reference number: 3.2.2
Process guided by: Activity 3 Plan

Process notes: Apply any logical modifications to the Current Logical Specification to produce the New Logical model.

This may involve adding, updating, and possibly deleting portions of the data flow diagram, data dictionary, and process descriptions that make up the Current Logical Specification. This task involves simply merging any new functions and data analyzed in the preceding task into the Current Logical model and resolving any interface problems.

After the modifications are incorporated to form the new logical model, you should have resolved all partitioning problems by having already applied business event partitioning to the total logical model.

This process may introduce some new stores into the model. If so, determine whether they have data that is redundant with existing stores. If new data is introduced, the specification for it will be included in the new system Data Dictionary during a later task.

Note:

1. At this point, you should see another advantage of studying the current system: any detailed modifications should fit inside the Current Logical Model; that is, the modifications should be completely bounded by the area of study of the project. If they are not, you did not study far enough. If you find that the modifications "touch the edge" of your current model, you should study one process beyond the modifications into the existing system to ensure that there are no problems introducing the new system into the current environment.

2. It is useful to highlight the modifications in the New Logical Model to easily identify them in the future.

3. In this process, you are actually developing a separate model, not modifying the Current Logical Specification, because the Current Logical Specification will be needed for reference in future processing.

Process name: REFINE MAN/MACHINE BOUNDARY FOR
NEW SYSTEM
Process reference number: 3.2.3
Process guided by: Activity 3 Plan

Process notes: Identify refinements to the automation boundary developed at the preliminary level.

At this detailed level of study, you identify a definite boundary between the manual and automated portions of the system. For example, having developed detailed process descriptions, you may have found judgmental actions guided by weak policy or a nonsystematic procedure, which you would exclude from the new automated system.

You could end up modifying the boundary from preliminary study but note that you should inform User and DP management before too much more project progress, if this is the case. The preliminary automation boundary formed the new system option selected by management from the feasibility report, and any change needs to be approved.

The main source for the final automation boundary is the project goals, especially those goals that apply to the requirements for the physical environment. As stated in the equivalent preliminary-level process, you may want to use the Current Physical Specification as an overall aid in this process, especially to identify physical interface characteristics.

You may have to introduce some redundancy in stores that will have to be in both the manual and automated portions of the system. For example, in an inventory system, the actual material will obviously be in the manual environment and you would also have an inventory file in the automated system. The logical DFD would show only the logical inventory store. Usually for presentation purposes, I show the automation boundary line drawn right through the middle of the store symbol on the DFD model. The New Physical Specification will show the store duplicated in the manual and automated environments.

Your task in this process is to use the greater amount of detail in the new logical model, along with any project goals that may affect this level of detail, to refine the automation boundary identified in the preliminary Bounded New Logical Specification.

The Bounded New Logical Specification is the new logical model with an automation boundary identified. Do not worry if this boundary forms many "islands" on the data flow diagram, as the next task is to repartition this model, separating the automated portion(s) from the manual portion(s). Additional repartitioning should facilitate both the presentation and the design of each of these areas.

Note:

1. To identify the detailed automation boundary, use an expanded data flow diagram made up from all the lowest-level data flow diagrams in the new logical model. The resulting model will show the automated and manual portions identified on one complete diagram. On this diagram you can also show the physical interfaces defined on the automation boundary, e.g., equipment, physical files, message queues.

2. For any project goals that can be partly or completely satisfied in this process, document the goals solutions in the Project Charter.

Process name: PROTOTYPE DETAILED NEW SYSTEM
Process reference number: 3.2.4
Process guided by: Activity 3 Plan

Process notes: Prototype those areas of the manual and automated parts of the system that were identified as suitable candidates for prototyping during the Preliminary-level activity.

Use the New System Project Goals and Bounded New Logical Specification to prototype the detailed inputs and outputs between the manual and automated portions of the system which were identified at the Preliminary level. Present prototyped options to the User for selection and use the selected prototype(s) to define how inputs and outputs should be processed for manual and automated areas. For significant parts of a system, you should document the above features in the data flow diagrams, data dictionary, and process descriptions of the New Logical Specification and use them as input to the Information Modeling process. In effect, you are using the results of prototyping to refine the Bounded New Logical Specification and to move towards New Physical.

Alternatively, if you used prototyping at the Preliminary level to extract new requirements, then a Bounded New Logical Specification for the detailed level will not be available to guide detailed prototyping. (The Preliminary-level activity simply identified those areas where prototyping would be used at the detailed level.) Iterate through those areas that are completely new and obtain User agreement as to the nature of the new system. Use this final prototype to back up to the previous process and develop a New Logical Specification showing the Automation Boundary interfaces as screen and report layouts.

Process name: CREATE DETAILED TEST CASES FOR THE
NEW SYSTEM
Process reference number: 3.2.5
Process guided by: Activity 3 Plan

Process notes: Develop the new system test cases using the detailed test cases for the current system. Not all current system test cases may be usable. This depends on how much modification was made to the Current Logical Specification. If there were no modifications, then all the existing test cases can be used.

If modifications were made to the Current Logical to form the New Logical Specification, then the current system test cases will need to be changed or added to accordingly. You can consider these tests as logical tests, that is, they do not pertain to the design or implementation of the system. (See the process notes for creating detailed test cases for the current system—process reference number 3.1.6—as they apply here also.)

The test cases created in this task will be used later to develop system and acceptance tests. The preliminary new system test cases will act as a guide for the detailed test cases, but they must be validated if the area of study for the detailed level is not the same as for the preliminary level.

You now are at a point in development at which you can create all test cases that apply to the business data and functions, that is, those that apply to what the new system must accomplish, but not to how it will accomplish it. Therefore, detailed test cases can be developed to field level. Later, you will add physical details such as record layouts and field values which will be used to form part of the machine-executable development test library.

Note:

The Test Specification rides through the whole methodology, being created and used in increments. It's a good idea to start to form the test cases early in the project because testing usually suffers from lack of resources (e.g., time) later in the project.

Process name: CONDUCT REVIEW OF DETAILED BOUNDED NEW LOGICAL SPECIFICATION
Process reference number: 3.2.6
Process guided by: Activity 3 Plan

Process notes: Identify any problems, inaccuracies, ambiguities, and omissions in the Bounded New Logical Specification.

This is the final deliverable from the analysis activities at the detailed level. Since this specification is going to be used to develop the detailed new design, it has to be complete and correct. You should have conducted walkthroughs on the intermediate deliverables up to this review. Therefore, this task formally reviews the Bounded New Logical Specification as a whole.

The agents reviewing the specification should be the project manager, User or User representative, project analysts, and, optionally, the designer. You should use the new system project goals and their solutions as well as the new system test cases to help validate the Bounded New Logical Specification.

(See Appendix E for Rules for Standard Review.)

Process name: VERIFY OR REVISE DETAILED CORPORATE
DATA DICTIONARY
Process reference number: 3.3.1
Process guided by: Activity 3 Plan

Process notes: Validate the data dictionary within your Bounded
New Logical Specification with the Corporate Data Dictionary, focusing on the corporate data items from other systems with which your
system interfaces.

The information-modeling tasks in Activity 3.3 refine and repartition the static data of your system just as Structured Analysis and
Design refine and repartition the active data of your system; they go
hand in hand.

Now you are at the detailed level of study; confirm the specification of the data. At this level you know:

- The detailed usage of the data from the system's functional primitive data flow diagrams
- The detailed data content from the system's data dictionary
- The actual transformation policy of the data, as stated in the
system's process descriptions (minispecs) constituting User business policy

Review the corporate data dictionary and update it from the
system's data dictionary. You may need to resolve conflicting data
names (aliases) between the corporate data dictionary and the
system's data dictionary. At this level of detail, the policy statements
in the minispecifications should help to clarify any aliases.

Identify any detailed project goals relating to data capture. For example a project objective may be to identify the data fields that are
duplicated and would therefore require redundant updating on both
this system and others on our corporate database. Document the
solutions to such objectives in the Project Charter. (A solution for the
above objective might be to present a subset data dictionary to
management in the next review indicating the data items that were
found to be redundant in the system, and that these will need to be
maintained in the future in the corporate database).

Note:

1. This process is aimed towards producing a companywide data dictionary that supports one or more common databases to reduce, if not eliminate, redundancy, multiple updating, inconsistency, and other potential data problems between systems. This process and the next two processes take a companywide view, whereas all other processes in this methodology have concentrated on the project's area of study. Data should not be looked upon as just the property of one application because most data tends to span many systems.

2. I have shown this and the other data specification processes fed by the Structured Analysis process, i.e., the Structured Specification forms what is known as a "User view" for Information Modeling.

   Another view is that Information Modeling can be the initial activity of a project with an Entity-Relationship model being its deliverable which is then input to Structured Analysis. The Entity-Relationship model is a **static** view of a system from a data perspective, whereas a Structured Specification is an **active** view of a system from a data perspective.

   Information Modeling shows entities and relationships and can be validated for a particular business system with a Structured Specification, or Structured Analysis can feed Information Modeling with detailed User views embodied in the Structured Specification in order to form the Entity-Relationship model with its supporting documentation (the Information Specification).

   I have shown the latter case in this methodology as the book takes a single-project view, and I believe the rigorous detail of the structured analysis effort will be the best input to feed the information modeling activities.

3. An agent outside the project team, such as data administration personnel may perform this process.

Process name: CREATE DETAILED INFORMATION
SPECIFICATION
Process reference number: 3.3.2
Process guided by: Activity 3 Plan

Process notes: Based on the Data Categories defined in the Preliminary-level and the Bounded New Logical Specification, prepare the Information Specification for the system.

The Structured Specification input to this task contains:

• A set of data flow diagrams showing how and where stores and their data are used in the system
• A data dictionary of detailed data content definitions for data flows on each DFD
• Minispecifications specifying business data transformation policy

With these and the Data Categories from the Preliminary level necessary to support your system, you can build the Information Specification consisting of:

• An Entity-Relationship diagram showing the entities and relationships between them
• Entity, relationship, and attribute specifications

Entities in our models represent actual objects in the business (people, roles, events, contracts, etc). They are refined by studying the information in **your** system's area of study. (Don't usurp the Structured Specification here; that is, don't document the information already gathered and recorded from an active view of the data. The system DFD shows a flow of information through the system and the transformation policy on that data; therefore, information flow and transformation policy don't need to be documented as part of the Information Specification. That information is the property of each application system and will vary for each application.)
You can refer to the Preliminary-level Data Model as an aid in this process, but the partitioned data stores on your Structured Specification DFDs are usually your best source for identifying specific entities.

Relationships are associations, between two or more business objects, needed to satisfy a specific piece of business policy. Our models must show such associations.

Some relationships that are already supported for other applications in the corporate information model may correspond to the similar relationship needs for your system; if so, they will be a starting point for identifying relationships specifications for your data model. Your system, though, may require different relationships among the same entities.

With the detailed information you have available to you at this point of the project, you may find that the data categories identified at preliminary study should be decomposed and refined into entity subtypes. For example, the data category Customer Account may actually be a supertype of: Savings Account, Loan Account, and Trust Account subtypes. Each of these may have their own detailed data needs, based on your discoveries during detailed-level analysis. Split these subtypes out as specific separate entity types because each view contains different data and is viewed separately by different Users of the system.

To avoid major duplication of effort, you should correlate the Entity-Relationship Diagram (ERD) entities or groups of attributes within an entity to the data stores identified on the Structured Specification and achieve a match between ERD entities and DFD data stores.

However, if you identified overly global stores in the Structured Specification, you may need to revise your DFDs, and Data Dictionary.

The steps in this process are:

- Identify all stores and their attributes on the Bounded New Logical Specification using the DFD stores and all data flows to and from those stores.
- Remove any leftover design data containers. You may find that attributes about an entity are scattered among stores on the DFDs, for example, PRICE LIST contains Product Price which is an attribute of the entity PRODUCT. Delete any such physical data containers and assign their attributes to the correct entity(s).
- Identify associative entities. Entities can be associated by a relationship. If we need data about the relationship, this will reside in an associative entity.

For example, the attribute GRADE would not sensibly reside in either of the two related entities—STUDENT or SEMINAR. It is, in fact, an attribute of the intersection of the two in the relationship STUDENT "ATTENDS" SEMINAR. The intersection data is discovered by examining the minispecification policy that states something like: "If final exam score greater than seventy points, inform student of passing grade and update Grade indicator in...?" You can form and associative entity called, for example, ATTENDANCE in which to keep intersection data such as GRADE.

Interrogate all stores on the DFDs and their associated processing to discover intersection data and create appropriate associative entities.

• Identify the relationships between the entities using the policy statements in the mini-spcifications.
• As a verfication step, apply the principles of normaliztion to the resulting Entity-Relationship Diagram to ensure that all entities are fully decomposed and their attribute correctly assigned, and will support all parts of the business applications.
• Annotate the Entity-Relationship Diagram to indicate the cardinality of entieis around a relationship (one-to-one, one-to-many and many-to-many).

You may find similar entities and relationships in the Corporate Information Model (also known as the Corporate Entity-Relationship Diagram) to those in your project's Entity-Relationship Diagram. Verify that these are the same by bringing the appropriate information from the Corporate Information Specification into this process.

Document the entities and relationships in the Information Specification and Data Dictionary using entity and relationship specifications.

The new system's entities will encompass the functional stores declared on the Bounded New Logical DFD. The Information Specification will be used to implement these stores in the new system, for example, via a corporate database.

Note:

1. Highlight the new or modified entities, especially those that require significant change to the corporate data dictionary, as they will affect the cost/benefit analysis for the system.

2. An agent outside the project team such as data administration personnel may perform this process.

3. This is one place in the system development effort where we must cycle back to update a previous deliverable, assuming that the Information Modeling activities are not being performed at the same time as the Structured Analysis. Use the result from these Information Modeling activities to cycle back and amend the stores in the New Logical Model and the Bounded New Logical Model. In effect, entities are simple stores that when "replaced" into the data flow diagram, should make it easier to read from a business point of view.

4. In my Information Modeling Seminar I actually propose a four-step procedure for conducting information modeling. These four steps parallel the structured analysis procedure:

   A. Develop Current Physical ERD:
      • Analyze the business information to determine the significant objects (people, places, things) and their relationships using nouns and verbs from User statements and/or automated documentation.
      • Create the Current Physical ERD from the above and existing data stores.

   B. Develop Current Logical ERD:
      • Remove business and physical objects which are not in the scope of study.
      • Remove "data containers" created because of old design partitioning and merge their attributes with the entity.
      • Examine processing conveniences such as sort/merge and extract files and assign to an entity, associative object, or both.

   C. Develop New Logical ERD:
      • Add any entities, relationships, and attributes needed to support new business requirements.
      • Update Entity, Relationship, and Attribute Specs for new information requirements.

D. Develop New Physical ERD:
- Add any new data containers to support the new design. For example: Stores needed to support the interface of the manual/automated boundary and any new job/program/department boundaries.

Process name: CONDUCT REVIEW OF DETAILED
INFORMATION SPECIFICATION
Process reference number: 3.3.3
Process guided by: Activity 3 Plan

Process notes: Identify any problems, inadequacies, inaccuracies, ambiguities, and omissions in the Information Specification.

This specification documents the static data which the new system must support in order to satisfy the business requirements, and consists of:

* An Entity-Relationship diagram, showing the entities to be supported and the relationships between them
* Semantic specifications for the entities, relationships, and attributes
* Rules governing the creation, use, and deletion of data

The review body should include the project manager, and representatives from Data Administration and each User area. This is a technical review, intended to obtain concurrence on the Information Model before it is used as input to the logical access path and physical data-modeling processes.

Following successful review, update the corporate Information Model from the refined entities, their data elements (attributes), and their relationships. Document them in the Corporate Data Dictionary with specifications for entities, relationships, and attributes.

Note:

1. If the User community is unfamiliar with the conventions of Entity-Relationship diagrams, you may need to hold a prior session on this technique and its model.

2. See Appendix E: "Rules for Reviews."

Process name: PREPARE LOGICAL ACCESS PATH DIAGRAM
Process reference number: 3.3.4
Process guided by: Activity 3 Plan

Process notes: Create the Logical Access Path Diagram needed to support the business information and processing requirements documented in the Bounded New Logical Specification.

The Information Specification contains the specific business entities and their relationships to support the minispecifications of business policy in the system. It also shows the cardinality between entities (e.g., one to one, one to many, many to many). The Corporate Logical Access Path Diagram contains all necessary entities and their access paths for the whole corporation. Now you must map the necessary access paths through the Entity-Relationship diagram to satisfy your system's needs. The Corproate Logical Access Path Diagram will show whether an access path is already supported in the Current Implemented Environment.

You should produce a Logical Access Path Diagrams for each business event in your system, showing how each business event in the Structured Specification navigates through the corporate Entity-Relationship diagram to get its necessary data.

Form the Logical Access Path Diagram as follows:

- For each business event in the Bounded New Logical Specification, trace the path through the Entity-Relationship Diagram that its response would take to access all the data required. Each navigation path can show the key(s) used to enter the structure and the elements accessed, all connected by arrows.
- If the business event Logical Access Path Diagram is too crowded, you can form many Logical Access Path Diagram fragments, each one satisfying an access need for a minispecification within the business event response.
- Annotate the Logical Access Path Diagram with the frequency for each event, and within each event, show the relative frequency for each part of the path. For example, the event "Customer Pays Bill" may occur 500 times per day, and if the average number of line items per bill is five, then the relative frequency of the path from Invoice Number (key) to Line Item Number would be five.

Where appropriate, use the Logical Access Path Diagram to update the Corporate Logical Access Path models.

Note:

Because of the implications for the corporate data model, an analyst from Data Administration may execute this task.

Process name: EVALUATE/SELECT SOFTWARE PACKAGE(S)
Process reference number: 3.3.5
Process guided by: Activity 3 Plan

Process notes: Conduct a detailed evaluation of each suitable software package and select the one(s) that satisfies most goals and requirements.

If there is a project goal to consider a software package for implementing the new automated system, then at this point in the project, you have all the information needed to conduct a detailed evaluation of each suitable software package. Your evaluation will be based on responses from vendors of suitable packages to the Requests for Proposal you generated in the Preliminary-level activity, or on detailed data gathered in the preliminary process as well as on information in the Bounded New Logical Specification and the Logical Access Path Diagram.

Examine each package in terms of its overall match to the business data flow and processing in the Bounded New Logical Specification and the area of automation requested as well as in terms of data access needs in the Logical Access Path Diagram.

Also, consider such things as the following:

• Ease of installation (minimal in-house and/or vendor customization)
• Ease of use (contact existing clients if possible for their experiences)
• Quality of documentation
• Level of vendor technical support and training for User and technical staff

In addition to evaluating the package, it is important to evaluate the vendor in terms of:

• Ongoing business stability
• References from existing clients, if any
• Willingness to negotiate nonperformance contingencies in contract
• Licensing or ownership arrangements

Based on the above and on any project goals that may be satisfied, determine whether the use of one or more packages for some or all of the new system is appropriate. If so, select the package(s) that satisfies most goals and requirements and document your choice in the Project Charter along with detailed purchase and ongoing costs.

If you did not gather detailed-level package information from the vendor(s) at the preliminary level, do so now. The package documentation will be needed as input to all processes from here on. Depending on the extent to which the package covers the business requirements, the package documentation may become a major part of your New Physical Specification.

Note:

This process is positioned here because no detailed physical design has been done to this point. Therefore, we can use the business requirements of data flow and static data as objective selection criteria. You may want to cycle back to the Bounded New Logical Specification to identify the data flow interface changes to the Automation Boundary for any selected package.

Process name: DEFINE PHYSICAL DATABASE/ FILE
STRUCTURES
Process reference number: 3.3.6
Process guided by: Activity 3 Plan

Process notes: Identify the necessary packaging (new design) of the system's data into implementation structures (sequential, hierarchical, network, relational, etc.) to support the manual and automated portions of the system.

The Information Specification contains the entities and their attribute specifications and the Logical Access Path Diagram provides an implementation-independent view of the data needs for the system; these inputs provide us with the inherent structure of the data. For example, there may be a natural hierarchical structure in the model—one root source with dependent objects. On the other hand, the model may contain a complex network that would introduce accessing problems if forced into a hierarchical structure. The above example is true for data structures that will be implemented in both the manual and automated environments.

If a project goal constrains you to use a particular packaging solution (e.g., IMS or DB2), your task is to express the data needs in the Logical Access Path Diagram in terms of the structures supported by this solution.

If you are not restricted to a particular data packaging solution and have not been preassigned a data management system, the issue of data access for your system will be the key factor in packaging the stored data needs into implementable structures; therefore, the Logical Access Path Diagram will be of most help here.

A particular software package may also dictate a database/file structure to be used, with this and the above models you can identify the necessary packaging of the data into implementation structures.

Some packaging considerations might be restricted by project goals, such as an objective to interface with existing systems and centralize all division data, which may result in your adhering to a predetermined implementation structure.

For any project goals that can be completely or partly satisfied in this process you should document the goals solutions in the Project Charter.

Note:

Because of the need to integrate the results into a corporate database environment, an analyst from Data or Database Administration may perform this task.

Process name: DEFINE DATA STORAGE AND ACCESS
Process reference number: 3.3.7
Process guided by: Activity 3 Plan

Process notes: Driven by the physical database/file structures and any database management system (DBMS) identify the physical storage media and devices for your stored data, as well as the data management system to be used for accessing this data. You should also identify whether any existing corporate data storage and access method will accommodate the system's data needs.

If not already identified, indicate the parts of the Database/File structures model that do not currently exist in the corporate data model. They will be used to identify the parts for which you have to create new stores for your system and possibly identify conversion details. The data storage and access description output should indicate which parts are, or are not, accommodated by any corporate data storage and access description.

For those items not satisfied in the corporate environment, you can identify the physical placement of data on media and the method of access (data management system) of that data by using:

• The new system data flow diagram and Data Dictionary showing where and what data is used
• The volume and frequency of data (the Logical Access Path Diagram can be used for this, although not shown as input)
• Any project goals that apply to data usage, such as transaction throughput and response times

You could identify, for example, physical adjacency, pointer chains, or a randomizing algorithm for direct addressing in the automated environment; index files, sequential ascending key files, etc., for the manual environment. If a DBMS is utilized then it may govern the physical storage issues.

The Bounded New Logical Specification will be of importance here because it shows the partitioning into manual and automated environments, and will show the positioning of stored data. For example, some stored data may be needed only to support the automation boundary, or certain data may be used exclusively in either the manual or automated environment.

Obviously, the storage needs and data management system to support these physical stores will be drastically different in the two environments. In the manual environment, for example, you may identify that a card index file will contain a specific key that points to subset data in file folders.

The device that will store the data may also govern access capabilities; for example, in an automated environment, a tape device requires sequential storage, but disks allow direct access for faster data retrieval. In the manual environment, index card files or display boards may speed data access. Hence, the New Physical Specification and the Hardware/Software Specification may provide guidance on selection of particular characteristics of a device, as well as supply information on vendor data management systems. You may also discover hardware/software support needs for the data storage and access.

Notice that the above specifications haven't yet been addressed at the detailed level. Your need to identify the physical characteristics of the data before confirming storage requirements is, again, a perfect example of the need for iteration in the methodology — this task needs to be performed iteratively with the development of the New Physical Specification in Activity 3.4.

Note:

1. You will need to update the data storage and access description after creating the New Physical Specification later in the project. For example, you will need to describe field lengths, data backup/recovery needs, etc. Such details will be required at least for new data; for existing data in the corporate storage and access descriptions, you can use the existing physical characteristics to aid identification of these physical details.

   In creating the storage and access description based on data usage, you may need to modify the database/file structures. For example, if the selected storage and access method cannot support the necessary access speed, then you may decide to introduce stored total amounts (data redundancy) instead of recalculating at access time; or you may duplicate stored data in order to save accessing multiple objects. Of course, the reverse may be necessary: to reduce overhead in pointers, you may access objects through other objects not directly needed by a particular request. These changes could cause data integrity constraints.

2. For any project goals that can be completely or partly satisfied in this process, document the goals solutions in the Project Charter.

3. I have shown the review process (in Process 3.3.3) applying to the Information Specification but not to the storage and access methods. This is because the latter are typically internal data processing deliverables and, as stated before, you should conduct internal walkthroughs on intermediate deliverables. However, you should show the packaged data model(s) to User and DP management and explain the advantages of the assigned data management system. Even at this point, talking to the User may reveal additional goals or provide the way to achieve some existing goals because of the broader and clearer view of data. Again, you may have to cycle back through previous activities if new goals are identified.

4. This task may be performed by an agent outside the project team, such as data administration personnel.

Process name: CREATE DETAILED HW/SW SPECIFICATION
Process reference number: 3.4.1
Process guided by: Activity 3 Plan

Process notes: Complete the specification of the hardware/software needed to support the manual and automated portions of the new system.

The Hardware/Software Specification must be completed before detailed design, as the hardware/software used will affect the "edges" of the new design; that is, it will affect the way in which you retrieve and store data. For example, particular support software may take care of error processing when an output device is not available, thus eliminating the need for your new design to get involved in the details of it.

In this process, you should first validate and, if necessary, correct the information identified in the preliminary Hardware/Software Specification (you may have a smaller area of study at the detailed level, which may change this specification).

If a software package has been identified as a solution, then it will already be documented in the New Physical Specification. Simply incorporate the software package documentation as part of the HW/SW Specification.

Next, identify any project goals that can be completely or partly satisfied in this process; for example, a goal might be satisfied by ordering a specific item of hardware, such as a dedicated communication line. In fact, you may have a project goal stating that you must use the existing system or company hardware/software. In such a case, the task of confirming availability and allocation of hardware/software will be very simple because the preliminary design and automation boundary will have had to accommodate this goal, too.

If you do not have such restrictive goals, you can use the following resources to complete the hardware/software specification:

• Bounded New Logical Specification, which shows the detailed automation boundary and which may already identify physical support characteristics on this boundary.

- Assigned data management system, for which you will need to specify support requirements; for example, a requirement might be to have a minimum amount of core to support the assigned data management system. (The assigned data management system should be documented in the hardware/software specification.)
- Data storage and access description, which will specify storage needs as well as access needs for permanently stored data.
- Production Hardware/Software Inventory, which identifies all companywide hardware/software, of which the current system's hardware/software is a subset.

You can select hardware/software by identifying the following:

- The portions of the existing system's hardware/software that can be reused for the new system.
- Additional portions of the company hardware/software that are available for use for the new system.
- The requirements for new hardware/software that cannot be satisfied by the above two items.

You are specifying the detailed requirements for hardware/software here. This may involve specifying the actual make and model of hardware, the name and release of support software, the interdependencies between them, plus the environment and maintenance needs. (Although you may not have a project goal stating it, you may want to ensure compatibility of all hardware/software in the system.)

This specification should cover all system hardware/software needs (manual and automated) regardless of whether the HW/SW is reused from the existing system, already company owned, or new (although these three categories should be highlighted separately).

For any project goals that can be completely or partly satisfied in this process, you should document the hardware/software goals solutions in the Project Charter.

Note:

You may want to iterate through this process and the detailed design of the new system; they can affect each other.

Process name: CREATE DETAILED DESIGN MODEL FOR
NEW MANUAL ENVIRONMENT
Process reference number: 3.4.2
Process guided by: Activity 3 Plan

Process notes: Specify how the data flows, data stores, and processes within the manual portion of the Bounded New Logical Specification are to be physically implemented.

As stated in the preliminary-level equivalent process, the design of the manual system is normally given little attention in data processing even though the manual system is just as important as the automated system for accomplishing business functions.

The design of the new manual environment will be mainly governed by the project goals. For example, if a project goal is to identify an efficient means of performing the business functions, then the functional partitioning (based on business events) on the data flow diagram should translate easily, from the point of view of document flow, to the new manual design.

However, if the goal is to develop an automated system with as little disruption of the manual activities as possible, the **current** manual system model can be used (along with the cross reference in the Bounded New Logical Data Dictionary) to identify the original physical data and functions and to see how and where they interface with the new computer system boundary. (Usually, the manual environment has much less flexibility for change than any existing automated environment. In this case the current manual model will be of greater use for designing the new manual environment.)

The modeling tools used so far (DFDs, Data Dictionary and mini specifications) are excellent tools for depicting the new design of the manual environment.

The manual design will consist of identifying any new job or title boundaries within sections or groups, and even allocating functions and their data from the Bounded New Logical Specification to individuals. It will also involve identifying the control (assignment to managers) and timings. You may even introduce additional processing into the physical model for such features as error conditions and data transportation processing which were not shown on the logical model (e.g., entering and retrieving data to and from the automated system). Then identify any physical interface characteristics such as forms or documents between the new partitioned boundaries.

If a software package(s) was identified earlier as satisfying some or all business requirements, introduce it into your design model to show the interface with the manual portion of the new system. The package documentation will already be in the HW/SW Specification, and this can be used in the above task.

When the automation boundary was identified, you highlighted modifications to the existing environment on the data flow diagram. Such modifications to the environment will be key areas of change on which to concentrate in this task. The HW/SW Specification describes the hardware that people will use to interface with the new automated system. Use this information to complete the design of the physical characteristics of the boundary between the manual and automated portions of the system, for example, input/output layouts, media, field contents, and data communication and transmission devices, etc.

In addition, concentrate on any project goals that can be satisfied at this point. In this detailed-level study, you will probably find that you can satisfy many system goals here and in the equivalent detailed automated task.

As stated in the data modeling activities, the packaging, storage, and access of stored data may influence the physical partitioning and procedures in the new design. Therefore, you should iterate between this physical design process and the data-modeling activities.

For any new stores identified in the data-modeling activities, you will need to identify document layouts and the manual support procedures necessary for ensuring their data integrity, such as back-up/recovery, access management, and security. The data storage and access description will be of help here.

The Bounded New Logical Specification is being physicalized here for the manual environment, so this process is basically the reverse of logicalization. (To identify detailed physical data, see the "Sample Table of Contents for a Manual System Model" in the Addendum to Data Dictionary.)

For any project goals that can be completely or partly satisfied in this process, document the manual design goals solutions in the Project Charter. It is useful to highlight the areas of change in the new design model so that you can identify them easily in the future.

Note that in this process you are developing a separate model, not modifying the Bounded New Logical Specification. The Bounded New Logical Specification will be needed for reference in future processes.

Process name: PERFORM AUTOMATED DESIGN
PREPACKAGING
Process reference number: 3.4.3
Process guided by: Activity 3 Plan

Process notes: Specify how the data flows, data stores, and processes within the automated portion of the Bounded New Logical specification are to be partitioned into major design packages.

First, replace the repartitioned data stores in the Bounded New Logical model if you didn't do this during logical data modeling. Using the Bounded New Logical specification as input, begin to form the new physical design for the automated portion by plugging in (inserting and/or replacing) the Physical Database/File Structures identified during data modeling.

If you had earlier identified one or more software packages which will satisfy business requirements, the documentation for the package(s) will already be in the HW/SW Specification and you can use this to document the new design (or part of the design) of the automated system. In effect, the package documentation becomes the Automated System Model, and you will not perform the tasks in this methodology relating to new design and code for the area implemented by the package. The software package's design and code will replace these deliverables. You should evaluate all other tasks, however, for inclusion in your customized project methodology, e.g., hardware selection, conversion, training, installation.

Next, for those areas that are not satisfied with a software package, use the resultant DFDs and the New Automated System Model from the preliminary level to produce the Automated Packaged Specification for the automated environment by identifying obvious major design boundaries. Base this partitioning on:

- Time boundaries, e.g., different subsystems running annually, monthly, daily, ad hoc, on-line, batch
- Hardware boundaries, e.g., different subsystems running in different hardware configurations such as mainframe versus microcomputer
- Geographical boundaries, e.g., different subsystems at different sites

Also take into account partitioning for such issues as audit/security, backup/recovery, use of software packages, and local versus remote data access.

Identify the boundary support characteristics for the resultant partitions such as terminals and input/output media if they were not identified in the man/machine boundary activity.

As far as possible, try to keep a complete business event partition within a packaged area. This will be the best (most maintainable and flexible) design for the automated environment.

Remember that one of the reasons for logicalizing the current system model was to give you a pure business view of the existing specification. You are now performing the reverse of logicalization and should not ignore the insights you gained into the essential business data and functions of the system.

There may be some project goals that affect packaging the automated system here, for example, "Produce a monthly report showing each month's sales summary compared to the same month last year." Obviously this will require a store to be processed monthly, probably by a batch job.

For any project goals that can be completely or partly satisfied in this process, document the automated design goals solutions in the Project Charter.

Process name: CREATE AUTOMATED SYSTEM
ARCHITECTURE
Process reference number: 3.4.4
Process guided by: Activity 3 Plan

Process notes: Convert the data flow diagrams in the Automated Packaged Specification into a detailed system architecture, laying out the design of the automated portion of the new system and write pseudocode for each new module in the design.

First, for each boundary in the Automated Packaged Specification, identify whether design by data structure or design by data flow is more appropriate for producing the internal architecture for the new computer system. (These are the two most common Structured Design methods recommended today for deriving internal designs.)

Next, apply transaction and/or transform analysis to the data flow diagram of your system to create the new internal design. If you can identify a strong nonvolatile data structure in your system, then you can use design by data structure, relying heavily on the data dictionary as input to your design.

If you use the DFDs in the packaged specification to design by data flow, then first identify any transaction centers on the automated portions of the DFD model of the Packaged Specification. (Transaction centers are typically found in computer-assisted systems such as inquiry, file update, message-switching, and automated teller systems.) Look for multiple incoming business event triggers (cohesive data flows or time prompts) around each Bounded (Packaged) portion of the automated system. (A correct New Logical Structured Specification will already be partitioned by business events.)

For each transaction center you identify, create a "boss" module to coordinate the transactions, and for each DFD process that handles a specified transaction, designate a second-level "executive" module subordinate to the "boss."

Then, identify any transform centers on the automated portion(s) of the DFD model, either stand-alone or within a transaction center package. Stand-alone transform centers are typically found in "total" applications such as payroll, stock control, and billing systems. Each business event partition (containing either only one process or many connected processes) is a candidate for Transform Analysis and will form one structure chart in the detailed System Architecture.

For transform centers within a transaction center, look out for common modules—those that can be shared among separate transactions, for example, those that perform validation, error handling, common calculations, etc.

Document the logic for any newly created "boss" control module in the form of pseudocode, a documentation language that introduces logic rigor without concern for any particular computer language's syntax or grammar. Pseudocode is an intermediate step to final code; it should contain enough information to validate how the function will be implemented, as well as provide a nonambiguous document from which to code. (I recommend that pseudocode not be retained for maintenance unless the language used for implementation is a low-level one.)

Note:

1. An excellent structured design text is Meilir Page-Jones' book: *The Practical Guide To Structured Systems Design*—see Bibliography.

2. For more detail on performing Transform Analysis, see the example documented in Appendix C of this book.

Process name: ADD PHYSICAL ENVIRONMENT
CHARACTERISTICS
Process reference number: 3.4.5
Process guided by: Activity 3 Plan

Process notes: Complete the Automated System Model by adding physical implementation details to the Automated System Architecture for job and program boundaries, for accessing physical stores and input/output media, and for reusable current system components.

Using the detailed internal design in the Automated System Architecture and any project goals stating implementation objectives, validate and refine the jobs and program boundaries (identified at preliminary level) and develop the system flowchart. The system flowchart and the physical design names for executable units of the system will be used later for documentation in the system execution manuals.

The Physical Database/File Structures and the data management system in the HW/SW Specification will also be needed to identify data retrieval and storage logic in the above design architecture. This logic should only affect the lowest level modules in the design and possibly some of the newly created boss modules.

The last step of packaging, job/job step/program boundaries, may introduce additional intermediate stores that will be shown along with the new packaged boundaries in the New Physical Specification. These new stores will require some additional data retrieval and storage modules. Depending on security, timing and access requirements, you may need to include some of these intermediate stores in the corporate data model, which will make you cycle back to the Information Modeling activities.

Depending on the project goals in the Project Charter, you may want to use the Current Automated System Model to identify any salvageable portions of the current design, e.g., coded modules. Use the cross-reference feature in the Data Dictionary in the Bounded New Logical Specification as a pointer to the original physical processes and data, but do not just copy the existing design. (One of the reasons for logicalizing the current system model was to give you a pure business view of the existing specification. You are now performing the reverse of logicalization and should not ignore the insights you gained into the essential business data and functions of the system.)

For any project goals that can be completely or partly satisfied in this process, document the automated design goals solutions in the Project Charter.

Note:

1. To identify detailed physical data, see the "Sample Table of Contents for an Automated System Model" (Addendum to Data Dictionary)

2. As stated in the creation of the Hardware/Software Specification, the new design may depend on the selected automated support hardware and software; therefore, iterate between this process and the creation of the Hardware/Software Specification.

3. Conduct an informal walkthrough of the complete automated design.

Process name: CREATE DETAILED TEST CASES FOR NEW
DESIGN
Process reference number: 3.4.6
Process guided by: Activity 3 Plan

Process notes: Identify the test cases needed to validate, at a detailed level, the New Physical Specification and the Hardware/ Software Specification for the new system.

The preliminary test cases can be used as a guide here, but note that management may have selected a smaller area of study for the detailed level.

You can build on the test cases from the analysis activities to form the tests for the New Physical Specification by adding in physical characteristics such as field lengths, value ranges, and physical structures, identified in the New Physical Specification and the data-modeling activities. Additional test cases will be needed, though, to validate the additional design features such as coordination/control modules, error-handling, backup/recovery, and all control data (end-of-file flags, etc.).

Two key areas of testing that you are most concerned with here should exercise the interface between the manual and automated systems, and the valid operation of hardware and support software. (This is where you should anticipate the bulk of the new test cases. Also you now have the physical characteristics necessary to complete all your test cases.) All test cases developed here will be detailed individual tests that will become machine-executable test sets in Activity 4.

Your best source for identifying and defining test cases is the data dictionary of the New Physical Specification, with the physical data flow diagram (manual side) and design charts (automated side) as guides for flow of data through each packaged system. The size of the testing effort, and the types of tests used—for example, range tests, boundary value tests, and so on—will depend on project requirements such as reliability, cost, and time.

Note:

1. For objectivity, someone other than the designer should create test cases.
2. For the design of test cases I recommend that you read G. J. Myers' book: *The Art of Software Testing*—see Bibliography.

Process name: CONDUCT REVIEW OF DETAILED NEW
DESIGN SPECIFICATIONS
Process reference number: 3.4.7
Process guided by: Activity 3 Plan

Process notes: Identify any problems, inaccuracies, ambiguities, and omissions in the detailed New Physical Specification and the Hardware/Software Specification. These specifications are the final deliverables of the detailed design activities. They will be used to develop the implementation specifications and to build the system (code and installation); therefore, it is vital that they are complete and correct. Walkthroughs should have been conducted on the individual deliverables during and after development.

This process is an internal data-processing review for the project team, the project manager, and optionally a hardware/software planning representative, but the Users may be involved in reviewing the manual design. You should also try to keep the Users involved throughout all of the system development effort.

You should use the design project goals and their solutions and the design test cases to help validate the design specifications.

Note:

For standard review rules and procedures, see Appendix E.

Process name: CREATE DETAILED PROCEDURES MANUAL
FOR NEW MANUAL ENVIRONMENT
Process reference number: 3.5.1
Process guided by: Activity 3 Plan

Process notes: Create the procedures necessary for the Users to work with the manual portions of the system and to interface with the automated portions.

The Preliminary-level activity did not identify a Procedures Manual because the new design was not specific enough. However, if the development of the procedures manual is going to be costly — for example, if it is going to be produced in foreign languages for distribution to overseas divisions—then the cost should be estimated at the Preliminary level, as the system's cost/benefit analysis and feasibility will be affected.

At this point, the Users should be fairly familiar with the modeling tools used in the analysis activities. If they like the nonredundant graphical means of specification that the modeling tools provide, then you might consider using the data flow diagram, data dictionary, data models, and minispecifications for documenting the procedures manual.

Derive the procedures manual from the New Physical Specification. The physical data flow diagram, data dictionary, and process descriptions of the manual system model, as well as the Hardware/Software Specification, have now been developed to the detailed level. You should use all of them to complete the detailed procedures manual as follows:

- Document all transaction flows through the system, plus any associated data preparation and distribution procedures. You may want to partition the data dictionary by transaction, putting together all fields and possible error messages for a particular transaction, in order to aid the Users' operation of the system.
- Document the operating instructions for interface hardware and/or software (such as terminals with program function keys) and for embedded manual hardware or software (such as special typewriters and microfiche equipment).
- Physically package the manual.

The information for this manual is mostly in the new manual system model, with the exception of operating instructions for the manual hardware and software. Therefore, this task mainly involves reformatting information into your company's particular standard layout for procedures manuals. The physical process descriptions and data dictionary for the manual system model can probably be used for documentation of specific procedures.

To complete these procedures you may want to use the information about particular equipment in the Hardware/Software Specification to support the processing of a transaction. If it is available, the current procedures manual may be helpful as a source for any reusable portions of it, or for identifying formatting conventions.

Although not shown on the methodology's data flow diagram, it is possible to have project goals that relate to this process; for example, documentation for the system may have to be developed using specific company standards, or it may need to be compatible with an interfacing systems documentation standard.

Process name: CREATE DETAILED OPERATIONS MANUAL
FOR NEW AUTOMATED ENVIRONMENT
Process reference number: 3.5.2
Process guided by: Activity 3 Plan

Process notes: Create the operations procedures necessary for the operations staff to operate and control the automated portions of the new system.

The Preliminary level did not identify an Operations Manual because the new design was not specific enough. However, if the development of the operations manual is going to be costly—for example, you may need to provide many operations manuals per site in an extensively distributed system—then the cost should be estimated at the preliminary level, as the system's cost/benefit analysis and feasibility will be affected.

This manual will be created from the automated system specification but will be affected by the operations environment itself; e.g., the environment may be centralized in the DP area or distributed under the Users' control. The operations manual could be partitioned using the system flow chart, which shows executable units for the new system. Also, the Hardware/Software Specification will help to identify equipment procedures. You should use all of these forms of documentation to develop the detailed operations manual, as follows:

- Document operations support staff and skill level needs that are relevant to the computer system partitioning, such as batch/on-line processing or daily/weekly/monthly processing, and relevant to hardware/software requirements for the new system.
- Complete the run schedules and procedures needed to control the new system; for example, job and job step dependencies on tape and disk loads, parameter updates for system control, security of system media, and data preparation/distribution schedules, etc.
- Document backup and disaster recovery procedures (if not already identified on the New Physical Specification).
- Physically format and package the operations manuals.
- If it is available, the current procedures manual may be helpful as a source for any reusable portions of it, or for identifying formatting conventions.

Although not shown on the methodology's data flow diagram, it is possible to have project goals that relate to this process; for example, documentation for the system may have to be developed using specific company standards, or it may need to be compatible with an interfacing systems documentation standard.

Process name: CONDUCT REVIEW OF DETAILED SYSTEM
EXECUTION MANUALS FOR NEW SYSTEM
Process reference number: 3.5.3
Process guided by: Activity 3 Plan

Process notes: Identify any problems, inaccuracies, ambiguities, and omissions in the procedures and operations manuals.

These manuals will support the new system; therefore, if they are not complete, correct, and readable, the new system may not be accepted by the working Users. Interim project team walkthroughs should have been conducted on the individual manuals after their development.

The review body should be the project manager, a representative from each area (if possible) that will receive the manuals, the developers of the manuals, and, optionally, other project team members.

To assist the review, you may also want to have available any project goals that governed the development of the manuals.

(For standard review rules and procedures, see Appendix E.)

Process name: PREPARE DETAILED SYSTEM INSTALLATION
SPECIFICATION
Process reference number: 3.6.1
Process guided by: Activity 3 Plan

Process notes: Prepare the detailed procedures and support requirements for installation of the new system's application software and manual procedures.

At this level of study, you have all the information necessary to complete the System Installation Specification. The main sources to consider are the process descriptions and detailed boundaries in the manual portion of the system, and the pseudocode and program boundaries in the automated portion (which are shown on the system flowchart).

First, identify the detailed area of change between the current and new systems (including changes to the way a function is performed). This area of change should already be indicated in the New Physical Specification; if it isn't, the Current Physical Specification can be used for comparison. The Bounded New Logical Specification may also be helpful in this task (although not shown on the methodology's data flow diagram).

Then identify any project goals that can be completely or partly satisfied in this process; e.g., there must be minimal interruption of the office operations when transferring to the new system. Along with these goals, you should identify your own system installation goals and document them in the System Installation Specification. Then, using these goals and the preliminary System Installation Specification as a guide, do the following:

- Review the detailed area of change in the New Physical Specification for the manual portions of the system and complete the procedures and support required to accomplish this change. The review includes installation of procedures manuals, relocation of staff, placement of new staff, and collection of old documentation.
- Review the detailed area of change in the New Physical Specification for the automated portions of the system and complete the procedures and support required to accomplish this change. The review includes changes to production library names, transfer of software and system controls from development libraries to produc-

tion libraries, installation of operations manuals, and deletion of old system application software.
- Complete the installation procedures for the maintenance information for the whole system. For example, transfer documentation and materials to the maintenance libraries.

For any project goals that can be completely or partly satisfied in this process, document the implementation goals solutions in the Project Charter.

Note:

You will probably find some overlap between this and the following implementation specifications; try to keep this redundancy to a minimum.

Process name: PREPARE DETAILED HW/SW INSTALLATION
SPECIFICATION
Process reference number: 3.6.2
Process guided by: Activity 3 Plan

Process notes: Using the preliminary Hardware/ Software Specification, complete the environment and support requirements for installation of the new system's hardware and support software.

First, validate the preliminary Hardware/Software Installation Specification. If there are any changes based on the detailed study, note that the cost/benefit report may be affected and that some long-lead-time hardware may already have been ordered during preliminary study.

During this process, you will concentrate mostly on the new hardware and software and on any in the existing environment that requires modification. The Hardware/Software Specification describes all hardware and support software needed for the new system and identifies the portions that are new. You should confirm that the existing environment can accommodate the new system's hardware/software needs and identify any support requirements. (The Hardware/Software Specification will identify the hardware/ software needs. This task identifies the support environment needs; for example, additional computer room space may be required to accommodate the new system.)

You should identify any project goals that can be completely or partly satisfied in this process; for example, there may be an objective to house all new hardware in an existing data center. Using these goals, review the hardware/software environment data in the production hardware/software inventory store and determine if an existing environment or portions of it can be used for new hardware/software. Use this detailed data to complete the information in the Hardware/Software Installation Specification as well as in the existing environment's documentation. For environments requiring modification or for completely new environments, you should specify the necessary environment description and configuration chart.

For all hardware/software, complete the installation support requirements. For example, acquire vendor installation procedures and support documentation and include them in the Hardware/Software Installation Specification.

For any project goals that can be completely or partly satisfied in this process, document the implementation goals solutions in the Project Charter.

Note:

You will probably find some overlap between this and the following implementation specifications; try to keep this redundancy to a minimum.

Process name: PREPARE DETAILED CONVERSION
SPECIFICATION
Process reference number: 3.6.3
Process guided by: Activity 3 Plan

Process notes: Complete the procedures and support requirements needed during the conversion of data for the new system.

First, validate and, if necessary, correct the preliminary Conversion Specification, as you will be using it to form the detailed Conversion Specification. Next, identify the detailed area of change (specifically, the change of stored data) between the current and new systems. This area of change should be indicated in the New Physical Specification (in the data dictionary); if not, the Current Physical Specification can be used for comparison.

Identify files containing data that requires a change of format, representation, or content, new files that must be created, and files that need a change of order, access, or media. This involves looking for change in the manual system as well as the automated system; for example, you may need to convert manual data based on a new forms design.

At this detailed level of study, you have all the information necessary to complete the Conversion Specification. Your main sources of information are the detailed data dictionaries in the Current and New Physical Specifications; the data storage and access description may also be of help, as it shows the physical placement of stored data. Some of the new data may need to be converted into the corporate data base format; as a result, features of the data management system may need to be taken into account in this process, although that information is not shown on the methodology's data flow diagram.

You should identify any project goals that can be completely or partly satisfied in this process; for example, there might be a goal to archive all customer records that have been inactive for more than six months. For these project goals, document the implementation goals solutions in the Project Charter. For example, a solution to the above goal could be identified in the conversion effort and documented in the Project Charter by including a statement that the initial conversion programs will separate and save all nonactive customers prior to converting data.

If the conversion effort is going to be a complex task, you may have already identified it as a small system in itself at the preliminary level. Here you would create a conversion requirements model (using such tools as DFDs, Data Dictionary, data models, and minispecifications) and a design model (perhaps with pseudocode, for example), for nonsimple data calculations. You may find that you can extract some of the Conversion Specification (such as the Conversion Data Dictionary, a subset of the Current and New Physical Data Dictionaries) from the New System Specification.

You can probably use the new system's application code and procedures to create new files. For example, you could enter current system data into the new application code as a way to add new records to an empty data base.

As the conversion of production data is critical, it is a good idea to create detailed test cases to validate the conversion procedures and their results. You can use the preliminary conversion test cases as a guide for these.

Note:

1. You will probably find some overlap between the implementation specifications; try to keep this redundancy to a minimum.

2. This task may be performed by an outside agent such as a Database Group analyst.

Process name: PREPARE DETAILED TRAINING
SPECIFICATION
Process reference number: 3.6.4
Process guided by: Activity 3 Plan

Process notes: Here you complete the specification of the requirements and support information that is needed for training the Users and operations staff for the new system.

First, validate and, if necessary, correct the preliminary Training Specification, as you will be using it to form the detailed Training Specification. Next, identify the detailed area of change between the current and new systems, as this is the area you will concentrate on in this process. The area of change should already be indicated in the New Physical Specification; if not, the Current Physical Specification can be used for comparison. You should also identify the area of change in the Hardware/Software Specification. You are looking for changes of function, changes to the interface with hardware/software, and changes to interfaces with data. These areas of change apply to the operations and User areas.

At this detailed level of study, you have all information necessary to complete the Training Specification; your main sources of information are the process descriptions that support the new manual environment, and the program/system boundaries (declared on the system flowchart and support documentation) for the automated environment, as well as the hardware/software operating instructions for both environments.

You should identify any project goals that can be completely or partly satisfied in this process. If, for example, it is a goal to utilize the company training facilities and support equipment as much as possible, then document the implementation goals solutions in the Project Charter; for example, the above goal can be satisfied by indicating that weekly hands-on workshop seminars will be conducted at the in-house training facilities using on-line equipment.

Using these project goals and the detailed area of change, complete the Training Requirements indicating such information as the exact number of people to train at each training level and the training support needed to satisfy these requirements. The training support can be as major as a series of courses or a pilot project, or as minor as instruction in modifications to existing procedures.

Use the detailed new system execution manuals as part of your training support materials, and to help identify training requirements. In fact, they will probably form the main documentation. Where possible, try to use the new application system itself and the new system hardware and software. You may find reusable training materials from the current system that can be modified as necessary. Highlight any training materials that must be specially created for this project, such as special workshop or on-line instruction courses, as these may be very time-consuming to create.

As part of completing the Training Specification, confirm the availability of training support: facilities, materials, vendor-provided training, and so on.

Note:

You will probably find some overlap between the implementation specifications; try to keep this redundancy to a minimum.

Process name: COMPLETE TEST SPECIFICATION
Process reference number: 3.6.5
Process guided by: Activity 3 Plan

Process notes: Identify and document any test cases that are not covered already in the Test Specification. These test cases will be concerned with the complete new system.

The Test Specification is different from other specifications as it is created in increments throughout the developing effort; the current system test cases are identified and are used to help develop the new system test cases, after which the design test cases are added. All test cases are developed through the preliminary and detailed cycles. At this point in development, you can view all of the test cases together and can consequently identify test objectives as well as test cases that were not covered by specific tests.

Identify any project goal that can be completely or partly satisfied in the testing effort, especially the testing goals for the total system, such as system performance tests; e.g., the system should be able to handle more than a quarter of a million transactions per day with on-line transaction response time of two seconds or less during peak periods. You may not be able to offer goal solutions at this point, but you can document test cases and special test environments to ensure that this goal is reached in the new system. You can develop your own testing goals here (for example, to test all execution paths in the system with at least one positive and one negative test) and document these in the Test Specification.

Using these goals, review the test cases in the Test Specification and verify that they satisfy the testing of the New Physical Specification. While doing this, identify and document the test cases required for a system test (the new system execution manuals should also be used for this task). Look for tests that satisfy criteria relating to volume, performance, security, recovery, interfacing, etc. Your test cases should apply to manual environment testing as well as automated environment testing, with special emphasis on the interface between the manual and the automated environments, the manual-to-manual interfaces, and the automated-to-automated interfaces. Having the total view of test cases, you can identify individual tests that can be satisfied by a single test case: One test case can satisfy testing a function, the design implementation of the function, and the function's hardware/software interface or manual-automated interface.

Also specify the total testing support needed. This can be identified by the individual test dependencies documented in each test case.

Process name: CONDUCT REVIEW OF DETAILED
IMPLEMENTATION SPECIFICATIONS
Process reference number: 3.6.6
Process guided by: Activity 3 Plan

Process notes: In this review, identify any problems, inaccuracies, ambiguities, and omissions in the Implementation Specifications for this level of detail.

These specifications document what is required to support the implementation of the new system, so they must be complete and correct. This should not be a "marathon" review, because you should have been conducting walkthroughs after development of each specification.

This review can involve a number of groups; for example, a planning group for hardware/software installation, the Users and operations staff for training, the database group for conversion, and the project members for installation. Each group, as well as the developers of the specifications and the project manager, should be represented. Each specification can be reviewed individually with the agents concerned. Note that there will be overlap in these specifications; for example, as stated in the process notes, the training support may include part of the new system hardware/software and actual system documentation.

The project goals applicable to implementation and their solutions should be used to validate these specifications.

(For standard review rules and procedures, see Appendix E.)

Process name: VERIFY AND UPDATE IMPLEMENTATION
PLANS
Process reference number: 3.7.1
Process guided by: Activity 3 Plan

Process notes: Verify and update the preliminary Implementation
Plans based on your detailed knowledge of the system.

The Implementation Plans show how the system implementation
will be conducted, that is, the strategy for system, HW/SW, conversion, training, and testing implementation.

First, confirm that the preliminary Implementation Plans still
apply. If any boundaries have changed, the Implementation
Specifications will have been updated and these can be used to
modify the Implementation Plans. Next, identify any project goals in
the Project Charter that can be completely or partly satisfied in this
process and document them in the implementation goals solutions.
For example, a goal might be that no backlog of processing should
occur during operations training. As a solution to this goal you could
offer a plan (for example, document in your plan that two extra
operators will be needed temporarily to support the operations staff
during training).

Using these project goals and the Implementation Specifications,
update the strategies as necessary and complete the specifications of
the individual detailed tasks, resources, dependencies, and schedules
for meeting these goals and specifications. Then, confirm that the
plans for the Implementation Specifications are synchronized with
each other (if a separate plan is created for each) by reviewing:

- Lists of tasks and identifying any tasks that can assist or replace
  tasks in other plans
- Detailed dependencies and schedules, confirming that there are no
  conflicts, and identifying any improvements that can be made
- Support material and resources and confirming that there are no
  conflicts in allocation and availability

Finally, project/calculate the cost for each task in the plan for
cost/benefit purposes.

This process will need to be iterated through with process
reference number 3.7.2, which produces the plan for coding the
automated portions of the system. The iteration is necessary because

the plan (or portion or the plan) to support the System Installation Specification is obviously dependent on the projected or actual schedule for the coding effort in Activity 4. This process and the next can be significantly helped by the results of the Survey/Probe projection technique described in the Appendix of this book.

Although you do not have any acceptance test cases to work from in the Test Specification, you need to allocate data processing resources to aid the User in acceptance testing. (You may also need to identify the User resources required.) Proper allocation, of course, requires knowing the level or amount of testing to be performed, as this may affect the project's schedule. If a User representative is a member of the project team, he or she may be able to provide reliable testing information; otherwise, you will need to consult with the User to get this information.

Note:

This task is identified as a managerial task, because the agents performing the task are the project manager and management; obviously the members of the project team, having developed the detailed documentation, should help with the Implementation Plans, as they are familiar with the effort involved.

Process name: COMPLETE ACTIVITY 4 PLAN
Process reference number: 3.7.2
Process guided by: Activity 3 Plan

Process notes: The plans for many tasks in Activity 4 are covered in the previous task, but there are some Activity 4 tasks for which you will have to produce detailed plans during this task. These are the coding, walkthrough, and management processes.

For the coding processes, use the following planning resources:

- The new automated system model of the new physical specification, containing the system architecture, pseudocode for modules, coding language(s), etc.
- Figures for projected and actual resources used for developing the pseudocode, which can be a guide for determining coding complexity
- The System Installation Plan, which identifies the schedule needed for installing the automated and manual portions of the system
- Survey/Probe metrics and projections of coding productivity

Using these factors, prepare the plan for developing the code, establishing the system controls such as Job Control Language, and performing the walkthroughs.

For the managerial processes in Activity 4, you can prepare the plan using figures for estimated and actual resources for similar activities in Activity 3.

Note:

This process uses the System Installation Plan as an input. In fact, this process and the one that produces the Implementation Plans are performed together (you should iterate through both these activities). Since you have done so much precoding development, you can, if necessary, make the coding effort fit the implementation plan. Using the design chart of the new automated model, you are able to delegate efficiently, because each module in the chart can stand alone. Hence, you have more flexible use of time and people.

Process name: ANALYZE DETAILED COSTS/ BENEFITS AND
PREPARE FINAL PROPOSAL
Process reference number: 3.7.3
Process guided by: Activity 3 Plan

Process notes: Produce a final proposal containing sufficient information to allow management to decide whether to approve the resources for further study of the project. This report will provide:

- Summary of the actual resources used in detailed study compared to what was estimated from the Project Plan.
- Overview of the system documentation developed so far from the current and new descriptions.
- List of the project goals (you should highlight any goals that have been added or modified at the detailed level of study) from the Project Charter, in which you may also list your own objectives, for example, you may wish to specify that structured techniques will be used for development.
- Analysis of the costs and benefits for the new system, along with any limitations and risks in producing it from the cost data in the specifications of the current and new system descriptions and from cost and benefit information in the Project Charter. Add any benefits and risks that you may have identified, such as a need for less operator intervention or the advantage of using state-of-the-art equipment, as well as any cost savings or increases. (If the new system description shows a software package solution(s), the Project Charter will contain information about the package solution(s). Extract any pricing information required for cost comparisons against the current system and any solutions involving in-house development.)
- Summary of the plans for Activities 4 and 5 with a detailed projection of resources needed for Activity 4 and your best projection for resources needed for Activity 5 from the project plan.

Since you produce the information in this final proposal from your detailed study, it should be accurate. Your projections at this point should be accurate within five percent; this degree of accuracy should be stated in the final proposal with a comment that the accuracy is true only for factors within your control. Factors that are uncontrollable are:

- Hardware/software being delivered on time
- User availability at presentations and reviews, and so on

Note:

Now that you have gone through the detailed tasks in Activity 3 you can evaluate the accuracy of the projections from the Survey/Probe technique by comparing them with actual resources used. If there are any variations, document them and the reasons, and use them to refine this projection technique for your particular environment.

Process name: PRESENT FINAL PROPOSAL TO
D.P. MANAGEMENT
Process reference number: 3.7.4
Process guided by: Activity 3 Plan

Process notes: Your goal for this presentation is to make data processing management aware of the progress to date, to report on the resources used, and to get a commitment for the resources needed for Activity 4.

This should be a formal presentation of all the information in the final proposal.

This presentation is part of keeping data processing management informed of the project progress so that if a slip in schedule is necessary, you may avoid data processing management's cancellation of resources. (If the project is an internal data processing project, such as a rewrite of an unmaintainable system, data processing management will be the same as User management. This presentation, therefore, would be the main presentation.)

In this presentation, you should also raise any issues that may adversely affect the progress of the project—for example, lack of department resources, or hardware delivery problems—and, if possible, resolve the potential difficulties.

Process name: PRESENT FINAL PROPOSAL TO USER
MANAGEMENT
Process reference number: 3.7.5
Process guided by: Activity 3 Plan

Process notes: Your presentation of the final proposal to User
management serves many purposes such as to:

- Report on the resources used so far.
- Give an overview of the system documentation completed to date.
- Present a detailed cost/benefit report of the new system option or
  its release for which you have completed detailed study.
- Obtain approval for, and commitment of, resources needed for Ac-
  tivity 4.

As the name of this process indicates, this is the final presentation
of the new system option or its release that you are going to implement. This should be a formal presentation of all the information in
the final proposal. It is possible that you may have identified necessary modifications (from hands-on Users) to the system requirements
at this level of detail, to this option, or to its release. These modifications should be pointed out in the presentation if they have already
been incorporated into the system documentation. Approval of these
modifications should have been received from individual User
managers during the detailed study.

If any serious modifications are necessary to this final proposal,
cycle back through the affected activities in the detailed study.

Since most of the new hiring and contracting needs should have
been approved at this point, revise the overall data processing plans
and resources to reflect any reallocation of resources.

Process name: PLACE HARDWARE/SOFTWARE ORDERS
Process reference number: 3.7.6
Process guided by: HW/SW Installation Plan

Process notes: With the management approval of resources, prepare and send out the orders for hardware and/or software that cannot be provided in-house.

Having evaluated the vendor hardware and/or software proposals along with the data contained in the Hardware/Software Specification, and having selected a vendor(s) to supply the hardware and/or software, use the detailed requirements presented in the Hardware/Software Specification and the Hardware/Software Installation Specification, the schedule requirements indicated in the Hardware/Software Installation Plan, and the Software Package(s) information in the HW/SW Specification to develop and negotiate a contract or order with the vendor(s). The contract or order will probably have to be signed by management before it is sent to the vendor(s).

Note:

1. This process may be performed by an agent outside the project team, such as a planning support group.

2. The orders for new hardware and/or software with long lead times may have been sent out during preliminary study. If this is the case, then this task should confirm the details of those orders and place any remaining short lead-time orders.

Process name: PREPARE TEST MATERIALS
Process reference number: 4.1.1
Process guided by: Test Plan

Process notes: Develop the executable test sets and the scaffolding needed to support them.

Your resources for this process are the Test Specification (containing the overall testing objectives and individual test cases) and the Test Plan (containing the testing strategy and resources). Form the test sets from one or more test cases. For example, to define a top-down, incremental testing strategy for programs in the automated system, you should identify all test cases that apply to

- the system as a whole
- each packaged subsystem
- each program in the system
- each module in a program

and form test sets for the units at each level. After you have identified the test sets needed to completely test a unit, create the actual test data and scaffolding required such as program/module stubs, Job Control Language, and manual procedures. These test sets and scaffolding should identify the original test case(s) from which they were derived. Your tests should encompass manual procedures as well as computer code. You may want to partition the tests by the type of test, such as normal, exception, performance, etc.

Note:

1. An automated test generator will significantly aid in creating test sets. If the old system had a regression test library, you may find reusable testing materials that require no change or only minor changes; the test specification should already identify these. The conversion effort is another source for testing support; it can probably produce test files to support your test sets.

2. As mentioned earlier, the developer of the unit being tested is perhaps the worst person to produce test cases—and in this process, test sets. Therefore, it is a good idea to conduct a walkthrough on the results of this process.

3. Unless a separate testing group is performing this process, you do not have to build all test sets at one point in time; the test plan may phase in the testing along with the code development effort.

Process name: PREPARE TRAINING MATERIALS
Process reference number: 4.1.2
Process guided by: Training Plan

Process notes: Prepare the User and Operations training materials needed for the new system training effort.

The resulting materials can also be used for ongoing training, for example, to train new support staff hired once the system is in production.

The Training Specification and the Training Plan guide this process.

- Obtain the reusable training materials from the maintenance library and, if necessary, modify them.
- Schedule any vendor-supplied and in-house-built training by means of the Training Plan.
- Obtain support materials, such as precourse reading or handouts for vendor-supplied training.
- Create any new training programs, such as an on-line training support program, plus associated presentation and student materials.

The Training Specification should also identify any reusable training materials, as well as identify actual application programs, testing materials, system execution manuals, etc., that will be used for preparing the training materials.

Note:

An agent outside the project team, such as a training department, may perform this process.

Process name: WRITE APPLICATION CODE
Process reference number: 4.2.1
Process guided by: Activity 4 Plan

Process notes: Create compiled application code and the development and production system controls, e.g., JCL (Job Control Language), for the automated part of the new system.

The Activity 4 Plan which guides this process, the new automated system model, and the Hardware/Software Specification should contain all the information needed for this task.

The New Automated System Model is the main source document for building the new application code. It contains:

- The portion(s) that need to be coded versus those that need to be satisfied using a software package.
- Structure charts indicating the detailed system architecture (modularity) with each module's data/control parameters (coupling).
- Pseudocode (detailed process descriptions) showing the logic that needs to be put into computer code.
- The source language to be used for each module.
- System flowchart and the data dictionary containing the information needed to create the system controls.

The Hardware/Software Specification also shows building requirements. It contains:

- Documentation for any software package.
- Any compiler requirements and operating software for system controls.
- The hardware for any necessary program documentation.
- The packaged data model and data management system needed for defining data access syntax and control, such as database search arguments, data store read/write keys, and status/return codes, etc.

The Activity 4 Plan contains the strategy for developing the module such as top-down and/or bottom-up development.

If the total system is to be implemented with a software package with no changes, this process is empty. Otherwise develop the new code or changes to the software package code using the principles of structured programming to obtain readable and understandable program code.

Notes:

1. Cycle through this process and the next two processes for each module specified in the New Automated System Model.

2. Because of all the up-front work in the project, this task of building the actual system should be straightforward.

Process name: WALKTHROUGH THE APPLICATION CODE
Process reference number: 4.2.2
Process guided by: Activity 4 Plan

Process notes: Code walkthroughs identify any problems, inaccuracies, ambiguities, and omissions in the application code and system controls.

During the walkthrough, look for readability and logic errors in the code and judge readability according to your company's standards. Verify logic by comparing it to the detailed process descriptions (pseudocode) in the new automated system model, and by human simulation of the test cases in the test specification. (Unlike manuals and specifications, programs can be, and often are, installed without any other person seeing them, so this process provides the last and possibly the only time that code can be independently confirmed as meeting requirements and being up to company standard. For this reason, this walkthrough is shown as an explicit process in the methodology, whereas others are not.)

During the walkthrough, also ensure that the program and system controls are complete and correct—they too form part of the actual automated system. Since the computer is incapable of finding programming logic errors (i.e., "bugs"), you have to rely on this walkthrough and the testing effort to detect them.

As you iterate through this process with the preceding and succeeding processes, bring together and review other major portions of the system where possible. For example, you might review a whole program to verify interfaces (coupling) after completing its individual module walkthroughs.

Note:

1. The code author's peers should perform this task because they not only are technically the most qualified but will get to know each others' code and thus be better able to take on other modules in an emergency. A designer and an analyst could also be of assistance in this walkthrough.

2. The author of the code being reviewed but should be deterred from explaining any assumptions in the material under review—the material will have to stand alone as maintenance documentation in production.

3. The walkthrough can be held before compilation of code, but is probably better held after compilation to avoid having participants looking for minor syntax errors.

Process name: PERFORM TESTING OF APPLICATION CODE
Process reference number: 4.2.3
Process guided by: Test Plan

Process notes: Test each application module and the system controls.

This process mainly involves program/module function testing, such as logic testing (white-box) and interface testing (black-box), but can include some performance testing on critical areas. The main performance testing will be done on the complete system during the system test.

You can test the application modules and their system controls using the test sets for each module in the development test library, the Test Specification (containing the individual test objectives and expected results), and the Test Plan (specifying the strategy for testing, such as incremental, top-down testing with critical areas to be tested first).

Note:

Because this and the two preceding processes are performed iteratively, you may also perform subsystem or integration tests after all modules composing the subsystem have been individually tested.

G. J. Myers' book *The Art of Software Testing* focuses on testing procedures—see Bibliography.)

Process name: CODE AND TEST THE CONVERSION
PROGRAMS
Process reference number: 4.2.4
Process guided by: Conversion Plan

Process notes: Write and test the programs and system controls needed to support the automated portions of the conversion effort.

This process for conversion programs corresponds to those for application code (see process reference numbers 4.2.1, 4.2.2, and 4.2.3 for more detail).

If the conversion effort is large and complex, you probably will have developed a system model just for conversion. Use this model, the Hardware/Software Specification, the Test Specification (for conversion test cases), the conversion testing materials, and the Conversion Plan to develop the conversion modules/programs and their system controls.

Process name: COMPLETE ACTIVITY 5 PLAN
Process reference number: 4.3.1
Process guided by: Activity 4 Plan

Process notes: Plan for the five processes in Activity 5 which are not covered by the Implementation Plans.

Use the previously created Implementation Plans and the Activity 5 Plan created so far as input to this task. Synchronize the output from this task with the total Activity 5 Plan.

The five processes that need planning are:

- Regression Test Specification and Library creation—use the Test Specification and the test material to identify the resource needs for creating these.
- Maintenance Plan preparation—use the new system description and your knowledge of the resource needs identified in other plans to identify the resources needed to create the Maintenance Plan.
- Preparation for the next release—the preliminary system documentation and Implementation Plans should already show the partitioning for the next release and, therefore, provide the necessary input for its resource needs.
- Production monitoring—this depends on the type and execution frequency of the new system; this part of the plan relies on your knowledge of the User environment.
- Project Completion Report preparation—the resource needs for this task depend on the size and complexity of all technical, managerial and political aspects of the project.

Process name: PREPARE IMPLEMENTATION REPORT
Process reference number: 4.3.2
Process guided by: Activity 4 Plan

Process notes: Produce an Implementation Report to provide management with a summary of the project's progress to date and to document the resources, including User resources, needed to accomplish Activity 5. The report should include:

- A summary of the actual vs. projected resources for Activity 4. Resource projections were presented at the last approval process and can be extracted from the Project Plan.
- A summary of the plans for Activity 5 with a detailed projection of resource needs (with User resources highlighted). This summary can be prepared from the Activity 5 Plan and the Implementation Plans.
- Issues not included in any previous report that have, and will continue to have, an impact on the project's progress.

Note:

If possible, show User management the test results from the program function tests or even present a portion of the working system in a test environment in order to keep User commitment and interest high at a time of low User contact. At this stage, following coding and system testing, the User would probably welcome any communication about the system's progress.

Process name: PRESENT IMPLEMENTATION REPORT TO
D.P. MANAGEMENT
Process reference number: 4.3.3
Process guided by: Activity 4 Plan

Process notes: This presentation makes data processing management aware of your progress to date, reports on the resources used, and seeks commitment to, and approval for, the data processing resources needed for Activity 5.

This process formally presents the information in the Implementation Report. It is especially important to keep data processing management informed of the project's progress now that you have given your final proposal to them. Identify any DP issues that can affect future progress, especially schedule slippage or changes, and if possible, propose solutions in this presentation.

Process name: RESENT IMPLEMENTATION REPORT TO
USER MANAGEMENT
Process reference number: 4.3.4
Process guided by: Activity 4 Plan

Process notes: This presentation makes User management aware of your progress to date, reports on the resources used, and seeks commitment to, and approval for, the User resources needed for Activity 5. (If the User is responsible for the project budget, this also includes project resources.)

A major goal here is to get approval for the significant User resources required in Activity 5.

This process formally presents the information in the Implementation Report. You may also present some program test results to keep open the communication about the project's progress. Identify any changes or slip in schedule during Activity 4 as well as any issues that may possibly affect progress during Activity 5. Whenever possible, recommend solutions to potential problems.

After you receive resource approval from management, revise the overall data processing plans and resources to reflect any reallocation of resources. You should also get commitment and approval for outside resources needed in Activity 5, such as hardware movers.

Process name: INSTALL HW/SW
Process reference number: 5.1.1
Process guided by: HW/SW Installation Plan

Process notes: Install the hardware and software required to support the new system.

The Hardware/Software Installation Plan guiding this process identifies whether you install all the hardware and/or software at one time or in stages by iterating through this and other implementation processes.

Using the Hardware/Software Installation Specification, confirm that all environments, new and reusable, are ready for both the new and reusable hardware/software and that the new hardware/software has been received from the vendors and is ready for installation. In addition, identify the existing hardware/software that requires relocating and confirm that it is ready.

Install this hardware/software in the production area using the support procedures and materials identified in the Hardware/Software Installation Specification.

After installing and testing the hardware/software, complete the Hardware/Software Installation Completion Report and update the production hardware/software inventory for new, reused, and reallocated hardware and software.

Note:

An agent outside the project team, such as a planning support group with vendor engineers, may perform this process.

Process name: PERFORM DATA CONVERSION
Process reference number: 5.1.2
Process guided by: Conversion Plan

Process notes: Convert current production data to a new format and/or storage and access technique, and create the data needed for the new production system.

The Conversion Plan indicates whether you convert all data at one time or iterate through this and other implementation processes to convert in stages.

Using the data dictionary in the Conversion Specification, confirm that the data is available and, if necessary, gather the source data for the new data needs. Then execute the conversion programs and procedures against this data using the procedures and support identified in the Conversion Specification.

After converting the data and conducting walkthroughs, testing and reviews to obtain User agreement that it is correct, produce the Conversion Completion Report.

Note:

Some of the agents performing this task may not be members of the project team. For example, they could be data administration staff setting up a new database or adding to an existing database, and, of course, the User should verify the conversion results.

Process name: CONDUCT TRAINING
Process reference number: 5.1.3
Process guided by: Training Plan

Process notes: Train User and Operations staff to run the new system.

Conduct the training for both staff and management using the training support identified in the Training Specification and the system development training materials. The system execution manuals make up the major documentation for training, but the Training Specification may also identify actual application programs and system controls to assist in the training effort.

The Training Plan identifies whether you train staff all at one time or in stages.

After the training is completed, produce the Training Completion Report for management.

Process name: PERFORM SYSTEM TEST OF MANUAL AND
AUTOMATED SYSTEM
Process reference number: 5.2.1
Process guided by: Test Plan

Process notes: Ensure that the new system, or this release of it, meets the system and business objectives.

This process represents the "trial run" of the entire new system in which the automated part is treated as a "black box." You are now testing that the system as a whole satisfies all the inputs and outputs, and that the interfaces between programs, subsystems, and procedures are correct. Since you have already tested the individual functions, the test sets from the Test Specification will concentrate on integration, performance, volume, security and recovery capabilities of the system.

Use the system execution manuals to guide this testing effort according to the Test Plan's testing strategy. The Test Specification provides the individual test objectives for the test sets in the development test library.

Also, for this to be a complete system test, use the trained data processing operations staff, application programs with their system controls, and the actual production environment.

This is the DP test of the new system, so operations staff, analysts, designers, coders, and the project manager should perform this process. User representatives should participate if they are members of the project team, but full User acceptance testing comes later.

Because the new system should stand alone, avoid letting any project team members who worked on a particular piece of the system test that piece.

After completing the system test, produce the System Test Completion Report.

Note:

Remember that at this point, not all objectives can be verified by a system test. For example, you cannot verify the goal to reduce production costs in a certain department; you can only verify this by monitoring production.

Process name: PREPARE REGRESSION TEST
SPECIFICATION AND LIBRARY
Process reference number: 5.2.2
Process guided by: Activity 5 Plan

Process notes: Create a regression test specification and library that can be used to verify that modifications applied in production do not inadvertently affect other parts of the system.

- From the Test Specification identify a minimum set of test cases and their test materials that can be used for regression testing.
- Examine the individual inputs (based on business events) to the system and identify their test objectives in the Test Specification.
- Extract the corresponding test materials from the development test library.
- Make any necessary modifications to the test materials such as changing the test scaffold for the production environment.
- Build the regression test specification and library.

You may need to include additional backup documentation in the regression test specification, such as expected hardware/software, to meet performance tests.

Process name: PREPARE AND PRESENT MAINTENANCE
PLAN
Process reference number: 5.2.3
Process guided by: Activity 5 Plan

Process notes: Prepare and present the Maintenance Plan required to support the new system or this release of the new system in production.

Unfortunately, the word "maintenance" has become a synonym for dealing with "bugs" which should not have been introduced to the system in the first place since we have the tools and techniques available to build "bug-free" systems. The Maintenance Plan is concerned with the inevitable modifications to the production system as the business evolves. These are rightly termed "enhancements."

The new production system must have future enhancements applied using the same concepts, tools, and techniques that were used to build the system.

• Review any accumulated change requests received during system development and identify those that apply to the data, functions, or support equipment and material in this system or release. (Changes to be included in another system or release will be covered in the area of study for that system or release.)
• Identify the data processing maintenance staff who will modify the system or release.
• Identify the ongoing requirement for hardware/software and training support.

Prepare the Maintenance Plan based on the above information, the new system description and the actual and projected resources used in the Project Plan, and present it to management.

Process name: TRANSMIT SYSTEM TO PRODUCTION
Process reference number: 5.2.4
Process guided by: System Installation Plan

Process notes: Install the new production system software, production system controls, and system execution manuals into the production environments.

Use the system installation procedures and support in the System Installation Specification.

- Transfer the new system software and system controls from development libraries to production program libraries.
- Transfer the system procedures manuals and operations manuals to production procedures libraries. (The system execution manuals may have already been transferred to the User and operations staff during training.)

Output program listings/source files and document system controls for maintenance documentation purposes.

Process name: TRANSMIT SYSTEM MAINTENANCE
INFORMATION
Process reference number: 5.2.5
Process guided by: System Installation Plan

Process notes: Transfer the system maintenance information to the maintenance library to support the new production system.

Use the maintenance installation procedures described in the System Installation Specification to move the following to the maintenance library:

- Regression Test Specification and library
- Training Specification and materials (ongoing portions)
- Maintenance Plan
- Hardware/software inventory (this may be just an update)
- Bounded New Logical Specification
- New Physical Specification
- New system execution manuals
- Copies of the program listings and system control documentation

Process name: CONDUCT ACCEPTANCE TEST
Process reference number: 5.3.1
Process guided by: Test Plan

Process notes: In this process, Users operate the system without it yet actually being "in production." The Users' main task is to execute manual procedures and automated system facilities and controls, and to approve the new system execution manuals.

By now there should be no errors, omissions and certainly no "bugs" in the new system. Although this task is just one more quality assurance process, DP management and system developers have often mistakenly used it to catch what they missed during the requirements definition phase. Up to now, we have been using "paper models" (structured specifications, design blueprints, etc.) for clarity of communication, but now it's much too late and costly to be defining requirements.

Users of the system execute this task aided by trained operations staff who were not involved in the system development effort. Project team members should not even assist because the system should stand alone. It has been installed in the production environment and the User and operations staff have been trained, so no assistance should be needed. Also, project staff may inadvertently bias test cases to their understanding of User requirements.

If human error has caused something to be missed or misunderstood in development and it is caught in this process, it will be necessary (and costly) to cycle back to the point in the methodology where the omission or problem occurred and repeat all steps for the omission/problem back to this point.

Recommend to the Users that they execute tests to make the system fail in all conceivable legitimate and illegitimate situations and combinations of situations. The Users' best source of test objectives is the Project Charter and the new system execution manuals.

Execute the system performance tests now that we have the system installed in the real production environment. You should also test the production hardware/software for usability at this point. (The training environment may have been the only time that Users have had hands-on use of the equipment prior to this time.)

After acceptance testing completion, produce the Acceptance Test Completion Report for management.

Process name: PREPARE FOR NEXT RELEASE
Process reference number: 5.3.2
Process guided by: Activity 5 Plan

Process notes: Prepare for the next release, if any, and archive the old system documentation:

- Document that the project goals stated in the Project Charter for the current release have been achieved. Include the Acceptance Test Completion Report in the Project Charter to verify this. (The methodology's DFD shows this as a "prompt" activating this process.)
- Identify the project goals for the next release in the Project Charter and document them as being "active". Reconfirm that these goals are still valid if a significant period of time has elapsed since receiving them or if User management has changed during the life of the project.
- Archive the current system description. (Murphy's Law says as soon as you throw it away, you will need it to answer some question.)
- Retain all project documentation in a Project History database for metrics on future projects.

To continue the development effort for the next release, cycle back to the process "Identify Preliminary Releases" (process reference number 2.7.1). However, if the next release's project goals have been modified during development of this release, you may have to cycle back even further in order to update the Project Charter.

Note:

To aid in developing plans in the next release, use the applicable portions of this release's plans.

Process name: RUN AND MONITOR PRODUCTION
Process reference number: 5.3.3
Process guided by: Activity 5 Plan

Process notes: Monitor the new system/release during its initial production period.

I look on this as the system's warranty period, which is why it is included as a system development activity. The length of this time period depends on the execution frequency of the system (or portion). For example, a quarterly batch system should be monitored over a longer period than an on-line system.

After the system's cutover to production, monitor the User's normal production execution of the new system, noting any problems with

- Usability
- Performance
- Accuracy
- Security
- Hardware/software ease of use, downtime, and support, etc.

After this initial production period, prepare a summary of initial production information for use in evaluating the new system.

Note:

Look out for any changes in the system usage pattern. For example, because the new system helps Users to run their business more effectively, they may make more use of the system than originally thought. Therefore, the number of input transactions may exceed your projections, thus requiring more hardware or a faster access technique to maintain the necessary response time.

Process name: PREPARE PROJECT COMPLETION REPORT
Process reference number: 5.3.4
Process guided by: Activity 5 Plan

Process notes: Evaluate the whole project and prepare the Project Completion Report based on monitoring the new system in production for an adequate length of time.

The monitoring period should have allowed you to determine whether the system satisfies its long-term goals, such as ease of maintainability, lower production cost, or less system downtime.

In order to repeat system development successes rather than failures, gather opinions on the project (e.g., ease of system installation, degree of disruption in changeover) and the new system or release from both DP and User management and staff via interviews and questionnaires.

- Document how well the project and system met their respective goals, based on User feedback, initial production information, and goals and solutions as defined in the Project Charter.
- Compare User feedback with the initial production information and document how well the new system is performing in production.
- Based on projected and actual resources used in the project plan, document how well the project team performed and how accurate the planning process was. (Use the Activity reports presented at the end of each Activity to assist here.)

This report should honestly and accurately document what happened in the project and why, both positive and negative. For example, if you found that the project team took longer than expected for certain activities (because of, say, a learning curve on new techniques or hardware/support software), then document that in the completion report so that other managers can anticipate it in future projects.

Also document such issues as User and support group cooperation that may have helped or hindered the development of the system. This type of information should not be lost as it will greatly help future project planning.

You can use the opinions and the data in the project plan to suggest improvements in tailoring the methodology and in project development techniques (such as the Survey/Probe projection technique).

When complete, distribute the Project Completion Report to management and file a copy in the Project History database together with other project information that may help future projects.

Afterword

I believe that the development of a system should be iterative and should evolve with use and experience. Therefore, I issue a call to those of you who are concerned with developing quality systems to provide me with input and suggestions.

System development techniques continue to evolve, and because a methodology is a "system to develop systems," the principle of evolution also applies. This book has gone through many iterations to get to its current form. Most of the ideas in this book have been "fleshed out" at corporations using the methodology over the past few years.

For any methodology to be accepted, it has to stay current and flexible. For example, I removed the three-level cycling from the first edition of this book and made only two levels because too many people were using this book for only large-system development instead of adapting it to any size of project. Users of the methodology fell into the trap of thinking that three iterations of analysis and design were mandatory, and therefore the approach was deemed suitable only for large development efforts.

If you have any suggestions concerning your experience with this methodology and other system development techniques, please send correspondence to:

Brian Dickinson
Logical Conclusions Inc.
450 Kings Road
Brisbane, CA 94005 U.S.A.
(415) 468-1880

Appendix A

Overview of the Structured Tools and Techniques

Structured Analysis

Structured Analysis is the activity of communicating a system's requirements from a user to an analyst and from an analyst to a designer. It uses four basic tools to accomplish this:

- Data flow diagrams (physical and/or logical)
- Data dictionary (logical)
- Data model
- Minispecifications

Structured Analysis discovers and models essential business requirements, i.e., **what** business data the system should accommodate and **what** business functions it should perform.

Structured Design

Structured Design is the activity of developing a flexible and maintainable computer solution to a well-defined set of system requirements. The intent is to maximize the useful life of the system and

303

minimize the overall system lifetime cost. The main Structured Design tools are:

- Hierarchical structure charts (system architecture)
- Data flow diagrams (physical)
- Data dictionary (physical)
- Pseudocode (module procedural logic)
- Quality evaluation criteria
- Packaging criteria

Structured Design determines **how** we organize a solution that satisfies requirements, i.e., the internal architecture for the computer system.

Structured Programming

Structured Programming is the activity of implementing a design solution in a readable, understandable style. The tools of Structured Programing include conventions for readable program layout and limiting program constructs to:

- Sequences of statements, tasks, and instructions
- Decisions (singular or multiple, e.g., **IF ELSE** or **CASE** statements)
- Iterative loops (e.g., **DO WHILE** or **REPEAT UNTIL** statements)

This activity can be considered **building** nonidiosyncratic programs from a given solution of a system.

Incremental Implementation

Incremental implementation is a technique of successively building and testing versions of a computer system having a hierarchical design. Implementation tools include:

- Hierarchical design charts (e.g. Structure Charts)
- Drivers/stubs (simulation modules)

This process is one of **putting together** and **testing** a system.

Information Modeling

Information Modeling is the activity of analyzing the business data needs of an environment and specifying them in a model. This activity uses two tools:

- Data models (e.g., Entity-Relationship diagrams)
- Data dictionary (which for this activity contains a superset of the analysis and design data dictionary documenting entity, relationship and attribute specifications)

Information modeling specifies the **static data needs** of a system or enterprise by focusing on the business meaning of data without regard to implementation details.

Database Modeling

Database Modeling is the activity of developing information structures for stored data. The results of Information Modeling are used as input to this process which packages the Information Model into a particular data structure implementation intended to provide flexible and efficient service for all applications. The tools used for this activity are:

- Logical access path diagram
- Database schema/structure

Walkthroughs/Reviews

A **Walkthrough** is a peer-group activity conducted to find errors, omissions, and ambiguities in a deliverable and to ensure conformance to company standards. Walkthroughs can be thought of as informal reviews.

As the name suggests, a walkthrough is conducted by the deliverable author who leads the group step by step through the deliverable, explaining its structure and content. Although it is advisable for the author to have distributed the deliverable in advance, the participants need not have examined it beforehand.

A **Review**, on the other hand, is more formal. The participants, who can include users, auditors, and QA (quality assurance) staff, examine the deliverable thoroughly beforehand. A moderator calls for their comments a section or model at a time. The author's presence is not mandatory, although most attend for the immediate feedback.

Neither approach attempts to solve problems during the meeting but confines itself only to identifying them. Corrections and improvements are made out of the review, and, if they are significant, another review may be scheduled.

Managers attending walkthroughs and reviews should refrain from using them to evaluate staff performance; otherwise their staff may become defensive. This would negate one of the principal benefits— feedback on the deliverable early enough in its life to save significant cost later in the system development life cycle.

Walkthroughs and reviews serve as **quality assurance** tools during system development and should be performed for all project deliverables.

Appendix B

Installing a Methodology

Introduction

I look upon this methodology as a system to develop systems.[1] Because it is a system itself, albeit mostly a manual one, a methodology should pass through the same development activities as any other system—from identifying the project goals to installing the system.

My main project goal for developing this structured methodology was to formally integrate all the structured techniques into a set of practical guidelines—a system for developing systems. Other project goals for this methodology were to provide the developer with:

- Accurate project metrics and improved system products
- System quality control
- Tools for communicating new development techniques and for documenting systems
- Ways to improve the efficient use of development staff and other resources

---

[1] This Appendix is based on a talk entitled "Implementing a Management Discipline: A Case Study" which I gave during a panel session at the 1980 National Computer Conference in Anaheim, CA. A version of it was published as "Committing to a Systems Methodology" in The Yourdon Report, Vol. 6, No. 1 (January—February 1981), pp 3-4,7. Copyright 1981. Reprinted by permission.

- Effective responses to system change requests
- Guidance in the use of state-of-the-art techniques
- Ways to identify and determine the degree of project risk
- Ways of declaring the modern system development life cycle for educating all participants in projects

In summary, the methodology should impose order on the development process, standardize its activities, and enhance communication between all members of the project team. However, more important is the proper installation of the methodology itself. (Any system not correctly installed may not be used at all!)

There are four major factors to consider when installing a methodology. Listed in order of importance, they are:

- Political/psychological considerations
- Installation and training
- The training medium used
- Ongoing support and monitoring

Let me expand on these and offer some recommendations for controlling them.

Political/Psychological Considerations

Political and psychological factors can profoundly affect a User's acceptance of the methodology. The most important consideration is high-level management's commitment to the installation of the methodology. In order to enlist their backing, educate managers in the advantages of a company-wide methodology. It is important that the methodology be adopted throughout an organization, because isolated groups using the methodology, or part of it, will not be able to communicate effectively and the benefits of the methodology may not be fully realized.

The second consideration is the potential feeling of loss of freedom or power, as well as the natural resistance to change, on the part of new Users of the methodology. I have found in my teaching career that DP folk are just as reluctant to give up old ideas as members of any other profession, even though DP is considered a fast-advancing profession.

To combat this resistance, the methodology must assist people in their work, be practical, and appear simple to use. This, of course, will depend on the methodology training and support tools, such as an automated data dictionary or a good comprehensive CASE (Computer-Aided Software Engineering) tool, provided to support the methodology. The quantity of forms and control procedures that a company assigns to go along with the methodology will also affect complexity. Too many forms to fill out or complex adherence procedures will hinder acceptability, leading to the problem of the developers' having to support the methodology instead of the methodology supporting the development process.

Finally, there is the possibility that Users' acceptance of the methodology will go to an extreme, and that the methodology will be taken too literally. Some people may look upon the methodology as a "cookbook" solution to all their problems, instead of as an aid to their own thought processes.

Aware of these considerations, you can take several steps to minimize their effects. First, you can classify the methodology as a guideline rather than as a standard and allow Users of the methodology to customize it whenever problems are found in its use. Thus, the methodology can be viewed as a help, not as a restriction. Of course, customization must be accompanied by an explanation; random customizing is not the goal. I have found that a separate quality assurance group or support individual (who has good communication skills) assigned to a development team can help overcome initial resistance.

Second, you can predispose acceptance of the techniques by setting up a review/User group that consists of managers whose departments will use the methodology. By doing so, you give them ownership in advance and a part in the decision to accept the methodology. Beware, however, that reluctant managers may make any meeting of this group their political battleground. I have found that the best proof of the benefits of the methodology comes from showing the successful results of an actual project in your own company, possibly from the results of a pilot project.

If you decide to test the methodology on a pilot project, choose such a project carefully. It should not be critical to the company's business, nor should it be overly complex. The learning curve for Users of the new methodology will compound the complexity and critical nature of the project and may prove fatal to the pilot project and so to the methodology. Even if not fatal, a too complex pilot project is not useful as a learning example.

Finally, carefully consider methods of training new Users to apply the methodology, as discussed in the next section.

Installation and Training

There are four general strategies that I see regularly implemented to install a methodology and to train its eventual Users: the Pilot Project approach, the integrated and Bottom-up approaches, and the Sheep-Dip approach. I briefly discuss each in the following paragraphs.

The PILOT PROJECT strategy: The methodology is tested by providing the necessary training for a small project team and applying any new techniques and the methodology on a reasonably sized pilot project. The resulting documentation from the project is used as support for other projects to adopt the methodology. The developers of the pilot project can assist or even train members of other projects by either being assigned permanently to the project or participating in its plans and reviews. These project members then can be appointed to aid other projects and so on in a pyramid implementation throughout the company.

The INTEGRATED strategy: Training in the methodology consists of teaching only those techniques that will be used immediately by the members of any new projects. For example, a course in the methodology's recommended analysis techniques is held before analysis activities, a design course before design activities, etc. This training is repeated as required.

The BOTTOM-UP strategy: Training courses are held for each category of employee (for example, analyst, designer, coder, or database developer), starting with the course applicable to their specific role and proceeding to courses on activities with which the employee may need to interface. A programmer, for instance, would take a course in coding techniques first, and a design overview course later. This is a realistic strategy for integrating new techniques into groups that are not scheduled for any new projects.

The **SHEEP-DIP strategy:** In this approach, all available staff members are trained at the time a course in any of the techniques is scheduled, regardless of whether they will need to use the techniques in the near future. This term is also used for the strategy that advocates training every employee in all of the techniques at once (a version of the six-week in-depth training course of everything you wanted to know about "getting structured" but were afraid to ask).

Realistically, a combination of the above strategies will be needed for most (large) environments. For example, combining the Pilot and Integration strategies is probably the best combination, but it could take years to train all of the groups involved. Moreover, neither strategy takes into account the training of new employees and maintenance groups. For this, the Bottom-up strategy is necessary.

In this regard, some people truly understand only those courses in subjects most applicable to their background. For example, programmers readily appreciate structured coding concepts and, when introduced to structured design, can see how its concepts aid the coding activity.

The Sheep-Dip strategy may actually be of some use, but only as an overview of different techniques to upper-level managers and other generalists. In general, it is best to give a person only the knowledge necessary to do his or her job well. For example, high-level management may require only an overview; middle management may require an overview and possibly an introduction to the deliverables or products; project leaders may require a working knowledge of the complete methodology; and technical project staff may require a detailed working knowledge of the activities for which they are responsible and possibly an overview of other activities.

As with any system development effort, a plan should be developed to monitor and control the installation of the methodology and its associated training.

Of course, how the methodology is installed cannot be separated from the medium chosen for training, as discussed below.

Training Medium

How the methodology is taught will greatly affect its understandability and, therefore, its acceptability. Although cost will probably determine the training medium used, some options include a workshop course, a lecture course, a self-study audiovisual course, and books or training documents. Any and all of these training devices can be backed up with assistance from consultants and with on-the-job advice of experienced personnel. In my consulting work, I have seen the best results come from using a combination of training vehicles, such as a workshop course with follow-up project consulting.

A workshop course is one of the best forms of training, as it provides staff with hands-on experience in applying a technique and with immediate feedback to questions. A lecture course also provides immediate answers to questions and is usually easier and cheaper to present, but doesn't offer participants the chance to practice using the techniques. A self-study audiovisual course allows a person to learn at his or her own pace. A combination of these training mediums will probably be best to support the whole training plan.

A final point to be made about training media pertains to the importance of the packaging of the support material. Careful consideration should be given to the way in which documentation is stored and accessed, so that it is easily usable. An easily referenced pilot project result that shows an example of each of the intermediate deliverable and final deliverables will help newcomers to the methodology. They can then compare a previous in-house project with their own project.

Ongoing Support and Monitoring

The methodology, like any system, should be modified to keep it from becoming out of date. A support group or even one individual part time, should have this as one of their responsibilities. The importance of this task should not be minimized, however, for the data processing industry is developing rapidly. New software development and support techniques are constantly being introduced in virtually every phase of system development, especially with CASE tools available through the proliferation of microcomputers.

For the methodology to survive, it needs to accommodate pertinent innovations, but the process of incorporating them must be controlled according to the same principles used in the original methodology. Unfortunately I have seen redundant tools and techniques included in customized versions of this methodology only because they were a "good idea" in the old methodology.

The effectiveness of the methodology should be tracked and compared with results using the old techniques to determine the cost-effectiveness of the methodology. Based on these results, adjustments to the methodology should be made when necessary. Consequently, an important task in any DP shop should be the gathering of metrics. Any good methodology should assist this task by introducing the basis of metric accumulation with measurement of specific deliverables, not phases.

Finally, a point I want to stress relates to the need for support consulting. An expert in the methodology—someone who has used the techniques, say, in a pilot project or in the original training group—should be available to help out on new projects to insure that the methodology is being used correctly. This can be accomplished simply by the advisor's being available during reviews and/or walkthroughs. I would like to stress that I believe any person charged with this responsibility should have good communication and technical skills.

In summary, the installation and ongoing support of any system requires commitment. This manual system—this methodology—is no exception.

Appendix C

Model Transformation— A Small Case Study

In this methodology, I have provided a description of what I believe to be the essential activities and data needed in system development. In this Appendix I would like to present an example of a small system application to demonstrate how the methodology would actually be used. My example focuses on what I believe are the most important technical activities, i.e., analysis and design.

I have concentrated mainly on the graphics models in this appendix although the analysis and design specifications should also be supported by a full set of deliverables, e.g., data dictionary, minispecs, physical dictionary, control module pseudocode, etc.

We are asked to study a small organization called "Consultant Services Inc." The company basically deals with customers (who request warm bodies to fill projects) and consultants (the warm bodies whom the company employs and contracts to the customers). The company is constantly searching for consultants who meet its high-quality requirements. The company obtains new consultants from personnel agencies because doing its own recruiting takes too much time away from their other important business activities. (Actually I found showing all aspects of the real company took away from showing the important points that I wanted to make in this small case study.) Customer bills are sent to the financial service division of the company's bank for collection and accounting.

The reasons for doing the project, that is, project goals, are as follows:

1. To eliminate or considerably reduce redundant data and processing between the existing automated and manual portions of our company systems. The number of errors and business costs caused by this are becoming intolerable.

2. To identify a way of reducing the computer time taken up by the customer billing run, which is steadily becoming the longest-running job in the data processing shop and is increasing with each new project and consultant.

3. To integrate the edits performed manually on the consultant time allocations with the existing automated edits; many times the automated edits overrule the result of the manual edits.

4. To allow a different rate to be charged for a consultant depending on the projects that he or she works on; currently the rate is fixed for a consultant regardless of the project.

The first model we produce from high-level discussions with the client is a context diagram (see Figure C-1) which bounds and identifies the area of study. It shows the net incoming and outgoing data flows of the system and the outside interfaces of these data flows (i.e., the edges of our world as far as this system is concerned).

We validate this high-level model (the Context Diagram) with the requestors of the project and ensure that the boundary and data interfaces to the outside boundary are correct. The Context Diagram once verified with the users will declare all the events stimuli that trigger our system into action. The Data Dictionary can show the breakdown into individual stimuli for "net" (compound) flows shown on the Context Diagram.

Next, we study the design of the current manual environments (i.e., the manual system that is in place today) and produce a number of "physilogical"[1] data flow diagrams, which we ensure the Users are able to validate. Because the Users of the current system have been using their manual procedures for so many years and are not

---

[1] See Glossary for a definition of "physilogical."

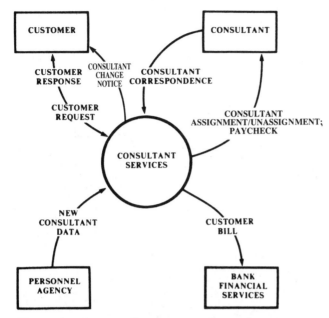

Figure C-1 Context diagram.

knowledgeable of physical-logical concepts but are knowledgeable about the business, we decided to produce a physilogical model as our communication and documentation tool rather than a pure logical model.

To get a complete picture of the system, all the detailed processes (i.e., functional primitives) and their data for the manual operation have been connected and shown together. The current automated system has yet to be partitioned. The current physilogical diagram is backed up with its data dictionary and process descriptions, and should be physical enough for the Users to validate as being complete and correct.

These data flow diagrams, when connected together, form the diagram shown in Figure C-2. Observing the model in Figure C-2, we can spot some obscure old physical packaging of tasks (no doubt the designer of this manual system had reasons for this packaging):

1. Multiple functions: Many environments have people who perform more than one function. For example, in Figure C-2, Mary handles "terminations" in her consultant relations role and also

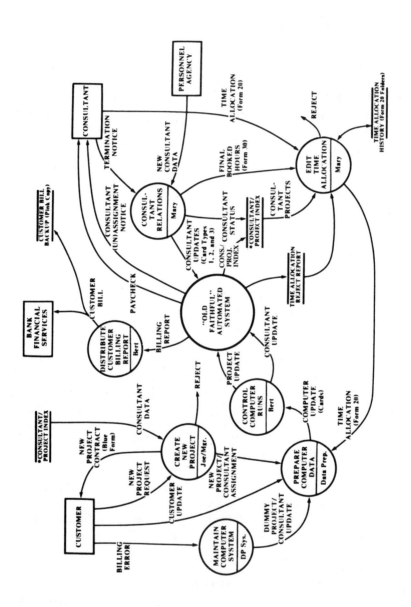

Figure C-2 Current Physilogical DFD for manual environment.

edits the daily "time allocation" forms. In our logical model we will split these "lumped" tasks and concentrate on data and its specific functions rather than on people's old roles or duties.

2. Split functions: In contrast to multiple functions, some cohesive functions have become the responsibility of more than one person. For example, "Create a New Project" in the example is split between Joe and the company manager.

3. Design stores: Stores/files that were created by the old system designer and that have no business need can be represented as data flows. For example, stores that are used to hold data between departments or between the manual and automated systems are only physical time delay stores. In Figure C-2, the paychecks are produced in the form of one report; later they are separated, but here they are shown as a data flow. We have left some manual stores and backup stores deliberately in the model for User validation purposes.

Other physical details (physical User signposts) remain in this model for our User validation purposes (for example, backup names like Mary, Joe, Blue Form, and Form 20 Folders). But ones we felt the User could spot as obvious old design boundaries, such as special locations and section names, were removed during development of this model.

In the example, many of the manual functions interface with an existing automated system that the employees affectionately call "Old Faithful" (because of its habit of blowing up regularly). In studying the design of this automated system, we identify four programs that have various qualities of structure, discussed as follows.

Program 1 (Figure C-3) has a fairly bad packaging (i.e., everything to do with handling projects): it was forced into a HIPO structure. There is no documentation other than the crude program boundary diagram which the computer system maintenance group validated as a reasonable representation of the program structure.

Program 2, depicted in Figure C-4, isn't too bad. It was developed during a modularization fad and had the typical pancake structure of that fad: one "mainline" module with all other modules immediately subordinate to it. It also typically didn't identify the data passing be-

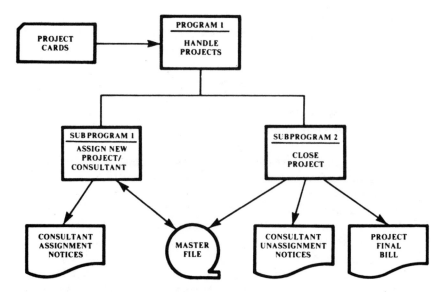

Figure C-3 Current design chart for automated environment: daily batch program.

tween the modules. This program structure was validated against the program code.

Program 3 was developed with a report writer package and was driven with parameter cards, but it basically consists of only one function (see Figure C-5). Program 3 produces bills for any customers that had hours of consulting time booked to them in the last month. Unfortunately, because of the file structure (defined later in this example) and the processing to "get around" this structure, the program takes forever to run. It has to scan the whole master file (defined in a data dictionary entry on the following page) accumulating "hours billed this month" for a particular project from each consultant record.

Program 4 (see Figure C-6) also has poor structure; it combines three functions connected only because they use the same file. The functions are triggered by input card types. If card type 1 is present, an index list of all consultants and their assigned projects is produced. This index list is updated by hand until the next list is requested. If card type 2 is present, it is used to delete a consultant (actually a change of status) from the master file. If card type 3 is present, the specified new consultant data is used to add a consultant to the master file.

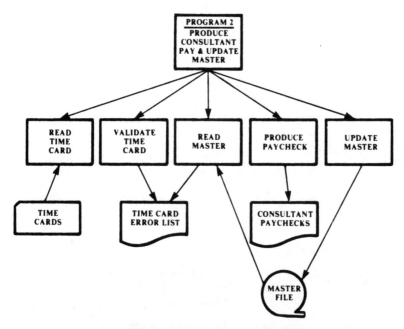

Figure C-4 Current design chart for automated environment: Nightly batch program.

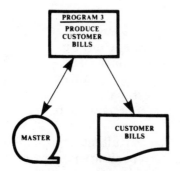

Figure C-5 Current design chart for automated environment: Monthly program.

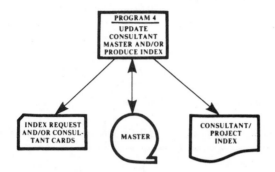

Figure C-6 Current design chart for automated environment: On-request program.

Figure C-7 Current system entity-relationship diagram.

The Master File is defined in the current data dictionary as follows:

= (consultant ID + consultant status + consultant address +
consultant skill + consultant rate + days per week available +
12(pay period + pay hours + pay amount)12 +
5(project ID + project status + project name +
project address + project cost estimate +
hours billed to date + amount charged to date)5)

So the Master File consists of consultant information keyed on "consultant ID" with two internal repeating groups: one for pay histories (a minimum and maximum of twelve sets of history kept) and one for projects (five sets of project data kept). This data dictionary information is confirmed by ensuring that all of the data is still in use via the data flow in the data flow diagram. We produce the following simple entity-relationship diagram from this information and from a User interview where we were informed that a project typically has more than one consultant contracted to it.

From our system point of view, Figure C-7 states that the stored data consists of two entities, one for consultant information and one for project information. The rounded boxes are entities and the diamond is a relationship. The one inside the circle indicates an anchor point from which to read the relationship, and the "N" indicates a many occurence. Therefore, this reads that a consultant "contracts to" one or more projects and a project "contracts" one or more consultants. We need to back this model up with two entity specifications and one relationship specification.

The logical data dictionary entries for these entities (functional simple stores) become:

CONSULTANT = {consultant ID + consultant status + consultant address + consultant skill + consultant rate + days per week available + {pay period + pay hours + pay amount}12}

PROJECT = {project ID + project status + project name + project address + project cost estimate + hours billed to date + amount charged to date}

The data dictionary entry for the "consultant" entity, above, has an internal repeating group; that is, it is not fully normalized. I have not separated the internal repeating group from "consultant" because it is not a stand-alone entity; that is, there is no business need for this data by itself.

Note also that the business policy of this company states that only twelve pay periods of history will be kept; therefore, the two data attributes of **"hours billed to date"** and **"amount charged to date"** are not actually derivable items for projects over one year in duration. Therefore, I left these data elements in the definition. The entities (functional stores) can now be plugged back into the logical DFD and connected up with the data flow that use these objects.

Before going further, I want to present what I call the logical-physical spectrum (Figure C-8).

I use the idea of such a spectrum to illustrate the need to address different degrees of logical and physical representations of models depending on the reason for a project. For example, if the aim of a

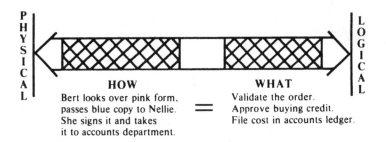

Figure C-8 Logical-physical spectrum.

project is to completely understand the underlying business functions of a system so that we can invent a completely new design for improving the business, then we will need to logicalize more than for a project that aims to identify better computer hardware for a system. There is precious little reason for developing a completely current physical model (i.e., design model of the current system) when the aim is to ultimately produce a new system design. Thus, the degree of logicalization in analysis should be considered before deriving physical or logical models. This should be addressed in the Project Plan.

After User consensus that the model in Figure C-2 really represents the current environment, then further removal of the physical characteristics from the model of the manual environment in Figure C-2 produces the diagram in Figure C-9.

Deriving the model in Figure C-9 from Figure C-2 involved the following:

1. Removing data transporter processes because they perform no data transformation; that is, there is no change to data content or status. For example, in Figure C-2, the "Prepare Computer Data" process changed just the input media and the "Distribute Customer Billing Report" process just moved data around. (The minispecifications for these processes contain nothing.)

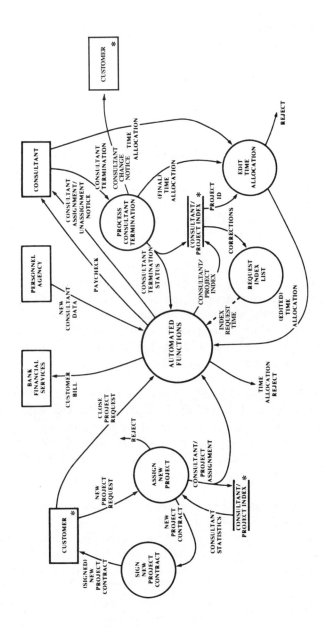

Figure C-9 Current logical DFD for manual environment.

2. Removing control/housekeeping processes and stores. They are old design features representing how the system is currently run. For example, in Figure C-2, the "Control Computer Runs" and "Maintain Computer System" processes and the "Customer Bill Backup" and "Time Allocation History" stores all supported the old system design, but did not support the business itself. These physical characteristics can and probably will change for the new design.

3. Policy-related processes such as "Sign New Project Contract" in Figure C-9 are physical tasks, but are shown because they are part of the company's essential business policy. The rule is, "If the current implementation of a portion of the system cannot change, then it's logical as far as the model is concerned." In other words, if you don't have the "Charter for Change," then it stays on the diagram.

4. Data flow alias names were resolved as the models were being produced. Data content and processing were also examined to reveal some of the non-obvious aliases. For example, in Figure C-2, "Final Booked Hours (Form 30)" and "Time Allocation (Form 20)" had the same data content and processing performed, so they became "(Final) Time Allocation" in Figure C-9.

5. The "Consultant Relations" process in Figure C-2 did nothing to "New Consultant Data." The data just took a sightseeing tour through the process so it could be manually entered into the computer system, but part of the consultant relations task—"Process Consultant Termination" in Figure C-9—does do some real work.

6. Prompts are triggers that contain no actual data but serve as initiators of a process. For example, in Figure C-2, a Card Type 1 (part of "Consultant Updates") was identified. It had no data content but served as a request for an index list from the computer program. It is represented as a dashed line in Figure C-9 to indicate that it is a prompt triggering the system at a point in time (i.e., anytime the new designer wants to invent).

7. I removed trivial reject processing—which does not require "backout" processing (reversing of previous business process-

ing). For example, to derive Figure C-9, I removed the store "Time Allocation Reject Report" which was input to "Edit Time Allocation" because it was there to support backup processing and a double check against the computer system for trivial time allocation rejects. Reject processing will be taken care of in the new system as appropriate to the new design.

The model in Figure C-9 will be refined further when both automated and manual system models are combined.

Next we use the four programs in the current computer system to derive a logical model for the automated environment. Removing the physical characteristics (such as subprogram/program boundaries, tapes, etc.) from the design models of the automated system and combining the results produces the diagram Figure C-10.

The important characteristics to note in Figure C-10 are as follows:

1. Group stores should be partitioned. The most obvious group store in the current environment was the Master File. This was really two stores (shown in the example) that were put together historically in the original automated system when that system processed only consultants' paychecks. The individual functional stores are shown on the logical diagram. (The manual environment may have the same problem with its stores.)

2. References to the media used for the stores or data flows should be removed, for example, references to cards, tapes, program, working storage. This is equivalent to the task we did for the diagram of the manual system.

3. Data transporters in the automated environment should be removed. These are processes such as read, write, display, etc. The data flow line itself serves to represent the movement of data.

4. Do not worry if there is no actual processing shown on a data flow once the data transporters have been removed (for example, the data flow into the stores indicating updating of "New Consultant Data" and "Project Status").

5. Remove control items (such as boss/coordination or backup modules as well as their backup stores and data in a design chart), as was done in the manual environment. Also, remove any control coupling (flags, switches, and end-of-file indicators, etc.) shown on the designs.

6. If necessary, prompts can be shown using a dashed line as in the manual environment. For example, the customer billing process in Figure C-10 is prompted by the end of the month. I labeled it "End of Billing Period" as the actual scheduled dates may change in the new design.

7. Functions should be separated. The model should show individual functions (especially at the detailed level). For example, in Figure C-3, the subprogram that closed a project contained two functions: one to release the consultants assigned to that project and one to produce the final customer bill. These two functions are shown separately in the logical model C10.

8. As follows from the previous characteristic, separating functions may reveal duplicate functions. For example, in the current system programs, C5, the billing functions are initiated twice in the system but should be represented once. The code for producing a customer bill was therefore duplicated in the current automated system, which caused maintenance problems. Showing it once in the logical model with two initiators (one at "End of Billing Period" prompt and one at the "Close Project Request" data flow) will ensure no duplicate code in the new system. Maybe we can use a reusable program to implement this process.

Now we combine the two models, the logical data flow diagrams for the manual and automated environments, to form a logical model for the total business system; the result after removing any remaining physical characteristics is the diagram in Figure C-11.

The characteristics to note in Figure C-11 are the following:

1. It may be common to find processes that are duplicated between the manual and automated environments. They should be merged as we remove the final physical aspects of the old

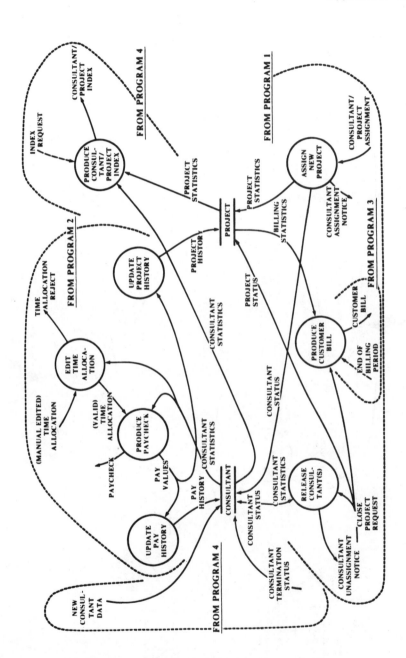

Figure C-10 Current logical DFD for automated environment.

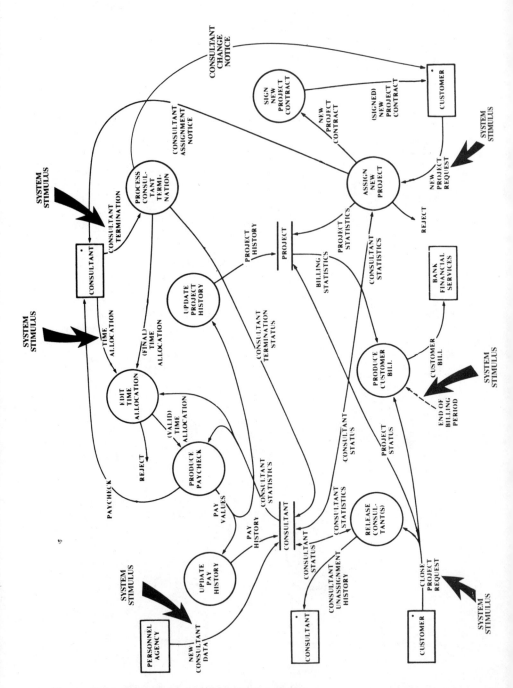

Figure C-11 Current logical DFD for total system.

implementation. For example, the current manual system assigns consultants to new projects and edits the data against the index file. The current automated environment performs the same edits against the Master File.

2. The previous designer may have created some control/backup processes and stores only to support the separation of the manual and automated functions. These should be removed when forming the total system logical model. For example, the consultant/project index file and its updating were used to back up the automated Master File and should therefore be removed.

Now that we have a complete view of the existing system, we can see what business event partitioning can do to show us the most functional breakdown of our business model. We see in Figure C-11 that in fact there are six stimuli created from outside business events.

The old partitioning "bunched" completely separate business events and processing together (possibly because of economies of scale or skill level reasons). This would be a very poor partitioning for a new computer system!

On the other hand, we can repartition the new design based on separate stimuli, their processing, and intermediate data to obtain a more maintainable, flexible new system—one that the User can even relate to the internal computer system structure (its architecture).

We can also see, way before we get to detail design and coding, that we can identify reusable modules (functions), e.g., the function "Produce Customer Bill" can be invoked from two separate system stimuli—"Close Project Request" and "End of Billing Period." Also notice that these two stimuli are different:

• One initiates a single customer bill to be produced (therefore, a data key will be needed as input).
• The other produces all consultant bills that have activity assigned to them since the past billing period (thus requiring just a time trigger and no input key or keys from outside the system).

They are best kept separate. If these two separate functions were pushed together in one program, some artificial parameter would have to be input to the program to separate them internally in the program, thus potentially causing a maintenance problem.

Other candidates for reusable modules are the two functions associated with the stimuli "Time Allocation." They are: "Edit Time Allocation," and "Produce Paycheck." Again these are triggered with two separate outside stimuli, but both would have the same input data content.

By the way, if we had produced a "business event Context Diagram" and used each stimulus on that diagram to partition and conduct our analysis effort, we could have traced through the system ignoring the old design partitioning and produced the DFD in Figure C-11 as our first system model. This would have probably saved significant time as long as the Users/clients of the system could validate this model without needing to see the physical view first.

As we are developing the data flow diagrams with our Users, we should also be documenting the Data Dictionary. When we reach the detail or functional primitive level of the DFD, we then have to produce minispecifications for the processes on this DFD. There are a number of tools we can use for this detail specification: graphs, charts, decision tables and trees, algorithms, structured English, or even just regular text if the logic being described can be read without ambiguity. We can use different flavors of textual documentation. For example, for the process "Assign New Project" in Figure C-11, we could develop informal or formal structured English as follows:

Informal structured English for "Assign New Project" process

Check the consultant list to see if there are enough available consultants to fill the new project request. (An available consultant is one who has available a number of days per week equal to or more than the number of days requested for the new project and whose city is the same as the new project city.) If there are not enough available consultants, then reject this new project request back to the customer.

If there are enough consultants, do the following three steps for each available consultant, starting with the highest-paid consultant, until the new project request is filled:

1. Reduce the consultant's days per week available by the days per week required in the new project request.

2. Check to see if the consultant's days per week available is now zero. If so, indicate that the consultant is no longer available by changing the consultant status on file.

3. Send a consultant assignment notice to the assigned consultant.

Finally, when the project request is filled, enter the new project in the project list and send out the new project contract.

Formal structured English for "Assign New Project" process

```
For Each CONSULTANT in Consultant store:
     If CONSULTANT-DAYS-PER-WEEK-AVAILABLE is greater than or equal to
         NEW-PROJECT-DAYS-PER-WEEK-REQUIRED
         and CONSULTANT-CITY is equal to NEW-PROJECT-CITY
     Then add 1 to AVAILABLE-CONSULTANTS

If AVAILABLE-CONSULTANTS is less than NEW-PROJECT-CONSULTANTS-REQUIRED
     Then issue NEW-PROJECT-REJECT
Else
     (conduct the following placement process starting with the consultant with the
     highest CONSULTANT-RATE until the number of
     NEW-PROJECT-CONSULTANTS-REQUIRED has been filled)
     For each available consultant:
         Subtract NEW-PROJECT-DAYS-PER-WEEK-REQUIRED from
             CONSULTANT-DAYS-PER-WEEK-AVAILABLE in CONSULTANT store
         Issue CONSULTANT-ASSIGNMENT-NOTICE
         If CONSULTANT-DAYS-PER-WEEK-AVAILABLE is zero
             Then change CONSULTANT-STATUS in CONSULTANT store to 'unavailable'
     Create new record of PROJECT-STATISTICS in the PROJECT store
     Issue NEW-PROJECT-CONTRACT
```

The same actual logic is in both the above process specifications but the former may be used if the User is "turned off" by structured english.

Next we look at the project goals and identify any that require logical modifications to the new system. (A logical modification consists of new or changed business data or functions, i.e., any changes to our current logical documentation.) It turns out that in the example of our consulting company, there is only one logical modification necessary to satisfy the project goals—modification to the entity-relationship diagram. The User's goal—to be able to charge a different consultant rate for each project—requires adding "intersection data" to the data specification, which results in an associative entity added to form the new diagram shown in Figure C-12. All other goals are new design-oriented.

Figure C-12 shows the same two entities and their relationships as does Figure C-7 but with a new entity "Assignment." This is where the rate attribute resides—at the intersection of project and consultant. This declaration states that rate is not dependent on just a consultant or on just a project, but on both, and if a new associative entity is implemented, it will have a compound key made up of the key for consultant and project. Its Data Dictionary definition is:

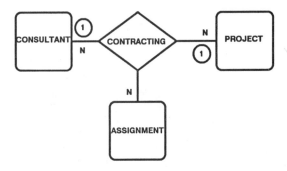

Figure C-12 New system entity-relationship diagram.

ASSIGNMENT = (CONSULTANT ID +
                PROJECT ID +
                ASSIGNMENT RATE)

We modify our definition of the entity "Consultant" in its entity specification to show that the attribute "Consultant Rate" has been removed and produce another entity specification for the "Assignment" associative entity containing this attribute.

We reflect this new entity in the DFD in Figure C-13 to show "Assignment" as a separate data store. We can now update the minispec for "Assign New Project" to show the User's new company policy for calculating the rate for a particular consultant assigned to a particular project when a new project request is processed. Note also, whenever a consultant is released from a project or a project is cancelled, data integrity provisions documented in the entity specifications should ensure that the occurrence of the associated Assignment entity is removed.

The choice of a solution for the goal that requests synchronizing automated and manual stores (notice the logical model already shows this because duplicated data is removed during logicalization) will depend on the usage of the data and the cost-effectiveness of the solution. For example, one possible solution would be a system that provides on-line data access, eliminating the need for separate

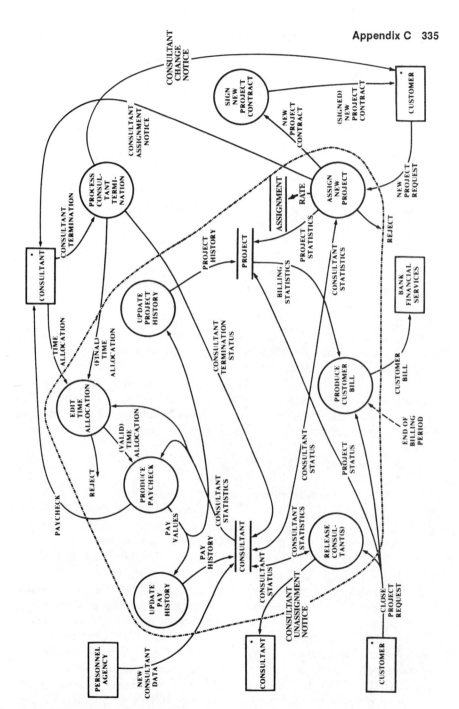

Figure C-13 Bounded new logical DFD.

manual and automated stored data. Another option could produce more regular reports on stored data to the manual environment.

However, if all the manual edits and new project assignment functions are automated, there is no need for a separate index file, which is the problem in the current environment. We can satisfy the goal to reduce the computer time used by the customer-billing run by a change in the old physical file structure, i.e., produce a data structure that allows direct reference to project information without accumulating project data via each consultant record, as is necessary in the current system.

Therefore, from the discussions above, it is apparent that because the goals require mostly "physical" changes to the current system, the New Logical DFD is the same as the Current Logical DFD except for the addition of the "Assignment" store. The Bounded New Logical DFD is therefore the Current Logical DFD of Figure C-11 overlaid with the Man/Machine Boundary, as in Figure C-13.

Note that our Man/Machine boundary indicated with a dashed line coincides with what was typically known as the area of study, only now all input and output data flows are known (declared in the data dictionary). It is also reassuring to know what functions originally created and finally used our system data. If we have the charter to change beyond the existing computer system boundary, we can now take the opportunity to improve the "total" system.

Forward into Design

We are on our own with design—the Users don't need to be involved. We use our knowledge of the technology to date to design the new system. We can now begin to identify the new design by identifying any obvious major packaged job boundaries. In fact, we have already performed some design by identifying the Man/Machine Boundary. (This is a design task because it requires invention.)

In our example, these packaged job boundaries will be based mainly on the periodicity of the functions. For example, the customer billing process will still be a monthly process because the User informs us that this is fixed business policy. So, the billing process (stimulated in our logical model by "End of Billing Period") becomes a separate job, but a customer will also receive a bill immediately when a "Close Project Request" is input. Therefore, we will implement the process of producing a customer bill as a routine that can be called from more than one program (a reusable module), thus overcoming the duplicate code that causes a problem in the current environment.

The same type of design can be used for processing consultant paychecks. The User wants the consultant paychecks (stimulated in our logical model by "Time Allocation") to be produced bimonthly except in the case of a consultant termination where a paycheck should be produced immediately; this latter case is stimulated by "Final Time Allocation."

The only requirement for the other three stimuli to our system is that they have fast turnaround times when input to the system. Therefore, we can propose an on-line system to our Users, with a menu screen choice prompted by one of the four stimuli. If the proposal is cost-effective and the User accepts it, we can then produce the internal architecture of our on-line system. The system can be viewed as a transaction center with a high-level design (see Figure C-14).

The structure in Figure C-14 shows a transaction-centered design indicated by the decision diamond under the "top boss" controlling module. This structure chart declares that a boss module is responsible for calling a module to get a transaction request and can then call the appropriate sub-module within the transaction center to process this request (i.e., one of the modules stemming from the decision diamond).

If an operator requests an unsupported transaction (i.e., an invalid request), then an invalid transaction message can be displayed by

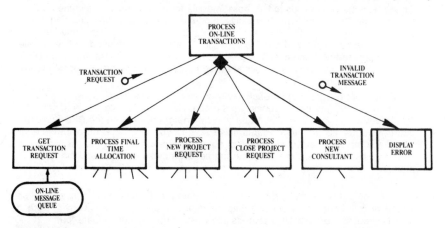

Figure C-14 New design chart for on line automated environment: top levels.

the library module "Display Error." Each transaction process sub-module can be further decomposed where necessary. For example, the module "Process Final Time Allocation" (processed on-line when a consultant terminates employment) performs a significant amount of work and is a good candidate to show the transition to design using "transform-centered" design techniques.

Transform Analysis

Let me now use this case study example to demonstrate a seven-step process for Transform Analysis that I have been teaching to my students for many years.

Perform Transform Analysis for each business event partition on the Bounded New Logical DFD as follows:

1. Identify the "real worker" process(es) on the DFD, i.e., that which performs the main processing on data which has already been retrieved, edited, and preprocessed but which is prior to any output formatting or regrouping. (Good verb/object process names on a logical DFD will help here. If in doubt as to whether a process is doing real main processing, leave it out.) Draw a boundary line around the process(es) to form the transform center. (Don't be concerned if no real processing takes place, i.e., no processes are in the transform center.)

2. Create a "boss" module. The name of this "boss" should be a summary of the processing it contains, i.e., its event partition name.

3. Create "executive" modules to the "boss" module for each process within the trans-form center. Create additional "executive" modules for each data flow crossing the transform center boundary. For each input data flow, create a module named after the data flow name prefixed with the verb "get," and for each output data flow, create a module named after the data flow prefixed with the verb "put." Use the actual DFD data flows to create the data coupling between these modules and the "boss" module.

4. Form the input hierarchy(s) for each newly created "get" module by converting each data flow coming into the preceding input process on the DFD into a subordinate "get" module. Then form another equally subordinate module from the DFD process that transforms this data flow. Repeat this step until you reach the source of the data flow (i.e., data store, outside interface or automation boundary). Again, use the actual DFD data flows to create the data coupling between these modules and the "boss" module.

5. Form the output hierarchy(s) for each newly created "put" module by forming a subor-dinate module from the succeeding output process on the DFD. Then convert each data flow output from this DFD process into another equally subordinate "put" module. Repeat until you reach the destination of the data flow (data store, outside in-terface, automation boundary). Again, use the actual DFD data flows to create the data coupling between these modules and the "boss" module.

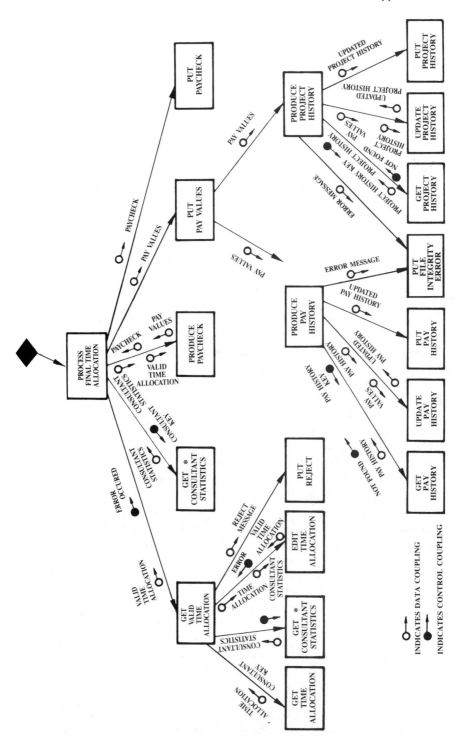

Figure C-15 Part of the lower-level new design for automated environment developed using Transform Analysis.

6. Add control parameters such as end of file, record not found, edit failure flags, etc. Also add initialization and termination modules if necessary.

7. Verify that the structure works, either by desk-checking or in an informal peer walkthrough. Check for such things as inverted authority (subordinate telling the boss what to do), coordination and timing issues, and the degree of coupling and cohesion.

Applying the above Transform Analysis procedure to part of our Bounded New Logical DFD produces the internal computer system design shown in Figure C-15. This is a structure chart developed from the business event stimulus " (Final) Time Allocation" and its associated processing on the automated portion of Figure C-13. The "get" and "put" modules corresponding to the input and output data flows have been introduced as part of the Transform Analysis design procedure used to turn packaged DFDs into Structure Charts. As only one paycheck is produced per invocation of this subprogram, no "End of File" control parameters are needed.

We can refine this model further, if needed, by breaking down (factoring) modules. For example, the edit module can be broken down to show the individual edits performed. We may need additional error processing to accommodate database errors, and other refinement criteria such as investigating the chart to insure that data is only passed between modules on a need-to-know basis.

Each of the items of coupling passed between modules on the design chart should be defined in the data dictionary. The data coupling, as opposed to control coupling, should already be in the data dictionary from analysis.

Each control module on the chart should have pseudocode developed for it. The minispecs from analysis should serve as is for "worker" modules, i.e., where a process on the DFD will be implemented as a module on the structure chart.

We may use pseudocode for our minispecs to be more specific. For example, we may want to "embellish" the minispec documented previously for the function "Assign New Project" especially as it contains some aspects of control, such as a loop for identifying the number of available consultants and reject logic.

Before we do the pseudocode for this function, we need to specify the design structure for the transaction stimulus that initiates that function. The diagram in Figure C-16 was produced using Transform Analysis on the stimulus "New Project Request" in our logical model.

The structure chart in Figure C-16 is "flat" because the DFD from which it was derived has only one process associated with it and this process is doing real work as opposed to input "cleanup" or output distribution. The "hat" on the module (process) "Assign New Project" indicates that we decided at design time to include this module's logic in its boss when we document its pseudocode and also when it is coded.

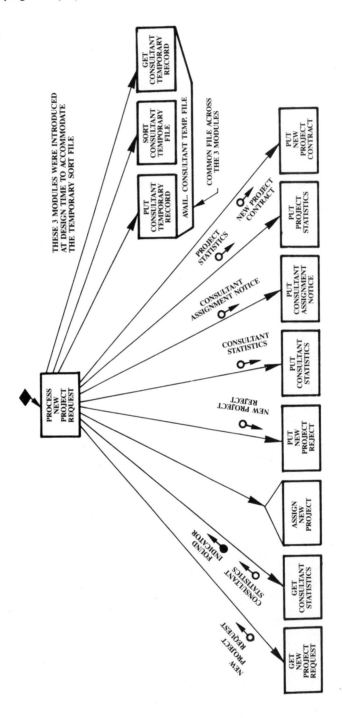

Figure C-16 Design chart for transaction "New Project Request."

Module: "PROCESS NEW PROJECT REQUEST"

*This module uses the on-line consultant database and requires an internal sort on a
*temporary file of available consultants. Data names beginning with CONSULTANT are
*from the CONSULTANT STATISTICS record and data names beginning with NEW
*PROJECT are from the NEW PROJECT REQUEST input (see Data Dictionary).

```
Begin module
    Set no-of-available-consultants to zero
    Perform GET NEW PROJECT REQUEST
    Set database-search-parameters for CONSULTANT-RECORD with
        CONSULTANT-STATUS equal to "A"
    Perform GET CONSULTANT STATISTICS
    Repeat while database-record-found-indicator is equal to "YES":
        If CONSULTANT-DAYS-PER-WEEK-AVAILABLE is greater than or equal to
            NEW-PROJECT-DAYS-PER WEEK-REQUIRED and CONSULTANT-CITY is equal to
            NEW-PROJECT-CITY
        Add 1 to no-of-available-consultants
            Perform PUT CONSULTANT TEMPORARY RECORD to available-consultant-temporary-file
        Else
        Do nothing
        Endif
        Perform GET CONSULTANT STATISTICS with database-search-parameters for
            CONSULTANT-STATUS equal to "A"
    Endrepeat
    If no-of-available-consultants is less than NEW-PROJECT-CONSULTANTS-REQUIRED
        Perform PUT NEW PROJECT REJECT
    Else
        Perform SORT CONSULTANT TEMPORARY FILE in descending order by
            CONSULTANT-RATE
        Set consultant-temporary-count to NEW-PROJECT-CONSULTANTS-REQUIRED
        Perform GET CONSULTANT TEMPORARY RECORD from
            available-consultant-temporary-file
        Repeat while not at end of available-consultant-temporary-file and
            consultant-temporary-count is not equal to zero:
            Subtract NEW-PROJECT-DAYS-PER-WEEK-REQUIRED from
                CONSULTANT-DAYS-PER-WEEK-AVAILABLE
            If CONSULTANT-DAYS-PER-WEEK-AVAILABLE is equal to zero
            Set CONSULTANT-STATUS to "U"
            Else
            Do nothing
            Endif
            Perform PUT CONSULTANT STATISTICS
            Setup CONSULTANT-ASSIGNMENT-NOTICE (See D.D. definition)
            Perform PUT CONSULTANT ASSIGNMENT NOTICE
            Subtract 1 from consultant-temporary-count
            Perform GET CONSULTANT TEMPORARY RECORD
        Endrepeat
        Setup PROJECT-STATISTICS (See D.D. definition)
        Perform PUT PROJECT STATISTICS
        Setup NEW-PROJECT-CONTRACT (See D.D. definition)
        Perform PUT NEW PROJECT CONTRACT
    Endif
Endmodule
```

By this point in design we should have decided the file storage and access needs. In our example we have chosen an indexed database for stored data.

Now we can see how the minispecification from analysis can be "embellished" to form the above design pseudocode. You will notice that I have used a particular form of notation in the pseudocode example. My intention here is that a code generator CASE tool would be able to create source code directly from the pseudocode using these conventions. Those shown here are for example only, and typically your organization would specify its own standards. The conventions I have used are:

- Data names in **UPPER CASE** are in the Analysis Data Dictionary.
- Data names in **lower case** are internal working storage items.
- Data in **"quotes"** are literal values.
- Module names are <u>**underlined**</u>
- All other words should translate into reserved words in the target coding language.

Alternatively, the same logic can be represented using a Nassi-Schneiderman diagram (with the same comments from the above pseudocode), as shown in Figure C-17. (I prefer Nassi-Schneiderman diagrams for pseudocode because they are graphical and make you think in block structured terms.)

You can now conduct a walkthrough on this pseudocode logic, and after acceptance, we can code the module. The previous pseudocode is "language-independent," that is, it can be implemented in any language. The coder (which may also be the author of the pseudocode) now need only concentrate on the implementation language's syntax and grammar without being concerned if the logic is correct. The pseudocode may actually be an overkill if a fourth generation language is to be used. If so those parts of the pseudocode that are taken care of by the languages need not be detailed out.

(You can see from this pseudocode example that the analysis minispec may "blossom" somewhat during the design activity as we get more rigorous with implementation-specific logic—in our example computer control logic was introduced.)

It is obvious how we can now easily proceed into the coding stage based on the quality deliverables produced in our analysis and design activities.

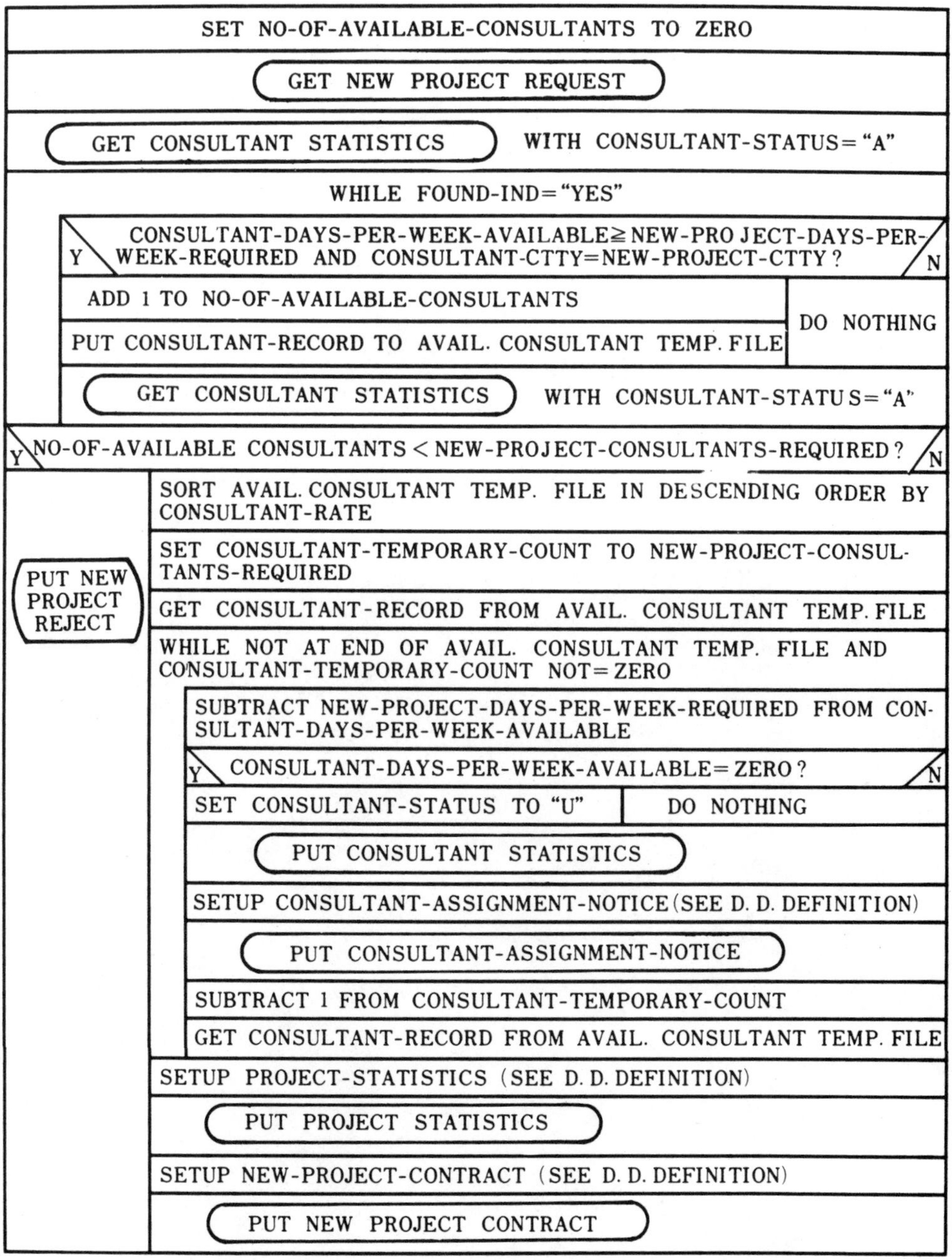

Figure C-17 Sample Nassi-Schneiderman diagram for "Process New Project Request."

Appendix D

Common Questions and Answers

Q. You state at the beginning of the book that this methodology works for system modification. How?

A. A modification effort (commonly combined with maintenance) can be classified as a small project. You can create a customized plan for the modification project from the methodology DFDs, e.g., you can compress Analysis and Design (Activities 2 and 3) into one activity, selecting applicable tasks and deliverables if the modification is not extensive. The existing documentation for the system to be modified will be the source for the current system study. If the system was developed using structured techniques, then you will just need to verify the documentation as up to date.

If your existing system is a nightmare, the best you can hope for is to put the modification into this system as a separate module or subsystem and then configure the current interfaces or coupling to this module/subsystem.

Q. You state that this methodology is just as applicable for software selection as it is for a new software development project. How?

A. Even though you may intend to use a software package, you still need to identify your requirements, that is, to conduct analysis. You may also need to analyze the package itself if the documentation supplied is not adequate, and then judge whether the package fills your new system requirements. By using a package, you may save on design and construction of the system, but you may also have to modify or add your own programs to the package. At least you will see where a software package is deficient or excessive.

Installing the package will be the same as for any system built in-house. So, you can customize the methodology to exclude the design and coding effort if the package really does fill your requirements for the new system. Alternatively, use a scaled-down partial plan if you need to design and implement requirements not covered in the package.

Q. Do we really need to study the following:

- The current environment if we already know what the new system must do?
- The manual environment if we are just rewriting the automated system?
- The current environment if we are implementing a complete new function into the company?
- Outside the actual area of change?

A. All the following answer these questions:

1. If the functions that the new system will perform are in an existing environment, whether automated or manual, then you certainly need to study them. Where else do you get your detailed requirements? Conducting a good analysis effort will save significant cost and effort later in the project.

2. Studying the current environment familiarizes you with the essential system and your User. Also, you must understand the current environment into which your new system will fit.

3. You must make sure that any new functions and the total new system are compatible with the existing environment. You may find that you can reduce costs and increase benefits by including a function previously thought to be outside the area of change. Also, by studying the current environment, you may

discover that some of the current input or output is not required in the assumed format, or is not required at all. (See Appendix C for examples of this.)

Q. Should we produce one data flow diagram for the total system?

A. I have found it does aid the developers of a system, especially the analysts, to see the system model as one complete detailed diagram—at least for areas that are truly connected by data flows. I believe the leveled set of DFDs is very helpful for partitioning the amount of information gathered and verified with the user when studying a large system, but I have also found that many project teams get too wrapped up in the upper-level DFDs, which to me are presentation levels.

With the introduction of automated software tools for the system development effort we can concentrate on the working level of a system—the functional primitive level. At this level all the interface data flows between any old designer partitions should connect. If they don't, it's a sign of missed data flows, miscommunication between team members, or old/out-of-use data that is still in the system. The important technical levels of the leveled set of DFDs are the Context Diagram and the functional primitive (lowest) level. Actually, I identify one other level as important to the project deliverables—the business event-partitioned level. (See Appendix C for examples of these.)

Q. Do we have to develop minispecifications for areas that we know will not change, i.e., areas that bound the system?

A. Let's define "change." If you modify any logic/business policy in the current system or if the new system will be implemented differently (e.g., manual to automated), then you will obviously need to create minispecifications for communication purposes. It's the "buffer zone" processes that are questionable. For these the answer is no in most cases. You can probably get away with rough draft minispecifications to understand what happens to the data before it comes into the system and what will happen to it when it leaves the system. Then if these processes are beyond your charter for change and do not affect your new system, don't put any further effort into them. A deciding factor would be the need for good documentation for new system interfaces to these areas. If this is a goal and time permits, you may want to prepare formal minispecs.

Q. Why should we conduct so many tasks in preliminary study, such as "develop test cases," "conceptual design," "conversion," "training," and so on, when we are just conducting a feasibility study and we may have the system size reduced anyway?

A. This is a Catch-22 situation. One of the reasons for conducting the total preliminary study is to determine whether the system is too large for one release. To not conduct all the tasks in the preliminary study would force you to guess at the feasibility of the new system. The cost of systems and their development efforts are too expensive to guess at.

Remember that in the preliminary study you are only "sizing" the project. Not much actual development effort is achieved at this level. Nevertheless, no work effort is wasted; the next release can validate the high-level documentation and build on it, decomposing and recomposing data and processing as necessary.

Q. Your methodology's data flow diagrams show hardware and software selection after identifying the system's man/machine boundary. However, our project must use existing company hardware and software. Will this be a problem in the development process?

A. No. Remember that the data flow diagrams are not flowcharts. The development effort of a project is a process of iteration. Although I have shown an explicit two-level iteration in this methodology, you should also iterate through processes within these levels of documentation. In your particular case, you may iterate through the selection of the man/machine boundary and through use of the hardware and support software on this boundary to facilitate entry and distribution of data until you are satisfied with the man/machine option(s).

You may also customize the methodology to show the hardware and software selections before the man/machine boundary selection. The methodology just shows the best case where you can select the most appropriate hardware and support software after you know your system requirements and are starting the new design.

Q. Can you really complete all the implementation specifications without knowing how you are actually going to accomplish the implementation activities, i.e., without implementation plans?

A. Not really. This question again raises the problem of looking at data flow diagrams as flowcharts. You will iterate through the specifications and plans, but you also have to acknowledge releases if they are necessary, because releases will have a strong effect on the implementation plans. Therefore, you must iterate through the processes that produce specifications, releases, and plans.

Q. Why do you identify releases as well as man/machine options?

A. The end of analysis is not the best place to identify releases, i.e., complete working partitions of a new system. On the other hand, you need to identify man/machine options at the end of analysis in order to proceed with designing the automated portion of the system. System releases are based on the analysis, design, and implementation activities. Releases may be based on which hardware can be installed or on the number of people or divisions that can be trained within a reasonable time period.

Releases can be perceived as a further installation partitioning of the man/machine option(s). Other kinds of partitioning (implementation partitioning), or versions (i.e., partially built functions), can be identified within a release. These are usually used for incremental testing purposes.

Q. You identify a monitored production period. When do we stop?

A. You should always monitor systems to ensure that they are still meeting User expectations and needs. This kind of monitoring can be sporadic. Intense monitoring to track problems and usage patterns should be conducted in order to produce the initial production report after most system conditions have been experienced, for example, after end-of-month processing, exceptional peak periods, and a sufficient amount of processing to identify any increase or decrease in system usage. Therefore, the period of time for intense monitoring of new systems will vary depending on how long it takes to experience all the system conditions.

Appendix E

Rules for Reviews

A **review** is a quality assurance/control procedure to find errors, ambiguities or omissions in a deliverable, to insure that company standards are observed in a deliverable, and to insure that a deliverable is readable and understandable by all who need to reference it.

The reviews referred to in this methodology are both internal project reviews in which the developers of the product participate and independent reviews in which the developers of the product do not participate. The procedures are basically the same for these two types of reviews. Reviews are shown in this methodology after a significant deliverable has been produced, but walkthroughs can and should be performed on complete intermediate deliverables such as DFDs, structure charts, or Entity-Relationship models.

Guidelines for **walkthroughs**, which are informal and more flexible than reviews, can be extracted from these procedures. Depending on the product and the stage of its development, you may need less lead time, a less formal presentation, no report, and so on.

The makeup of the review participants will depend on the material being reviewed but should mainly consist of the deliverable developer's peers such as other analysts or designers. The developer(s) of the deliverable can also attend providing they do not verbally add any assumptions that should have been in the deliverable. A User representative can be helpful, especially in the analysis, design, and implementation reviews, as these will, in various degrees, affect the User.

A feature I see being adopted frequently in reviews is to have what I call "someone borrowed," that is, someone from the activity on either side of the activity that produced the deliverable under review. For example, when reviewing an analysis specification, borrow a User and a designer; in a design review, borrow an analyst and a coder, etc.

The project manager may attend if he or she is involved in the technical side of the product, but no upper-level management should attend. When upper-level management is present, developers of the deliverable under review can unfortunately become defensive, and reviewers may try to look good by concentrating on how **they** would have developed the document or by inventing "instant" solutions to problems. For the same reason—that the product, not the developer, is being reviewed—a review or review report should never be used for personnel evaluation or salary review.

The review body may also include representatives from database administration, standards, auditing, maintenance, and so on.

A review must be cost-effective. Therefore, the time, number of reviewers, and degree of formality will depend on the amount and importance of the deliverable being reviewed. For example, a preliminary-level review will demand fewer resources than a detailed level review.

Suggested review procedures follow:

1. Identify the amount of material to be reviewed at one time and, if necessary, partition it and schedule multiple reviews. The material to be reviewed at one time will be based on the duration of the review and the time for the review, which will probably be allocated by the project manager. (The optimal duration for a review is twenty to thirty minutes; the maximum time should be one hour.) The detailed project plan will act as a guide for this partitioning.

2. Identify the location for the review, and ensure that it is conducive to the thinking process and free from interruptions.

3. Identify the review participants if they are not already identified in the project plan, and obtain commitment and approval from the appropriate managers for those outside the project team.

4. Assign participants to review roles. The main roles are:

   - "Moderator" to keep the review in order and look out for style arguments, never-ending issues, discussions and questions that veer away from the matter at hand, etc.
   - "Scribe" to take minutes and to document questions, comments, and issues that need resolving outside the review
   - "Presenter" (optional)
   - The objective reviewers

The presenter's presence is optional since the material should stand alone at the review stage. However, if necessary, a developer or someone who is familiar with the material but more objective than the developer can present the material. Individuals can take on more than one role.

5. Distribute the schedule and materials far enough in advance to give the reviewers time to look them over and to formulate review questions. Do this at least a day in advance, but give more lead time if the material is complex or if the reviewers' own work schedules are busy.

6. Have the reviewers raise issues and questions and comments as the material is presented or as the moderator requests them. The best review presentations are those that require minimum verbal backup of the product under review. After all, one of the aims of any documentation, from Project Charter to code, is that it can stand alone to aid system maintenance and modification.
   On the other hand, if the material is presented, the presenter should not add extra details that should already be in the product (especially if the developer is doing the presenting).

7. Do not try to resolve problems. Merely note them as review issues for the author's attention.

8. At the end of the review, identify the recommendations for the material. Based on any problems found, decide whether to accept the material "as is," to accept it with minor problems to be resolved outside the review process, or to reject it and schedule another review after the material has been corrected. (To emphasize the seriousness of this decision, I usually remind reviewers in my seminars that they are **each** responsible for the material under review and can be called in when future problems are found that this review should have caught!)

9. After the review, the scribe summarizes the minutes and combines them with the recommendations to form the review report, which can then be distributed to the reviewers and management. The review minutes are a good source for statistical data, which should be documented and used in future reviews and planning.

10. Solutions to minor problems can be incorporated into the material with verification (done outside of the review process) by the person who discovered the problem. Major problems may require cycling back to previous affected processes in the methodology to rework them and, of course, for another review.

A by-product of reviews and walkthroughs is that they serve as a training ground and communication tool for different development styles and as insurance that someone other than the developer is familiar with and can use a product if the developer leaves the team.

Appendix F

Survey/Probe Projection Technique

This appendix describes a technique to help the project manager avoid the nightmare of DP project estimating.[1]

I have found that most DP projects have a serious problem with estimating the resources required for development tasks. It is not uncommon to find projects that have cost and time overruns of 100 percent over their original estimates. It isn't hard to see why this happens when most estimates are given at, or before, the beginning of a project when the full scope of the requirements is not known and when there is no knowledge of the existing system. At this point, the system's complexity, the availability of the existing system User, the User's knowledge of the system, or how deeply the business policy is buried under the existing system design is largely unknown.

I ask students in my management seminars, "When can we give our best estimates?" The answer is always, "At the end of the project, when we're finished." Then I ask, "When can we give our worst estimates?" The answer always comes back: "At the beginning of the project." Between these two points, our estimate is an ever darken-

---

[1] I first presented this technique at a Southern California conference called "The Structured Development Forum" in 1982.

ing shade of grey; i.e., we get better at predicting a deadline the closer we get to that deadline.

In order to produce reasonable resource projections, we must acknowledge that we have to look at our system in some detail, noting such factors as DP staff resources and skill levels, User staff availability and their knowledge of the system, as well as customizing the methodology to be used on this particular project, selecting the tools and techniques to be used, and addressing factors that are difficult to predict in advance such as company politics, the project team's ability to interact well, and the User's attitude towards DP and DP staff.

I devised the following projection technique to allow the project manager to integrate the above factors in order to arrive at an accurate figure for project resources and delivery dates. Figure F-1 graphically indicates the increasing cost and effort distribution throughout the life of a project. The shaded area depicts the amount of effort we are going to undertake in producing accurate projections using this Survey/Probe technique.

The technique involves studying one or more small portions of the system, clear down through implementation, using the actual tools and techniques that we are going to use in the full project effort and, if possible, using the actual members of the project team.

Most systems have a varying complexity level. Some parts are simple; some are complex. Thinking of systems as being analogous to

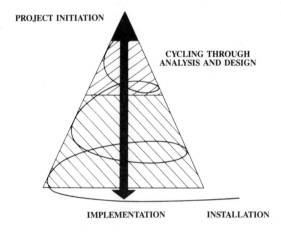

Figure F-1 Survey/Probe effort.

a lake works well for explaining these Survey/Probe ideas (see Figure F-2).

The lake perimeter is analogous to the system Context Diagram boundary, and its area to the size of the system. The varying lake depth equates to the system complexity. We need to "survey" the system's size and "probe" its depth in order to derive an accurate projection of resource needs.

Let us take an example of a project using software engineering tools and techniques. For all different deliverables produced in our project we must gather detailed metrics about actual resources used to produce those deliverables. After we identify a Context Diagram, let's assume we came up with a Data Flow Diagram one level below

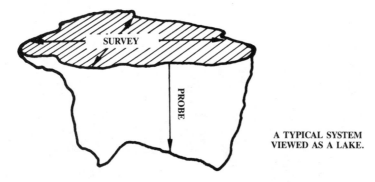

A TYPICAL SYSTEM VIEWED AS A LAKE.

Figure F-2   Viewing a system as a lake.

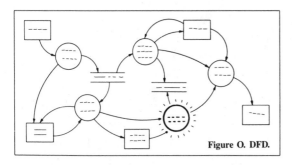

5 MAJOR FUNCTION/AREAS FOR STUDY IDENTIFIED DURING PRELIMINARY ANALYSIS

Figure F-3   Context diagram.

that Context Diagram, i.e., "Figure 0" shown in Figure F-3. This shows that we have five major functions/areas for future study in our system.

Now comes the practical and most critical step of this technique—finding a knowledgeable User, one who is working with the existing system and its manual procedures. If the system is already automated and, for example, we are upgrading from batch to on-line, also bring in a maintenance programmer from the current automated system and, if available, the analysts who produced the "Figure 0" diagram in Figure F-3. With these people decide which process (or, if a more accurate projection is needed, which two processes) could be classed as truly average in terms of total system complexity.

Next we model the chosen process(es) in further detail (e.g., to one more level of decomposition of Data Flow Diagram), and again the User, maintenance programmer, and analysts decide which process

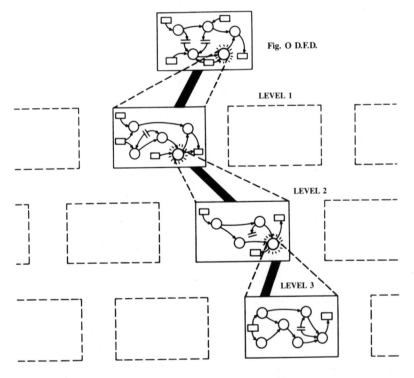

Figure F-4 Probing through to the detailed level of the system.

is average on this further detailed model. Repeat this procedure until you reach the functional primitive level of the analysis model (see Figure F-4).

The crux of this technique is that we gather **detailed metrics** from the people who are producing these deliverables. (Now you see why I call this a "probe"—because we're taking only a narrow sample slice to the bottom of the system.)

Now we keep going for just the slice of the system and use all tools that we intend to use in the actual project, producing at least two samples of each deliverable—two structure charts, two pseudocode specifications, and even two coded programs (see Figure F-5). We study two samples so that we can allow somewhat for any learning curve experienced by a project team member. We will use the second metric from each probe result for our projections. If possible, we should even install two programs on an actual test system.

Again the most important point is to gather metrics for these actual project deliverables. Notice that these metrics for **your** particular project are accurate. They were derived for **your** actual system with **your** users, with **your** staff in **YOUR** project environment, with **your** staff skill level, and with **your** existing system documentation, etc.

The process of producing an accurate projection (we no longer need to call it an estimate because it isn't vague anymore) is now simple. For example, in Figures F-3 and F-4, if this was our actual system, we can see that five major processes in the high-level model in Figure F-3 would potentially decompose on average to another three levels. Five Level 0 processes decompose to another five processes at Level 1, to four processes at Level 2, to six at Level 3.

If the user/maintenance programmer selected truly average processes (and we must rely on their knowledge of the existing system), then we can see that we should expect about 100 (5 x 5 x 4) total **Data Flow Diagrams** to be produced (plus one for Level 0) with approximately 600 functional primitive processes (100 DFDs x 6 functional primitive processes per lowest-level diagram).

Having drawn four different levels of Data Flow Diagram, made the associated data dictionary entries, and gathered actual detailed metrics for these, your analysts should have sufficient metrics to project the total resources required to complete the DFDs: the Context Diagram and "Diagram 0" resource (which can be counted as total actual production) **plus** five times the resource usage on the Level 1 diagrams (we have four more diagrams to do at this level),

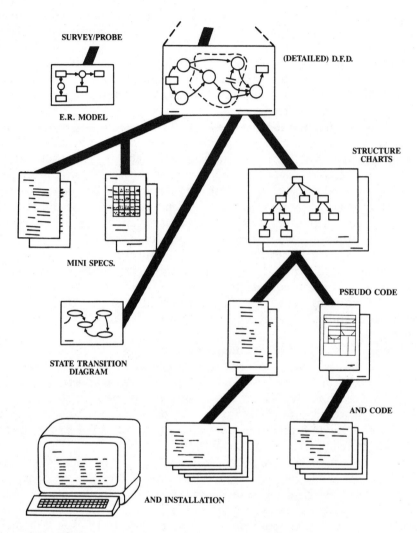

Figure F-5 Further probe through new system deliverables.

plus twenty-five times the Level 2 diagram resource usage (we have about twenty-four more to do at this level), **plus** 100 times the Level 3 diagram resource usage (we have about ninety-nine more to do at this level).

Next, we have 600 functional primitive processes. Simply multiply the time it took to do the second minispecification by 600 to give you the total minispecification resources projection (remember you did two of each deliverable so that you could use the second deliverable rather than worry about the learning curve factor on the first). Add these projections to the resources used for producing the Data Flow Diagrams and you have the total "analysis" resource projection for the actual project.

Repeat this procedure for all other types of deliverable in the project.

Now with some simple calculations, plugging in the available number of personnel for each total deliverable, also adding in outside support and material costs, realistic budget projections can also be derived. The sum of the projections make up the total resources needed for the actual project.

You will probably have to allow for some activities that could not be performed during the Survey/Probe, for example, hardware installation and system installation. This gap should be noted in your resource figures, and you may have to fall back on estimates for these.

A valuable fallout from this technique is that you produce **actual deliverables** which show a User new to structured methods just how you intend to conduct the project and the level of quality that you intend to deliver. And, of course, the User is involved in the projection process and therefore knows that you have produced a realistic figure and not just a guess.

The projections used from the Survey/Probe technique can now be used as realistic starting projections for management approval and as a starting point for further refinement and monitoring as the project continues. Again, the practical point to make for this technique is that it is using base metrics from **your** people, with **your** project and system, in **your** environment and **your** company politics, and using the **actual** tools and techniques that you will be using for the total project.

These initial projections should be constantly refined as each deliverable or significant intermediate deliverable is produced. Also, a formal review of the projections should be conducted at the completion of detailed analysis and design.

Appendix G

Business Event Partitioning (Logical Modeling)

Without any input data or stimulation, our systems have no meaning. If nobody requests whatever product or a service your organization delivers, your organization is out of business. Therefore, systems (manual or automated) all rely on outside stimuli as their reason for existence.

Stimuli arise from what we call "business events."[1] The system (a manual operation, a computer system, or even your whole company) has no control over outside business events. At the same time, it is obliged to respond to the arrival of the stimulus arising from an event. Therefore, a good place to start in a systems development effort is a Business Event Context Diagram (see Figure G-1).

A business event might be that a customer pays a bill. This event results in an input data flow (customer payment) that triggers the system into action. The data flow tells us perhaps two things about the event: (1) that is has occurred, and (2) information necessary to proceed with processing, e.g., Customer ID, payment amount.

Another type of event, say, the end of your organization's fiscal year, causes a stimulus prompt, such as automatic execution, or

---

[1] A similar term, "Event Partitioning," is well defined in S. M. McMenamin and J. F Palmer's book *Essential Systems Analysis*—see Bibliography.

generates instructions for a person to initiate some processing to trigger the system into action. Yet another event could be a pure prompt that has no data content and is not based on a scheduled point in time, for example, there might be a business need to summarize sales to date. These last two examples are what we call "business prompts."

I have found that many existing systems are partitioned for historical reasons (I usually use the term "hysterical" instead of "historical"). These reasons typically include creating system, subsystem and program boundaries based on the processor's operating system, a database management system, an "all edits together in one program" approach, the old system's department boundaries, old system job descriptions, IBM's old HIPO view, economy of scale, etc.

None of these characteristics lead us to a "functional" view of the system or portion of one and therefore tend to lead designers of new systems into cloning a bad design. In fact if we took an initiating stimulus and followed it through a typical traditionally partitioned system (a nonstructured system), we would probably find a ridiculous trail left over from poorly fragmented designs, poorly implemented maintenance fixes, and poorly planned system development efforts (see Figure G-2). Also we could probably find duplicate processing and mass redundancy of data along this trail.

There are still programmers and file designers who believe that "big is best" and that partitioning is a waste of time, leading to inefficient systems. With nonpartitioned designs, the situation gets

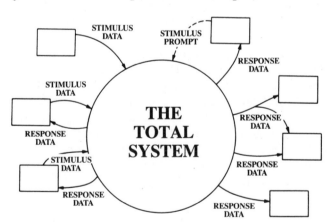

Figure G-1   Business Event Context Diagram.

worse when multiple stimuli are passed through common system partitions, such as one huge, monolithic edit program, one update program, and an "everything but the kitchen sink" program. Through these programs and systems, our "trail" diagram would look like the tracks remaining after a demolition derby!

A **functional partition** consists of an initiating stimulus and all its associated policy-based responses. The policy-based responses could be processing, intermediate data, interactions with data stores, issuance of outbound data, etc. These functional partitions should be void of old physical or old design issues.

If you have the opportunity to partition your new system by the business events it supports, then each partition should endure as long as its associated business does, rather than for the duration of the technology (hardware or support software) used to implement it.

The steps in business event partitioning (once you have verified the system boundary through the use of a context diagram) are:

• Select an initiating stimulus (an input data flow, e.g., purchase order, or a business prompt, e.g., fiscal year end) portrayed on the context diagram, and follow it through all of its associated trans-

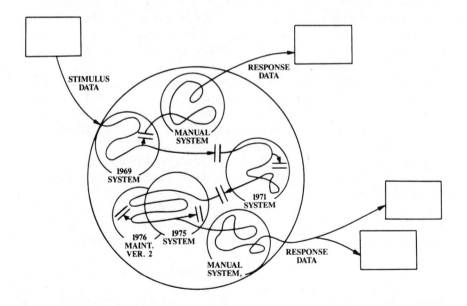

Figure G-2   System Archaeology.

formations (manual and/or automated). Ignore any old physical partitioning, e.g., job descriptions, departments, programs, job steps. Continue tracing until the system creates a final output (data flow to an external interface) and/or delivers its results to a data store.
- Perform this procedure for all initiating stimuli on the context diagram, and finally verify that the total system has been modeled by ensuring that all inputs and outputs on the context diagram have been accounted for.

Now we can identify the need for "logical data stores." The traditional definition of a data store was a "time-delayed repository of information." In my view, time is primarily a design characteristic. With business event partitioning, we can now see the true business need for data stores, or logical stores. These are necessary when the responses to two or more initiating stimuli need to share information. The shared information should reside in a data store on our logical DFD. This store is an essential element of the business.

Keep in mind that the business events or their stimuli arise outside our scope of study and that we have no control over them. Therefore, we must hold on to the data from certain events while waiting for the stimuli from others. If you see a "one data flow in, one data flow out" data store triggered by only one event stimulus, then replace this data store by a continuous data flow; it does not have to be a store on your logical model.

The result of this procedure will be sets of "functionally partitioned" individual models, each built around a business stimulus to the system. In fact, this is exactly what we intend to accomplish when we refer to a logically partitioned model, i.e., one partitioned by business events.

Now if we draw our new "trail" diagram, the model should show separate trails with connections via data stores to other stimulus trails (see Figure G-3).

If you install your new working system based on business event partitions and are not forced into any particular implementation technology partitioning, you can achieve a number of benefits:

- Clients and users will more readily understand the effects of potential changes to the system.
- When changes occur in portions of business policy, business event partitioning of our system model will make it easy to identify the

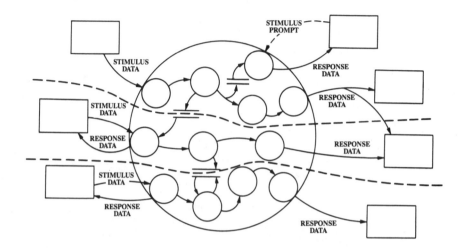

STIMULUS PROMPT

STIMULUS DATA

RESPONSE DATA

STIMULUS DATA

RESPONSE DATA

STIMULUS DATA

RESPONSE DATA

STIMULUS DATA

RESPONSE DATA

RESPONSE DATA

RESPONSE DATA

RESPONSE DATA

Figure G-3 A Business Event Partitioned Model.

location where the model needs to be modified and therefore will limit the scope of that change.

- Entire event partitions can be added or removed from the model with minimal confusion. For example, when the client says that we are no longer going to handle "special payments," with most nonfunctional system partitioning, a request of this nature would result in "dead code" and/or "dead procedures" or in changing the majority of the old system's programs. User changes such as adding a new transaction in a nonfunctionally partitioned system can make the maintenance programmers update their resumes.
- Reusable functions (that will later become common library modules) can be spotted easily and early in the project, usually during analysis, but by design at the latest.
- Changes to hardware or support software should have trivial effects on the business partitioned system.

You can also see the benefits of this technique for long-term systems planning. If all systems in the corporation were modeled and built with business event partitioning, then bringing systems together at some future date, or identifying the effect on all systems for some new business event, would be easy compared with traditionally partitioned systems.

BIBLIOGRAPHY

I have changed my bibliography from the first edition, having discovered that many DP people do not have the time to read stacks of books. Many of my students over the last few years have asked me for my essential, or "lazy person's" bibliography. Here is my limited set of reading materials. There are many other good books on the market—these are just my own favorites.

Block, R. *The Politics of Projects*. New York: Yourdon Press, 1983.

DeMarco, T. *Controlling Software Projects*. New York: Yourdon Press, 1982.

DeMarco, T. *Structured Analysis and System Specification*. New York: Yourdon Press, 1979.

DeMarco, T. and Lister, T. *Peolpeware*. New York: Dorset House, 1987.

Fitzgerald, J. & A. *Fundamentals of Systems Analysis*. New York: John Wiley & Sons, 1987.

Flavin, M. *Fundamental Concepts of Information Modeling*. New York: Yourdon Press, 1980.

Jackson, M. A. *Principles of Program Design*. New York: Academic Press, 1975.

McMenamin, S. M. & J. F. *Palmer Essential Systems Analysis*. New York: Yourdon Press/Prentice-Hall, 1984.

Myers, G. J. *Composite / Structured Design*. New York: Van Nostrand Reinhold, 1978.

Myers, G. J. *The Art of Software Testing*. New York: John Wiley & Sons, 1979.

Page-Jones, M. *The Practical Guide to Structured Systems Design*. New York: Yourdon Press, 1980.

Thomsett, R. *People and Project Management*. New York: Yourdon Press, 1980.

Yourdon, E. *Structured Walkthroughs*, 2nd ed. New York: Yourdon Press, 1978.

Additional Reading

To alleviate "people" problems in data processing such as personal or political game playing and poor communications, techniques like Transactional Analysis (TA) are applicable to foster awareness and sensitivity in interpersonal relationships. Because I feel this is such an important area, I recommend these additional books. The first and fourth are popular treatments of TA; the second and third are important because they stress the idea of quality, which applies to systems (and to life).

Berne, E. *Games People Play*. New York: Ballantine Books, 1964.

Crosby, P. B. *Quality Is Free*. New York: Mentor, 1979.

Persig, R. M. *Zen and the Art of Motorcycle Maintenance*. New York: Bantam Books, 1974.

Steiner, C. M. *Scripts People Live*. New York: Bantam Books, 1974.

Glossary

Agent — A person, group, or program that performs a process or function

Attribute — A property or quality of an entity of which the system must hold the actual data value

Backout processing — This is processing that upon finding an error, returns the system to its original state by undoing processing performed prior to the error

Bottom-up — A qualifier indicating that the product is developed or the process is conducted from a specific low level of detail to a gross high level of detail

Business event — A discretionary incident outside the context of study which causes a stimulus to which the system must respond

Cardinality — See "relationship cardinality"

Cohesion — The measure of how closely related—that is, how strong—is the association of instructions/functions that are packaged together; there are various levels of strength of cohesion

Complex store — A store of data that consists of more than one repeating data group or a store that describes multiple different entities

Coordinating module — A module that calls upon other modules to accomplish a function

Cycling — The act of performing similar activities at different levels of detail (see "iteration")

Data Capture — The act of gathering and storing information needed for a system

Data Coupling — The communication of data to and/or from a function; usually related to a design solution in which data parameters are passed between modules, indicating the dependence of one module upon another

Data Dictionary — A set of definitions for all data items (data flow, data element, data store, outside interface) declared on a data flow diagram; the data dictionary will also contain (later in the system development effort) definitions for control items and data on a structure chart and in application code

Data Flow — A pipeline of information between processes, data stores, or outside interfaces; an item of data is no longer available in the pipeline once it reaches its destination

Data Flow Diagram — A modeling tool used to represent the active data view of a system (automated and/or manual); it has four components—data flows, processes, data stores and outside interfaces; these components are represented graphically to model a system and to show its partitioning

Data Integrity — A feature of a data item or entity indicating that it is dependent or independent of another

Data Model — A component of the structured specification which graphically represents the static data of a system or enterprise; data models typically have two components—simple entities and the access paths required between them to satisfy the data needs of the system's processing

Data Primitive — A data item that does not require any further breakdown in order to be defined

Data Transformation — A change of status or content of an item of data

Data Transporter — A physical process that simply moves a data item(s) and does not change its status or content

Decision Table — A graphical tool used to specify decision logic by showing a matrix of all combinations of conditions and their results that can occur in a process

Decision Tree — A graphical tool used to specify decision logic by showing a hierarchy of all combinations of conditions and their results that can occur in a process

Deliverable — A product that has been rigorously defined and that meets the goal of an activity

Driver — A module that simulates a controller function on a design chart; usually used to aid incremental building and testing of a system

Entity — A stable and permanent component of the business about which data must be held

Entity-Relationship Diagram — A normalized and decomposed graphical, model showing the information entities within the system scope or enterprise and the associations between them that are important to the enterprise

Executable — A qualifier for a process or data, indicating that it can be executed directly by a person or a machine

Functional Primitive — A detailed-level, specific task that does not require further breakdown in order to be specified because it is small enough and simple enough to be understood and verified by any reader

Implementation — The process of building and testing a product prior to installing it; usually related to the writing and testing of code for an automated system

Incremental — An approach to system development that avoids giving premature commitment to a single inflexible estimate at the start of a project, but instead encourages a projection that is refined by the project team based on their level of knowledge of the system as system development progresses

Installation— The process of installing a product (system) into a production/operational (user) area

Iteration — The repetition of activities in order to develop and refine a product, as opposed to the creation of a deliverable in one linear effort; also known as explicit iteration (see "cycling")

Level of Detail — A range of specific information gathered during a given iteration of system development; the number of levels of detail will vary from system to system depending on such factors as system complexity

Logical — An implementation-independent view; a qualifier for data or processes indicating that all physical characteristics of the item have been removed except those needed for essential business reasons: for data, the composition is specified in the data dictionary, but its media or format is not; for processes, the essential logic is specified but not who accomplishes it or how it is accomplished

Logical Access Path Diagram — One or more implementation-free diagrams showing the access paths among the business entities about which the system holds data (access paths differ from relationships in that they show how processing navigates from one logical data group to another whereas relationships show the business associations between entities)

Logical Data Model — A data model that does not indicate its implementation structure such as relational, network, or hierarchical (see "data model")

Maintenance — (Bad word); the cleanup process performed on production systems to remove errors that were put in during their development

Methodology — A guideline identifying how to develop a system; as an object, a methodology is a product that shows managerial and technical activities and their deliverables needed to produce a working system; as a process, a methodology is the practical set of procedures that facilitates development of a system

Metrics — Detailed historical records of deliverable related usage of project resources, containing information as well as data

Mini-specification — The specification of a functional primitive which describes the policy or procedure necessary to transform incoming data flows into outgoing data flows

Model — A representation to be used as a pattern or guide for conceptualizing, specifying, planning, or executing a system or deliverable

Modification — The necessary change to a product initiated by the user of that product when business needs change

Module — A cohesive set of statements/instructions that accomplishes a specific function and that has known inputs and outputs

Nassi-Shneiderman Diagram — A graphical tool used to specify logic; usually used as a form of pseudocode in design

Negative Test — Type of test that is expected to fail; also known as an exception test consisting of data and procedures that are invalid

Physical — A qualifier for data or processes, indicating that implementation features are specified: For data, the definition/composition may include the media and format used for transmission and/or storage; for processes, the specifications may include the people or program IDs performing the tasks and how the processes are procedurally accomplished

Physical Data Model — A data model that identifies how the data structure will be implemented

Physilogical — A qualifier indicating the item being qualified is specified with a hybrid of a physical and logical characteristics; that the qualified item is mostly logical but will have as many physical characteristics included as necessary for user validation/approval

Physilogical Model — A logical model overlaid with physical characteristics, usually just enough to allow the user to validate the model. A physilogical model lies somewhere on the spectrum from complete physical to pure logical; its main use lies in avoiding the need to prepare a full current physical model of the system under study

Plan — A deliverable that identifies how the development of a project or deliverable is managed

Policy — essential business logic specifying the transformation of input data into output data

Positive Test — A test that is expected to work correctly; also known as a normal test; consists of data and procedures that are expected to be valid in the system being tested

Project — The total activity of developing a system, beginning with a formal acknowledgment of business objectives and related problems and ending with a formal acknowledgment that the solution to these objectives and problems has been implemented

Pseudocode — A graphical tool used to specify logic; forms a stepping stone between the analysis specification and implementation code. Pseudocode identifies (via spatially arranged logic) how a process is accomplished without the restrictions or formality of a particular computer language's syntax or grammar

Regression Test — Test that can be used to validate a portion of a production system after a modification has been made; also used to insure that portions of the system unaffected by a change still perform correctly

Relationship — An association between two or more entities which is important to the enterprise

Relationship Cardinality — The relative numbers of occurrences of each of the entities participating in the relationship, for example, 1-to-1, 1-to-many, many-to-many

Resources — Available or allocated time, money, people, or materials for accomplishing an objective

Review — A formal quality control/assurance inspection of a deliverable

Structure Chart — A graphical tool used to hierarchically model the design solution (architecture) of a system; used to show the partitioning and control structure of a system into modules (functions) and the data and control interfaces between these modules

Structured English — A spatially arranged tool used for specifying business policy during analysis. Structured English consists of a formal subset of the English language used with the constructs of structured programming

Structured Specification — A formal description of a system (manual and/or automated), which is the product (deliverable) of structured analysis; the specification is partitioned into a leveled set of data flow diagrams, a data dictionary, a data model, and minispecifications

Stub — Cryptic code that simulates a module on a design chart; used to aid the incremental building/testing of a system

System — A connected or related set of manual and/or automated activities that produce a desired result

Top-Down — A qualifier indicating that a product is developed or a process is conducted working from a high level of detail to a specific lower-level of detail

Transaction Analysis — A design strategy in which a design solution is developed by identifying a number of individual transactions in a system or portion of a system, and forming a transaction-centered design where a coordinating module invokes any one of a set of subordinate modules based on a transaction input

Transform Analysis — A design strategy in which the hierarchical design solution is developed by identifying a major data transformation point in the system or portion of the system specification, and forming a design structure chart around that transformation center

User — The requestor/recipient of project resources and its product—a system

Walkthrough — An informal quality control/assurance inspection of a deliverable in which reviewers are peers of the author of the deliverable

Worker Module — A subordinate module on a design chart that was derived from the analysis specification; it does not direct or coordinate other modules

Index

About the Author

Brian Dickinson is the founder and president of Logical Conclusions Inc., a training and consulting corporation based in Brisbane, California.

Brian has more than 22 years of experience in all areas of data processing, including consulting and teaching for many major U.S. and international corporations and governments. He has worked internationally, applying the structured techniques that took him to Yourdon, Inc., one of the first U.S. companies to offer education in the evolving software engineering disciplines. Brian was one of a handful of people who originally helped develop and spread the software engineering message across the United States.

After teaching the tools and techniques of software engineering, Brian saw that as these new ideas were being introduced into the DP profession, there was a need to bring all of them together under a new systems development life cycle methodology, so he wrote the first edition of this book, "Developing Structured Systems— A Methodology Using Structured Techniques," originally published by Yourdon Press.

His expertise covers education in: software project management and methodologies, and structured analysis and design, information modeling and programming to both User and DP communities. He has taught and consulted internationally and has been a speaker on quality system development to organizations such as NCC, DPMA, ASM, EDPAA and Data Training.

WOULD YOU LIKE "DEVELOPING QUALITY SYSTEMS" ONLINE?

YES! *I'm interested in getting all the* "DEVELOPING QUALITY SYSTEMS" *data flow diagrams, data dictionary, and process descriptions on a diskette plus the CASE tool* "VS DESIGNER"* *from Visual Software Inc. to run on my PC!*

* This version of "VS DESIGNER" gives you the ability to customize the "DEVELOPING QUALITY SYSTEMS" data flow diagrams, activities, and data dictionary entries, delete those you don't need, and add new activities and flows to produce your project's customized methodology.

Name _____

Company _____

Address _____

City _____ State _____ ZIP _____

NO POSTAGE
NECESSARY
IF MAILED
IN THE
UNITED STATES

BUSINESS REPLY MAIL

FIRST CLASS MAIL   PERMIT NO. 131   BRISBANE, CA

Postage will be paid by addressee:

LOGICAL CONCLUSIONS INC
450 KINGS ROAD
BRISBANE, CA 94005-9901